The Coach U Personal and Corporate Coach Training Handbook

The Coach U Personal and Corporate Coach Training Handbook

Coach U, Inc.

WILEY

John Wiley & Sons, Inc.

ISBN 0-471-71173-X

Printed in the United States of America

10 9 8 7 6 5 4 3

Contents

Acknowledgments

In 1992, the original curriculum for Coach U was authored by Thomas J. Leonard, the person recognized as the founder of the coaching profession. Since its inception, we have remained committed to regularly updating and improving our materials to remain the leading accredited coach training organization in the world. There are literally hundreds of seasoned coaches to thank for contributing to the quality of our training materials. One particular individual who deserves recognition is Jodi Jan Shafer, the training director for CoachInc.com. This book would not have been possible without her ongoing focus and dedication.

Each year, we receive many calls and e-mails from our students and graduates, who graciously and generously provide us with input on how to further improve our body of knowledge. Today, our materials truly embody the concept of collective wisdom at its very best. This book is a synergistic product of many minds coming together in collaboration. Although we cannot thank each contributor individually, we sincerely appreciate all of the support that you have given us throughout the years. The comments, suggestions, class facilitation and participation, and coaching experiences that you have shared with us have made a difference. We hope that you are proud of the role that you have played and the contributions that you have made.

Finally, we would like to acknowledge you for considering this book. We know that if you are reading this book, you have an interest in supporting others in their personal and professional development or supporting the growth of organizations. Our vision has always been to have all individuals and organizations on the planet take a coach approach in all forms of communication, whether at home or at work.

We have come a long way since 1996, when we started working together—there were fewer than 500 coaches worldwide. Now, it delights us to know that you, our readers, understand that coaching isn't found just in sports and that coaching is changing the world, one person at a time.

Sandy Vilas
Owner and CEO of CoachInc.com

Jennifer Corbin
Coach U and Corporate Coach U President

Preface

I began my journey in the coaching profession in 1989, when I took a course offered by Thomas Leonard and became certified as a life planner.

Over the next five years, I wrote a book, led workshops, and spoke to groups all over the country. During that time, Thomas started Coach U (along with being my own personal coach). I was using my coaching skills at every opportunity, and in 1994 I enrolled in Coach U and became a full-time coach. At that time, most people had no idea what coaching was or how it worked. With the support of my coach, I was coaching 80 people a week at the end of my first year.

I was having more fun and making more money than any other time in my life. Perhaps more important, I was deeply imbued with a sense of peace, fulfillment, and satisfaction that I had never before experienced. I had clearly found my passion and mission in life, or rather, it found me because I had done the work and was ready. Two years later, Thomas was ready to sell Coach U, and a week later I was the owner, amidst a great deal of excitement, mixed with a heavy dose of fear. The journey since has been full of lessons, growth, satisfaction, and joy!

Today we have 27 staff members working out of their homes in four countries, and they are the most dedicated, hard-working and creative people I've ever worked with. We have over 100 faculty members that are highly skilled at delivering our training and love giving back to this profession. We have more than 11,000 students and graduates from 51 countries who are making a difference, one client at a time.

I attribute my success as a coach to excellent training in the skills, language, and distinctions available in this book. As a result, I have a strong desire to continue supporting others in their success. One way to realize this goal is to give new coaches the benefit of not only my experience but also the expertise of the many coaches, graduates, staff members, and faculty of CoachInc.com. By using the material in this book and participating in our classes, students not only will develop as coaches but also will continue to create outstanding professional and personal lives. The principles and practices of coaching not only can transform the lives of coaches and coachees but also can transform the world.

As the reader of this book, you are most likely just beginning your journey as a coach and learning skills that will support you in any endeavor you choose to undertake. You may be a professional manager, entrepreneur, or consultant, or you may have a desire to become a full-time coach. Whatever motivation brought you to this book, I encourage you to immediately implement these principles in your own life. I hope it brings you the fulfillment that so many others and I have attained as a result.

Sandy Vilas
Owner and CEO of CoachInc.com

Part 1
Introduction

Chapter 1

New Coach Orientation

Overview

Benefits

Go to Page > 7

By fully participating in the material offered in this module, you will begin to understand the profession of coaching and evolve your own personal definition. You will gain an understanding of the coaching core competencies identified by the International Coach Federation and the steps involved in developing your coachees and providing continued structure for their growth. You will gain knowledge of the Coaching Ethics for Internal and External Coaches and learn how to apply these ethical principles in various coaching scenarios.

Definitions

Go to Page > 8

Collective wisdom, concepts, developing, seeding, distinctions, influence, problem solving, environment, coaching competencies, principles, coaching ethics, and mentor coach.

Concepts

Go to Page > 10

What Is Coaching?

Coaching is a catalyzing relationship that accelerates the process of great performance; it's about individuals' and/or organizations' identifying purpose and living out of that purpose.

Distinctions

Go to Page > 24

Developing versus parenting, developing versus growing, developing versus learning, distinction versus definition, competence versus mastery, and ethics versus morals.

Benefits

By fully participating in the material offered in this module, you will begin to understand the profession of coaching and evolve your own personal definition. You will gain an understanding of the coaching core competencies identified by the International Coach Federation and the steps involved in developing your coachees and providing continued structure for their growth. You will gain knowledge of the Coaching Ethics of Internal and External Coaches and learn how to apply these ethical principles in various coaching scenarios.

This course is designed to:

○ **Define** coaching as a profession

○ **Recognize** the emerging impact coaching is having on the world

○ **Identify** the importance of advancing the individual growth of each coachee

○ **Use** the core coaching competencies as a framework for what happens in a coaching interaction

○ **Understand** the importance of Coaching Ethics as guidelines for behavior in the profession, and as a means to deliver consistent value to your coachees

○ **Apply** the Coaching Ethics to various coaching scenarios

○ **Explore** the supportive role that a Mentor Coach can play in personal learning and how to select one

○ **Evolve** your own personal definition of coaching

Definitions

The following are common words used to gain a better understanding of the coaching process, particularly in regard to your beginning development as a coach.

Collective wisdom: The coaching interaction is different from many other interactions in that the wisdom and brilliance of the coach and coachee are included and honored in the overall process. Although both parties benefit from the engagement, of course the person being coached has the primary focus and gain. At CoachInc.com we built our entire curriculum using the collective wisdom model, utilizing the wisdom of thousands of masterful coaches who have come before you.

Concepts: A concept is a notion or idea about something, usually formed by combining all its characteristics, facts, and particulars. It is something directly conceived, either through outside influences or through intuition. It is a theme, or image—a packaged combination of thoughts.

Developing: To develop is to bring out the possibilities in someone or something. It is to progress to a more advanced, effective, or usable state; to cause to grow or increase; to elaborate on something and cause it to expand; to cause it to mature and evolve from earlier stages to more advanced stages.

Seeding: Literally, to seed means to sow or plant something. In the context of this module, seeding means to introduce something (information, suggestions, influencing requests, ideas) in the hope of increase. A farmer seeds in the hope of a great harvest. You practice seeding in the hope of increasing the coachee's awareness and development.

Distinctions: A distinction is a discrimination made between things as being different. It is the recognition that two similar-appearing or -sounding ideas, concepts, words, or other things actually have distinct differences.

Influence: Influence is the capacity or power to produce effects in others by intangible or indirect means. A masterful coach is constantly influencing a coachee's development process, through a number of direct and indirect methods.

Problem solving: Problem solving assumes that there is a problem. The focus of coaching is to enhance one's life, developing personal strengths, creating patterns of success, and building reserves as opposed to believing that life is a problem that needs fixing.

Environment: An environment is the aggregate or combination of surrounding things, conditions, and influences, including social, cultural, relational, personal, and professional forces that shape a person's life.

Coaching Competencies: The first major milestone in developing new skills or taking the skills you have to another level is to develop competency in using those skills. In coaching, we talk a lot about competency as a true measure of effectiveness and consistency in drawing distinctions between coaching and other ways of working with people.

Principle: A principle is an accepted or professed rule of action or conduct, a fundamental law, axiom, or doctrine. It can also be a personal or specific basis of conduct or management, or a guiding sense of the requirements and obligations of conduct.

Coaching ethics: As in any profession, there is a stated set of guidelines that clearly delineate and guide a coach's behavior. Coaching ethics help both the coach and coachee, because they allow all parties to assume that certain things will and will not occur in a coaching relationship. Coaches abiding by the ethics outlined build credibility in the profession for every coach. Ethics are not suggestions but a code to consider and commit to upholding in your professional interactions.

Mentor Coach: This is a seasoned professional coach that is hired by an aspiring coach to support him or her in developing his or her coaching skills and building a coaching practice. Typically, a mentor coach is hired for his or her level of experience and expertise, in addition to the other criteria one would consider when hiring a coach. CoachInc.com students and graduates have access to ICF-certified coaches who have met our qualifications for mentoring and are designated as Professional Mentor Coaches.

❝ Men can starve from a lack of self-realization as much as they can from a lack of bread. ❞ | **Richard Wright**

Concepts

What Is Coaching?

Coaching is a catalyzing relationship that accelerates the process of great performance; it's about individuals' and/or organizations' identifying purpose and living out of that purpose. When people are actively seeking meaning and solutions, they value partnership and support that assists them in accomplishing their goals and objectives. Historically, that kind of support has come from sources such as friends, parents, therapists, consultants, and advisors. Coaching has drawn ideas and techniques from many different kinds of support relationships and historical theories to create, formalize, and distill the best practices for masterful coaching.

Coaching is a journey of personal and professional discovery. To realize the true benefits of this journey, you must have the desire to risk, learn, and stretch to your potential, just as you will be requesting of your coachees. The skill set required to become a masterful coach is a skill set that is used regularly by people in all their interactions. This results in many people's coming into coaching claiming they have been "coaching" all their lives. We request that you let go of thinking you have been doing this all your life and consider the possibility of your own evolution and mastery of a skill set that will allow you to be with others, affecting their lives and the world at large in a profound manner. That is truly the possibility that coaching as a profession presents.

We welcome you into the global coaching community.
—The CoachInc.com community

The Process of Developing

To develop something is to bring out the possibilities within. The entire coaching process, and every coaching interaction, involves developing—a natural by-product of the coaching relationship. Developing also happens naturally in every moment of our lives. Although we continue to develop and grow all the time, often the development is "accidental," can be unhealthy, or at the least may not be intentional. As an example, humans need to eat to sustain life, but we have choices as to what and when we eat. When time is short and demand is high we may choose to eat fast food. Many people will not take time to begin their day with a balanced meal and find that late into the evening they are craving one more snack. Or we may exercise an intentional choice by eating a potato or a banana to enrich our potassium intake.

In a coaching relationship, you and the coachee work together to decide how and where a coachee can be developed, when it is appropriate, and the specific kind of developing that is needed to enrich them. The majority of the development that occurs in a coaching relationship is intentional, and there are specific coaching tools that you will implement to rapidly enhance or target the development of certain areas in the coachee when he or she is open to growth. Often, intentional growth will accelerate a coachee toward his or her stated goals, resulting in a more advanced, effective, and productive state of being. Intentional development releases possibility and creates sustainable growth, both for immediate goals and throughout the coachee's life. Developing is an aspect of the coaching process that creates an environment that stimulates, motivates, and sustains coachee growth.

Developing and Problem Solving

Coachees come to you for personal and professional development. They may come with immediate goals or problems, but they always want the development required to accomplish these goals or solve the problems more quickly, even if these requests are unstated. You will spend a percentage of the time focusing directly on the goal or problem and a percentage on development. As you grow in mastery, the time spent on development tends to increase. The advanced coachee knows, wants, and appreciates the value of development and the sustainability of the changes he or she makes because he or she is actually different, not just doing things differently. The beginning coachee usually needs more of a "goal" and problem-solving focus until the benefits of development take effect.

The Concept of Seeding to Develop

As stated in the definitions section, seeding is the practice of introducing something in the hope of increase. In this case, the hope of increase is the coachee's continued development and subsequent maturity and transformation from a lesser state to a greater, more fulfilling state of being and doing.

Seeding involves planting something in the hope that it will grow. You are forever planting seeds with your coachees. These seeds may be bits of information, correction of old ideas, requests, or any other number of plantings. In many cases the coachee expects and wants this to occur. You become adept at knowing the optimum moment of planting any variety of seeds. The analogy of planting and seeding, and the subsequent growth and harvest of those seeds, is an analogy that allows you to come to more fully understand the coaching process.

" To see things in the seed, that is genius. **"** | **Lao-tzu**

Much of the advanced work you do with a coachee takes time, sometimes years, to bloom into a garden. Some of the planted seeds will sprout in a week, others will poke up in the next "season," and others will miss the mark entirely and land on a rock. Sometimes the coachee wants immediate growth and will ask that sod or a tree be brought in. Soon, this transplant will become fully integrated with the coachee and will be part of his or her being. You plant seeds by asking questions, sharing suggestions, requesting change, pointing something out, and discussing concepts. Coachees will "get it" in their own time. You and the coachee can make sure the soil is tilled, fertilized, and watered, and that the weeds are pulled, but each seed has its own germination time.

Developing All Areas

A master coach seeks to develop the coachee in every sphere of influence and every part of their being and doing.

Developing the Whole Person		
Mind	Ability to think	○ Improving their good judgment ○ Reducing reaction time to events ○ Giving them new ways to make decisions ○ Expanding ways of thinking ○ Increasing their capacity to learn quickly
Heart	Ability to feel	○ Improving their ability to distinguish between a feeling and an emotional reaction ○ Increasing their ability to give and receive love ○ Expanding their ability to relate and connect with others
Spirit	Ability to enjoy	○ Providing expanded perspective ○ Increasing the capacity for inner peace ○ Helping them become more aware of self, others, and life in general
Business	Ability to succeed in business	○ Adding value to their customers faster than their competitors ○ Increasing their ability to enjoy work ○ Improving their innovative and creative abilities ○ Assisting with the balance of life and work
Environment	Awareness and control of surroundings	○ Increasing the awareness of surroundings and the ability to control them ○ Improve their available resources and network ○ Upgrading home and office environments ○ Improving health and wellness

Coaching Core Competencies

The coaching relationship is based on a set of guiding competencies that provide a framework from which the coach operates. Knowing that a coachee comes to you with the primary focus of creating significant positive change in his or her personal and/or professional life, it is useful to have directional signs as you navigate the coaching conversation. These competencies comprise the key features that define today's coaching environment, the elements that make up the coaching interaction. These key behaviors and skills are the basis for the International Coaching Federation's credentialing process, and are commonly known to create a solid foundation for effective coaching. Each competency listed has a definition and related behaviors. Behaviors are classified as either those that should always be present and visible in any coaching interaction or those that are called for in certain coaching situations and, therefore, not always visible in any one coaching interaction.

A. Setting the Foundation

1. Meeting Ethical Guidelines and Professional Standards
   An understanding of coaching ethics and standards and the ability to apply them appropriately in all coaching situations. A Coach:
   a. *Understands and exhibits the International Coaching Federation (ICF) Standards of Conduct in his or her own behaviors*
   b. *Understands and follows all ICF Ethical Guidelines*
   c. *Clearly communicates the distinctions between coaching, consulting, psychotherapy, and other support professions*
   d. *Refers coachee to other support professionals as required, knowing when this is needed and having the available resources*

2. Establishing the Coaching Agreement
   The ability to understand what is required in the specific coaching interaction and to come to agreement with the prospective and new coachee about the coaching process and relationship. A Coach:
   a. *Understands and effectively discusses with the coachee the guidelines and specific parameters of the coaching relationship (e.g., logistics, fees, scheduling, inclusion of others if appropriate)*
   b. *Reaches agreement about what is appropriate in the relationship and what is not, about what is and is not being offered, and about the coachee's and coach's responsibilities*
   c. *Determines whether there is an effective match between his/her coaching method and the needs of the prospective coachee*

B. Co-creating the Relationship

3. Establishing Trust and Intimacy with the Coachee

The ability to create a safe, supportive environment that produces ongoing mutual respect and trust. A Coach:

a. *Shows genuine concern for the coachee's welfare and future*
b. *Continuously demonstrates personal integrity, honesty, and sincerity*
c. *Establishes clear agreements and keeps promises*
d. *Demonstrates respect for coachee's perceptions, learning style, and personal being*
e. *Provides ongoing support for and champions new behaviors and actions, including those involving risk taking and fear of failure*
f. *Asks permission to coach coachee in sensitive new areas*

4. Coaching Presence

The ability to be fully conscious and create a spontaneous relationship with the coachee, employing a style that is open, flexible, and confident. A Coach:

a. *Is present and flexible during the coaching process, dancing in the moment*
b. *Accesses and trusts his or her own intuition and inner knowing—"goes with the gut"*
c. *Is open to not knowing, and taking risks*
d. *Sees many ways to work with the coachee, and chooses what is most effective in the moment*
e. *Uses humor effectively to create lightness and energy*
f. *Confidently shifts perspectives and experiments with new possibilities for own action*
g. *Demonstrates confidence in working with strong emotions, and can self-manage and not be overpowered or enmeshed by coachee's emotions*

C. Communicating Effectively

5. Active Listening

The ability to focus completely on what the coachee is saying and is not saying, to understand the meaning of what is said in the context of the coachee's desires, and to support coachee self-expression. A Coach:

a. *Attends to the coachee and the coachee's agenda, and not to his or her own agenda for the coachee*
b. *Hears the coachee's concerns, goals, values, and beliefs about what is and is not possible*
c. *Distinguishes between the words, the tone of voice, and the body language*

    d. *Summarizes, paraphrases, reiterates, and mirrors back what coachee has said to ensure clarity and understanding*

    e. *Encourages, accepts, explores and reinforces the coachee's expression of feelings, perceptions, concerns, beliefs, suggestions, etc.*

    f. *Integrates and builds on coachee's ideas and suggestions*

    g. *"Bottom-lines" or understands the essence of the coachee's communication and helps the coachee get there, rather than engaging in long descriptive stories*

    h. *Allows the coachee to vent or "clear" the situation without judgment or attachment, in order to move on to next steps*

6. Powerful Questioning

   The ability to ask questions that reveal the information needed for maximum benefit to the coaching relationship and the coachee. A Coach:

       a. *Asks questions that reflect active listening and an understanding of the coachee's perspective*

       b. *Asks questions that evoke discovery, insight, commitment, or action (e.g., those that challenge the coachee's assumptions)*

       c. *Asks open-ended questions that create greater clarity, possibility, or new learning*

       d. *Asks questions that move the coachee toward what he or she desires, not questions that ask the coachee to justify or look backward*

7. Direct Communication

   Ability to communicate effectively during coaching sessions, and to use language that has the greatest positive impact on the coachee. A Coach:

       a. *Is clear, articulate, and direct in sharing and providing feedback*

       b. *Reframes and articulates to help the coachee understand what he or she wants or is uncertain about from a different perspective*

       c. *Clearly states coaching objectives, meeting agenda, purpose of techniques or exercises*

       d. *Uses language appropriate and respectful to the coachee (e.g., nonsexist, nonracist, nontechnical, nonjargon)*

       e. *Uses metaphor and analogy to help illustrate a point or paint a verbal picture*

D. Facilitating Learning and Results

8. Creating Awareness

   The ability to integrate and accurately evaluate multiple sources of information, and to make interpretations that help the coachee to gain awareness and thereby achieve agreed-upon results. A Coach:

       a. *Goes beyond what is said in assessing coachee's concerns, not getting hooked by the coachee's description*

b. *Invokes inquiry for greater understanding, awareness, and clarity*

c. *Identifies for the coachee his or her underlying concerns, typical and fixed ways of perceiving himself or herself and the world, differences between the facts and the interpretation, disparities between thoughts, feelings, and actions*

d. *Helps coachees to discover for themselves the new thoughts, beliefs, perceptions, emotions, moods, etc., that strengthen their ability to take action and achieve what is important to them*

e. *Communicates broader perspectives to coachees, and inspires commitment to shift their viewpoints and find new possibilities for action*

f. *Helps coachees to see the different, interrelated factors that affect them and their behaviors (e.g., thoughts, emotions, body, background)*

g. *Expresses insights to coachees in ways that are useful and meaningful for them*

h. *Identifies major strengths instead of focusing on major areas for learning and growth, and what is most important to address during coaching*

i. *Asks the coachee to distinguish between trivial and significant issues, and between situational and recurring behaviors when detecting a separation between what is being stated and what is being done*

9. Designing Actions

The ability to create, with the coachee, opportunities for ongoing learning, during coaching and in work or life situations, and for taking new actions that will most effectively lead to agreed-upon coaching results. A Coach:

a. *Brainstorms and assists the coachee to define actions that will enable the coachee to demonstrate, practice, and deepen new learning*

b. *Helps the coachee to focus on and systematically explore specific concerns and opportunities that are central to agreed-upon coaching goals*

c. *Engages the coachee to explore alternative ideas and solutions, evaluate options, and make related decisions*

d. *Promotes active experimentation and self-discovery, where the coachee immediately applies what has been discussed and learned during sessions in his or her work or life setting*

e. *Celebrates coachee successes and capabilities for future growth*

f. *Challenges coachee's assumptions and perspectives to provoke new ideas and find new possibilities for action*

g. *Advocates or brings forward points of view that are aligned with coachee goals and, without attachment, engages the coachee to consider them*

h. *Helps the coachee "Do It Now" during the coaching session, providing immediate support i. Encourages stretches and challenges but also a comfortable pace of learning*

10. Planning and Goal Setting

The ability to develop and maintain an effective coaching plan with the coachee. A Coach:

a. *Consolidates collected information and establishes a coaching plan and development goals with the coachee that address concerns and major areas for learning and development*

b. *Creates a plan with results that are attainable, measurable, and specific, and have target dates*

c. *Makes plan adjustments as warranted by the coaching process and by changes in the situation*

d. *Helps the coachee identify and access different resources for learning (e.g., books, other professionals)*

e. *Identifies and targets early successes that are important to the coachee*

11. Managing Progress and Accountability

The ability to hold attention on what is important for the coachee and to leave responsibility for taking action with the coachee. A Coach:

a. *Clearly requests that the coachee take actions that will move him or her toward his or her stated goals*

b. *Demonstrates follow-through by asking the coachee about those actions that the coachee committed to during the previous session(s)*

c. *Acknowledges the coachee for what he or she has or has not done, learned, or become aware of since the previous coaching session(s)*

d. *Effectively prepares, organizes, and reviews with coachee information obtained during sessions*

e. *Keeps the coachee on track between sessions by holding attention on the coaching plan and outcomes, agreed-upon courses of action, and topics for future session(s)*

f. *Focuses on the coaching plan but is also open to adjusting behaviors and actions based on the coaching process and shifts in direction during sessions*

g. *Is able to move back and forth between the big picture of where the coachee is heading, setting a context for what is being discussed and where the coachee wishes to go*

h. *Promotes coachee's self-discipline and holds the coachee accountable for what he or she says he or she will do, for the results of an intended action, or for a specific plan with related time frames*

i. *Develops the coachee's ability to make decisions, address key concerns, and develop himself or herself (to get feedback, to determine priorities and set the pace of learning, to reflect on and learn from experiences)*

j. Positively confronts the coachee with the fact that he or she did not take agreed-upon actions

What Are Ethics?

It could be considered that the core competencies outline what happens in a coaching interaction and ethics provide guidelines for how the coaching interaction is to occur, including the manner in which you operate with your coachee during an interaction. Following the core competencies will allow for a very rich and solid interaction. Adhering to the ethics will ensure that the product of your interaction will actually be coaching in its most recognized and valued form, and not an interaction that is driven by the competencies of another profession more profoundly than by coaching competencies.

" Ethics, in the end, is not something we do. It is something we become. " | Art Kleiner

Ethics is a most important conversation to embrace and understand while developing yourself as a coach. Many people seek direction on how to coach, struggling to clearly define the profession and what happens in that brilliant coaching interaction. They are uncovering how to do coaching. The ethics conversation responds to an internal longing to be a coach, not just do coaching. It is the nagging internal process that drives us beyond the definition of ourselves as coaches to how we are as human beings with everyone we coach. Ethics drive us to want to coach very well, pursuing mastery of the art of coaching.

Coaching is a highly personalized business, due to the coachee's individual issues, challenges, wants, desires, and intended outcomes. Each coachee relationship is unique. Some of your coachees may work in the same environment or have familiar scenarios, but what they truly want from a coaching relationship will vary. As each relationship evolves, ambiguous issues will present themselves. As coaches, we want to provide high-quality, consistently valuable coaching services. By establishing standards of behavior, we create a compass to guide us in unfamiliar territory.

As in any business, reputation is everything. In establishing yourself as a coach, you build a strong reputation based on sound and proven business guidelines, aligned with recognized strong moral principles and fabulous work with your coachees. By establishing principles and guidelines now, you will be building on a foundation that will allow you to continually offer consistent service to a spectrum of coachees dealing with complex challenges.

By accepting and adhering to the ICF Code of Ethics, you will help build the coaching profession around sound principles of business practices. You may view those at www.coach federation.org.

Why Coaching?

We have begun discussing some of the definitions of coaching and coaching ethics and have presented a thorough review of the core coaching competencies associated with the profession. Hopefully, we have begun to unravel what guides a coach to behave in a specific way during a coaching interaction. To add another perspective to your understanding of coaching it may be useful to look at a question:

If coaching is the answer, what is the question?

Obviously, coaches are successful—because people hire coaches. What are people seeking when they enter a coaching relationship? Let's take a look at a variety of current life conditions that bring people into coaching.

To Make Significant Changes

Even though change is the only constant, the condition that can always be counted on, human beings seem to be challenged by the notion of change. A coach is uniquely trained to support people in making both fundamental and permanent change in all areas of life, business, career, relationships, and quality of life.

To Better Deal with Uncertainty

Flatter, leaner organizational structures mean that there is less day-to-day direction from the top. Individuals are expected to form networks within and outside their organizations, master the skills of creative collaboration, respond to frequently changing priorities, and assume personal responsibility for setting their own direction.

To Make Better Decisions

As life speeds up and becomes more of a luscious smorgasbord, we are presented with far more choices than our parents ever had, but who had Decision-Making 101 in high school or college? Enter the coach, who can help you learn how to make the best decisions for you, regardless of the circumstances and even in the most confusing situations. CoachInc.com-trained coaches help coachees make better decisions.

To Set Better Goals

The most important thing when setting goals is making sure that they're the ones that reflect your true values and that are a true joy to reach. The wrong goal, perhaps based on whims, advertising, or instant gratification, takes needless effort and often comes at a high cost to you, your body, and your soul. Coaches help each person discover what he or she REALLY wants, using the coachee's own values, needs, and vision as personal reference points. They help coachees eliminate the goals they've had forever that aren't really important but that they've always thought they should pursue.

To Reach Goals Faster

Who doesn't want to reach their goals faster, especially if it's possible to get there with less stress? A coach provides consistent structure of support and offers innovative strategies and approaches to help coachees and/or employees reach their goals in record time. CoachInc.com-trained coaches are familiar with performance and attraction approach models and share these with their coachees.

To Become Financially More Successful

Career advancement in the traditional organizational structure consisted of upward promotions throughout one's career. Leaner organizational structures preclude that expectation within twenty-first-century corporations. Instead, career advancement—indeed, the ability to add value to the organization—will increasingly be evidenced by "cross-functionality." Rather than following a vertical path to the top of the organization, people will develop a broader base of experience and more extensive networks by making a number of crisscross career moves. A coach can support you in navigating your way through the next right move within or outside your organization.

To Get Ahead Professionally

Organizations that survive and thrive in the twenty-first century will be those that are continually renewing and learning. People who work in or with them will be expected to assume full responsibility for managing their learning in response to changing organizational needs. Learning will be different from that in traditional organizations. Rather than prescribed curricula being handed down from "experts," people will be responsible for creating their own learning opportunities to harness their individual creativity and talents. Coaching can help you to realize your true strengths and passions and then go about developing them to maximize your potential.

To Deal with the Influence of Technology

The Internet is rapidly becoming the hub of the global marketplace, and the corporation's workforce will need to develop and maintain its proficiency in computer and telecommunications technology in order to be viable. With the growth of technology, people are challenged to clearly see their place in an organization or society in general. Technology has challenged our most intimate relationships, such as communicating with our kids only via instant messaging, even within the same household. A coach can help you see the effects of the world we are currently living in, helping you slow down enough to get to the source of what is holding you back from having the life you really want.

To Have a Collaborative Partner

When you have someone to toss ideas around with, someone who understands the creative process, someone who expands your thinking, you end up with synergy. And, in our view, synergy is the essential component of success in the next decade.

To Improve Their Relationships

Increasingly, organizations are entering into alliances, mergers, and joint ventures with former competitors. The ability to manage lateral relationships will be a critical determinant in people's ability to achieve results. Cross-functional work teams and matrix structures are becoming commonplace, and they require a more demanding set of interpersonal skills. This says nothing of the blended family systems that now are more common than the nuclear family, putting even greater demands on our internal emotional functionality. A coaching relationship provides a partnership to explore your true self, your limits and capacities, without the concern of reactions from others.

To Make a Bigger Impact on the World

People tend to be driven to want to make a mark on the world. Many people are working with coaches to identify their unique strengths and resources and a way to use these to make a local or global difference, without the traditionally high emotional or physical cost that comes with leadership.

To Be a Better Leader

Reshaped organizations will have fewer leaders at the top than traditional vertical organizational structures, and, given the rapidity of change, those at the top will be incapable of being the repositories of organizational knowledge and wisdom. In the new era, leadership will emerge throughout the organization, regardless of job title or status, and individuals will have relationships with "leader coaches" who will sponsor them in their development of new knowledge and achievement of evolution performance.

To Simplify Their Lives

You really can have "it all" and yet simplify your life at the same time. CoachInc.com coaches use coaching models and assessments that help people to simplify yet enrich their lives at the same time. It is one of the many proprietary methods and technologies that our coaches are trained to use with coachees.

To Reduce Stress

Stress comes with our times, but an increasing number of people recognize that the cost of stress is too high. Therefore, they seek out a coach to help them identify and reduce their personal stress levels, benefiting body, mind, and spirit. Learning to deal with life stresses in a healthy manner significantly improves a person's productivity and creative contributions. Many CoachInc.com-trained coaches also use the toleration-free approach. Identifying what you are putting up with and eliminating these tolerations instantly reduces your stress level.

To Address an Altered Reality of Employment

Contract work, outsourcing, temporary employment, telecommuting, and virtual organizations are but a few of the changes in the way people are redefining employment, as organizations are downsizing and restructuring to be more competitive. The workforce of the twenty-first century will not expect to have a lifelong relationship based on dependency with one employer. Instead, people will have a series of short-term relationships throughout their careers in which they contribute their knowledge and expertise in response to particular business needs. They will have to operate more like business owners whose customer is the corporation. This creates a significant opportunity for a coach to support people in developing the skills necessary to run their "professional life business" most successfully.

To Keep Up with the Speed of Life

Never has the pace been more rapid than it is in today's marketplace. Organizations must respond quickly and be innovative to survive, let alone have a competitive advantage. This requires a flexible, adaptable workforce. Corporations simply do not have the reserves to tolerate anything less. A coach can help develop a clear success strategy to keep your competitive advantage.

Distinctions

There are subtle yet important differences in meaning between the following closely related terms. Understanding these distinctions allows you to perceive new layers of meaning and offers you new choices for shifting your thoughts, attitudes, and actions.

Developing versus Parenting

Developing means bringing out the possibilities of something or someone and bringing them to a more advanced, effective state. When you are developing coachees, you are helping them grow, learn, build skills, make better choices, grasp concepts, recognize symptoms or opportunities and reality, and get to know themselves better. When developing, coachees develop on their own, in their own time, and by their own choice. A parent, however, has a responsibility—a social contract—to raise the child, whether or not the child wants to grow. If you are trying to get your coachees to grow, learn, and develop and they are fighting this or not responding, consider whether you have been parenting instead. It may be helpful to talk through this distinction.

Developing versus Growing

Growth is advancement, maturity, and increase—in any number of areas. Development implies not only growth but also a structure to sustain the growth. For example, a tomato plant will grow tall and keep producing tomatoes until the branch breaks from overload. Unless the gardener provides a support system, further growth is stunted, and the plant does not reach potential yield. The same is dramatically true in coaching. You and the coachee must devote time to building a support structure to accommodate further growth. It is possible for a coachee (and a business, etc.) to continue growing, only to have the existing infrastructure collapse under the weight of the growth. This can be a devastating setback. Anticipate and plan for building a supporting structure during the coaching process.

Developing versus Learning

Learning is the acquisition of knowledge. Information, or learning, while important for development, does not guarantee it. It is what we do with the learning that either hinders or enhances personal development.

Distinction versus Definition

A definition explains the meaning of something. A distinction compares one thing to another, similar thing, identifying the differences between them and providing context, which adds a richness of understanding to both items. Both are useful, but definitions provide knowledge, whereas distinctions provide clarity, understanding, and growth.

Competence versus Mastery

When one is competent in a particular skill, one is adequate at using the skill effectively. Mastery lives at the other end of the continuum, at the moment when the skill becomes perfected. Because of the dynamic nature of a coaching interaction, there is a constant interplay of skill level throughout the conversation, depending on various contextual factors.

Ethics versus Morals

Morals—the right, decent, and just way to behave—live within the definition of ethics. Ethics are actually defined as the science of morals in regard to human behavior. The repetitively systematic, observable manner in which successful coaches behave leaves an ethical pattern that can be replicated by others.

Application

The Coaching Code of Ethics for Internal and External Coaches

Listed here is the Coaching Code of Ethics for Internal and External Coaches. This is a more condensed and specific list of ethics that could be used when engaging in a coaching relationship, without specific reference to the ethical considerations of being a member of the ICF.

By reading and signing the Code, you as a coach agree to hold yourself to the highest standards possible.

1. Establish Sound Contracts and Business Practices

Establish, agree and honor the terms and conditions of the engagement. Provide specifics that include such items as (1) payment terms (external coaches); (2) time, frequency, and method of communications; (3) definition of services to be rendered; and (4) an agreement of the terms. Upon establishing this agreement, ensure that I operate out of sound business procedures (e.g., record keeping, how I do business in general).

2. Establish My Professional Competencies

Set forth the areas of competencies I have achieved. Include my coaching training, education, and credentials. Make sure that I have acquired high levels of competencies and have practiced sufficiently to do the work I am hired to do.

3. Adhere to the Limits of My Expertise

Coach only in my area of competence and where legally permitted to practice. Refer individuals to other specialists, such as financial planners, investment advisors, lawyers, doctors, and therapists, as needed.

4. Guarantee Confidentiality within Boundaries

Guarantee the confidentiality of information that the person being coached entrusts to me. Advise them of any circumstances that might influence my judgment or objectivity. Specify situations where confidentiality may be interrupted (e.g., legal subpoena, violation of federal law, company policy, etc.). This is particularly important when being hired for a company and working individually with the employee. Both the individual and I must be clear about the boundaries of confidentiality.

5. Be Respectful and Constructive

Respect the individual's needs, wishes, and differences. Make sure each person is honored and that I am constructive and honest with him or her at all times.

6. Respond Quickly and Responsibly

Set my own agenda aside in order to listen fully to what the individual says or means. Promptly respond in the moment of the coaching. Respond promptly as well to phone calls, faxes, or electronic mail and any request that the person being coached may make of me. Promise only those things that I fully intend to provide, then follow through.

7. Be Professional at All Times

Maintain the relationship on a professional basis. Associations that reduce objectivity (e.g., those of a romantic nature) are incompatible with a coach's professional role and will cause an end to the trustful coaching relationship.

8. Maintain Appropriate Distance

The coach does not invest capital in or make loans to the individual's business or projects unless both parties develop formal, written, and legally supported agreements. Even in the case of a formal agreement, I am aware that the coaching relationship may change.

9. Be a Model

Conduct personal and professional affairs with high standards and integrity so as to be a model for my clients and other coaches. I must live fully the values and beliefs I espouse to assure that those engaging my services may receive full value. Anything less is not coaching.

10. Be Coachable Myself

All masterful coaches have coaches themselves. I must continue to learn, grow and stretch just as I am asking my clients to do. I am willing to learn from those I coach as well.

By my signature, I commit to the highest of ethical standards in the practice of coaching.

_____

Signature   Date

The Ten Standards of the Code of Ethics

Ethics are a choice. They are not required or mandatory, nor will anybody make you adopt or adhere to them. Ethics are eloquently stated and are wordsmithed to sound really good, but then only become meaningful when challenged and put into action. If you are serious about coaching professionally, ethics are an absolute.

Consider the following coaching scenarios. These scenarios are meant to be discussed with a certified coach who has been actively coaching, abiding by the Coaching Code of Ethics. After adopting the Coaching Code of Ethics, what would you do?

1. Establish Sound Contracts and Business Practices

What's a coach to do when ...
Joyce has been coaching independently for about one year. When she first started her practice she decided that a verbal agreement was sufficient to work with the medical professionals in her niche market. Her initial coachees were people she knew well and had worked with for years. Therefore, she did not invoice her coachees, and they sent her checks or cash each month. She received a letter from the IRS about auditing her records. What should she do?

2. Establish My Professional Competencies

What's a coach to do when ...
Although Harry did not have a college degree, he had over 30 years of experience as a manager and left a company where his position was chief operating officer. Harry has all the natural characteristics and abilities you would expect of a coach. Should Harry get additional coach training as he begins to represent himself as a coach?

3. Adhere to the Limits of My Expertise

What's a coach to do when ...

Simon is a very good coach. He has studied many ways to grow and develop himself personally. He is also very easy to talk to, and his coachees trust him quickly. His new coachee seems to get tearful during each session. Should Simon help her discover what the tearfulness is about? Where is the ethical line for coaching?

4. Guarantee Confidentiality within Boundaries

What's a coach to do when ...

Sheila is a coach development leader who coaches and manages 18 direct reports. One of her employees, Judy, begins to confide some things about a man in another department who has been approaching her inappropriately. What should Sheila do?

5. Be Respectful and Constructive

What's a coach to do when ...

Timothy has just started coaching. He encourages people to take action and get moving. Tim will coach almost anyone who wants to be coached. However, one of his coachees is moving very slowly. Tim does not enjoy working with the coachee because he doesn't think the coachee is getting anything from the coaching. What should he do?

6. Respond Quickly and Responsibly

What's a coach to do when ...

Richard advises new coachees that he will promptly return their calls or emails. He believes in promptness as a good standard of doing business. Recently a coachee began placing emergency calls to him at least once a week. How should he respond?

7. Be Professional at All Times

What's a coach to do when ...

Marcia is an external coach. Even though she primarily coaches her coachees on business-related issues, her coachees talk about almost anything, even issues of a very personal nature. She is very attracted to an executive she coaches. Can she maintain her professional approach while hearing about very personal issues when she is attracted to him?

8. Maintain Appropriate Distance and Objectivity

What's a coach to do when ...

David coaches with technical entrepreneurs who are creative geniuses. One coachee has created a new Internet software program that appears to have a high dollar potential. The coachee has requested that David invest seed money in the project so that it can go forward. David could potentially earn millions of dollars from the investment. Should he invest?

9. Be a Model

What's a coach to do when ...

Mark espouses high standards as he coaches others. However, his own personal life is a mess, with high credit card bills and failures in his personal relationships. One of Mark's coachees asks how he managed to create financial reserves. Mark has indicated that having reserves is an important thing to do. Should Mark discuss finances or refer his coachee to a financial planner? How can this become a great coaching opportunity for both Mark and his coachee?

10. Be Coachable Myself

What's a coach to do when ...

Kathleen is an executive coach who has been hired to help an executive team learn to improve its public speaking skills. She has always viewed her inability to speak publicly as a deficit. What steps can Kathleen take to optimize her ability to more masterfully coach the team?

Application Exercise: Coaching Conversation

Review the following coaching scenarios. With the coaches' Code of Ethics in mind, consider your coach approach to each scenario. Be prepared to discuss the scenarios in class.

Scenario 1

You're just getting started with your coaching practice. One of your former colleagues left the company at about the same time you did, taking six talented marketing people with him. He wants you to come and coach the team. He sends you the following e-mail:

"Kyle, we don't have cash available, but we could really benefit from your team coaching talents. What do you say to an exchange of services—you coach at no charge, and we create free marketing materials for you?"

What is the ethical issue? How do you reply?

Scenario 2

One of your coachees is having work/life balance issues. She is an ambitious and successful executive who spends a lot of time at the office. Her home life is unraveling, and she is struggling with her feelings of failure. She tells you that you are the only one she really confides in because she doesn't have peers at work and has lost touch with her friends. Plus, she knows that you have gone through a divorce, so you can understand her situation. She announces the following during your weekly phone session:

"I'm asking for a separation. Marc and I have become strangers—strangers who fight whenever we're in the same room. Who was your divorce attorney? Was he any good?"

What is the ethical issue? How do you reply?

Scenario 3

You are on your way to a business lunch with a potential coachee when your phone rings. You pick it up and hear the desperate pleas of a valued coachee. He tells you:

"I am so glad I caught you! I am scheduled to meet with our regional manager in two hours. He wants to discuss last quarter's sales performance. I need a mental boost. What can you do for me?"

What is the ethical issue? How do you reply?

Application Exercise: I Know I Am a Coach When ...

In the listing that follows, determine how you would make such a shift in order to embrace the ideas in this and subsequent modules. Come up with as many examples as you can that will describe the difference you would see in yourself when you are truly being a coach.

Examples

I know I'm a coach when … I focus on listening to the total conversation before I decide what to say and resist the urge to solve problems.

I know I'm a coach when … I'm willing to risk the relationship to respectfully help my coachees see their truth.

How will you know when you are a coach?

I know I'm a coach when …

Mentor Coaching

By now you may be realizing that you were not completely accurate when you originally stated, "I have been coaching all my life." You may certainly be one of those people that others seek out because you are a good listener or you are empathetic to life circumstances or maybe even because you generate great ideas that vaguely represent solutions to others' problems. Beyond just defining coaching, our further intention in this module was to dispel the myth that everyone is a coach. For many, coaching is their calling. However, you now know that coaching is a profession with a highly specialized skill set oriented in core competencies. These competencies represent a compelling knowledge base driven by how to be a coach and a real treasure of the profession. Coaches perfect the ability to connect with other human beings in a profound way that motivates, inspires, and moves them to make significant changes in their life.

Just as many professions have a common set of competencies that lead to mastery and a set of guidelines that insure a consistent standard of product or service, most professions also have some implicit or explicit form of mentoring or apprenticeship. For the very same reasons that other professions support mentorship, we at CoachInc.com advocate for mentorship as you develop as a coach. We find that those who enlist the use of a mentor coach are more successful developing themselves as coaches and reach their intended goals more quickly. That sounds like a good reason to hire a coach.

We encourage you to explore the following questions for yourself when considering a mentor coach:

> What do I want to use my Mentor Coach to achieve?
> When would be the best time for me to have a Mentor Coach?
> What should I consider when selecting a Mentor Coach?

What do I expect from my Mentor Coach?
What about me would be helpful for my Mentor Coach to know?
Where do I find the right Mentor Coach?

CoachInc.com has created the industry's leading referral system, www.findacoach.com, featuring personal and corporate coaches from around the world. Each coach listed is a student or graduate of CoachInc.com's coach training programs. The site has been designed to respond to each visitor's unique needs. Unlike most directories, findacoach.com works with you to determine the coaches who will best be able to help you reach your goals. We do this in a unique environment that allows you to establish your own search parameters and the form in which you wish to view your results. The site is completely confidential, and it is up to you to determine if and when you would like to contact a coach and explore working with him or her. You can bookmark specific profiles, print out a listing of all the coaches you are interested in, or e-mail them directly for more information.

Here are some questions that you might want to ask a coach during the interview stage.

1. Tell me about your experience of coaching practice (listen for depth/breadth).
2. What is your long-term vision for your practice?
3. Describe the characteristics of coachees who relate best with you.
4. What is your specialty or niche?
5. Tell me about your background and experience. How will that help me meet my goals in my area of expertise and in what I want to achieve?
6. How long have you been coaching?
7. What is your involvement in CoachInc.com (and the coaching profession)?
8. What other activities are you involved in with your practice?
9. How many people have you coached? How many coaches have you mentored?
10. What value-added services do you provide for coachees?
11. Are you an ICF-certified coach (PCC or MCC)? Is your ICF certification current? (*Note:* Be sure to ask if the coach plans to work toward being a certified coach, as the ICF and CoachInc.com certifications require you to be mentored by an active ICF-certified coach.)
12. How would you describe your coaching style?
13. What is your coaching format(s)?
    Type? (One-on-one, group, combo, etc.)
    Frequency? (2x/month, 3x/month, 4x/month, etc.)
    Length? (20 min., 30 min., 40 min., etc.)
14. What is your regular fee or fee structure?
15. If I selected you to be my coach, what would we start working on first?

" No man who continues to add something to the material, intellectual and moral well-being of the place in which he lives is left long without proper reward. " | **Booker T. Washington**

Defining Coaching

So, what *is* coaching? We started this module by suggesting that your definition of coaching will be shaped by your personal journey. Some principles are basic and must be included in the definition, while others are specific to each coach, based on his or her life experience and what he or she has to offer. As stated previously, one of the main objectives of this module is to develop your unique definition of coaching, gathered from what we have learned together and what you bring to coaching. Your definition of coaching will continue to evolve throughout your coaching experience.

The Coach Approach

An individual's approach to coaching can be discovered by observing a coach's language, behaviors, approach to people, management of others, and, in general, his or her way of being. The CoachInc.com "coach approach" is distinctive because coaching is a way of life and not just a methodology. Coaching is not something you do 9 to 5, it's the manner in which you live your life.

Following is a suggested list of practices of "being" a coach.

- Set your agenda aside. Get yourself out of the way so others can grow.
- Create a partnering relationship in an environment of trust.
- Create discovery versus solutions.
- Listen.
- Encourage or request others to grow.
- Use the power of language and endorsement to help people make life shifts.
- Lead by being transparent so others own their progress.
- Make stretch requests.
- Live your life as a model of your own high standards.
- Celebrate your own life as you celebrate with others.

Resources

Attention Readers:

Thank you for participating in the collective wisdom of Coach U. Together, we all continue to learn. Additional resources and forms can be found in *Coach U's Essential Coaching Tools: Your Complete Practice Resource* by CoachInc.com.

Attention CoachInc.com Students and Graduates:

CoachInc.com students and graduates may find additional and/or more recent resources associated with this module in the resource area of the student-only web site. If you are a student or graduate of one of CoachInc.com's ICF-accredited coach training programs, you can access these by searching under the name of the course. When the course description page appears you may find a link to the list of additional resources. Each item is a live link to its actual location on the web site. Click on the item to access the information.

Do remember to take the associated online self-test for this module once you have completed the course in person or by TeleClass. The tests are required for coach certification with the International Coach Federation. Throughout the course or anytime you find valuable resources for a particular course please feel free to add to the value of our curricula by forwarding the resource to revampteam@coachu.com.

The Coaching Code of Ethics for Internal and External Coaches

1. Establish Sound Contracts and Business Practices

Establish, agree, and honor the terms and conditions of the engagement. Provide specifics that include such items as (1) payment terms (external coaches); (2) time, frequency, and method of communications; (3) definition of services to be rendered; and (4) an agreement of the terms. Upon establishing this agreement, ensure that I operate out of sound business procedures (e.g., record keeping, how I do business in general).

2. Establish My Professional Competencies

Set forth the areas of competencies I have achieved. Include my coaching training, education, and credentials. Make sure that I have acquired high levels of competencies and have practiced sufficiently to do the work I am hired to do.

3. Adhere to the Limits of My Expertise

Coach only in my area of competence and where legally permitted to practice. Refer individuals to other specialists, such as financial planners, investment advisors, lawyers, doctors, and therapists, as needed.

4. Guarantee Confidentiality within Boundaries

Guarantee the confidentiality of information that the person being coached entrusts to me. Advise them of any circumstances that might influence my judgment or objectivity. Specify situations where confidentiality may be interrupted (e.g., legal subpoena, violation of federal law, company policy, etc.). This is particularly important when being hired for a company and working individually with the employee. Both the individual and I must be clear about the boundaries of confidentiality.

5. Be Respectful and Constructive

Respect the individual's needs, wishes, and differences. Make sure each person is honored and that I am constructive and honest with him or her at all times.

6. Respond Quickly and Responsibly

Set my own agenda aside in order to listen fully to what the individual says or means. Promptly respond in the moment of the coaching. Respond promptly as well to phone calls, faxes, or electronic mail and any request that the person being coached may make of me. Promise only those things that I fully intend to provide, then follow through.

7. Be Professional at All Times

Maintain the relationship on a professional basis. Associations that reduce objectivity (e.g., those of a romantic nature) are incompatible with a coach's professional role and will cause an end to the trustful coaching relationship.

8. Maintain Appropriate Distance

The coach does not invest capital in or make loans to the individual's business or projects unless both parties develop formal, written, and legally supported agreements. Even in the case of a formal agreement, I am aware that the coaching relationship may change.

9. Be a Model

Conduct personal and professional affairs with high standards and integrity so as to be a model for my clients and other coaches. I must live fully the values and beliefs I espouse to assure that those engaging my services may receive full value. Anything less is not coaching.

10. Be Coachable Myself

All masterful coaches have coaches themselves. I must continue to learn, grow, and stretch just as I am asking my clients to do. I am willing to learn from those I coach as well.

By my signature, I commit to the highest of ethical standards in the practice of coaching.

_____

Signature   **Date**

Chapter 2

Guiding Principles

Overview

Benefits Go to Page > 43

By fully participating in the material offered in this module, you will gain an understanding of the Guiding Principles of Human Interaction. These represent the fundamental theories and principles about people in interaction, which coaches generally accept as true. You will recognize the existence of these principles in yourself and others whether in a personal or organizational setting.

Definitions Go to Page > 45

Guiding principle, collective wisdom, ground of being, life purpose, discernment, self-interest, awareness, and integrity.

Concepts Go to Page > 46

The Guiding Principles of Human Interaction
A guiding principle is a basic understanding of something fundamental about the human condition; a statement that a particular behavior or phenomenon always occurs, a theory that consistently explains the facts. Guiding principles are like living, breathing things that adapt and grow over time as others test and explore them further.

Distinctions Go to Page > 49

Guiding principles versus human laws and mastering versus gaining mastery.

○ **Application**   Go to Page > 52

The Nine Guiding Principles of CoachInc.com
1. People Have Something in Common.
2. People Are Inquisitive.
3. People Contribute.
4. People Grow from Connection.
5. People Seek Value.
6. People Act in Their Own Interest.
7. People Live from Their Perception.
8. People Have a Choice.
9. People Define Their Own Integrity.

○ **Resources**   Go to Page > 85

Benefits

By fully participating in the material offered in this module, you will gain an understanding of the guiding principles of human interaction which represent the fundamental theories and principles about people in interaction, and which coaches generally accept as true. These guiding principles are an essential and foundational base for coaching individuals as well as the individuals that make up teams or organizations. They guide what coaches do when they coach, and also who they are with their coachees.

This course is designed to enable you to:

O **Define** the nine guiding principles from a theoretical perspective as well as their relationships to specific human conditions

O **Explain** the difference between similar terms to uncover new layers of meaning for each principle

O **Describe** the relationship of each guiding principle to different types of coaching

O **List** the changes and attitude shifts required to move your coaching presence from disconnected to deeply rooted in the common ground of being between all human beings

O **Demonstrate** how the integration of these nine principles into your coaching practice evolves you closer to being a master coach

The nine guiding principles are universally true, but each individual will have a unique experience around them, based on their culture and personal history. They are going on all the time, in all our relationships with others, whether we recognize them or not. Working with the guiding principles allows you and your coachee to identify, appreciate, and embrace other dimensions of self, learning to create value and connect with others in a more powerful and authentic way.

The Guiding Principles of Human Interaction illuminate the typically ignored, yet constant effect, we have on ourselves, each other, and our circumstances.

They are not meant to be the final word, only a starting point in an ongoing conversation that includes everyone who encounters them. Some, most, or all of the guiding principles may seem obvious and simplistic. However, when you explore their implications in detail, you will find that they expand our capacity to live fully in the world.

Definitions

The following are common words used to gain a better understanding of the coaching process, particularly in regard to the Guiding Principles.

Guiding principle: A guiding principle is something fundamental about the human condition; a statement that a particular behavior or phenomenon typically occurs, a theory that consistently explains the facts. This particular set of guiding principles directs a coach's understanding of how people are in interaction with themselves, others, and circumstances.

Collective wisdom: Everyone's wisdom is woven together to benefit the learning of the whole. The guiding principles as well as the entire curriculum has been created using this collective wisdom process, tapping into the brilliance of each and every participant of the CoachInc. com programs. We model the value of the collaborative coaching process to offer thinking and understanding that benefit a vast majority.

Ground of being: The root system and common elements that make us who we are as human beings. Although there is a lovely uniqueness to every individual, understanding that we have common elements supports us in understanding and accepting others and ourselves.

Life purpose: The defining statement as to why we are on the planet. Often coachees enter the coaching relationship seeking articulation, understanding, and modification of their life purpose. Many people believe that whether we know what it is or not, we will live our life purpose. It is defined as how and why we live out our life.

Discernment: The process by which one perceives clearly through the mind or senses. Throughout a coaching relationship there will be many times when a coachee is seeking discernment or clarity around a certain topic or issue. Our lives often move too fast, making discernment a challenge.

Self–interest: Being invested in yourself and your thoughts, needs, values, emotions, feelings, and all that makes you the person that you are. This investment is your most valuable commodity in that it drives all your decisions. When linked with self-responsibility, taking full responsibility for yourself, including your actions and inactions, the quality of all your interactions improves.

Awareness: Conscious understanding and acknowledgment of the current reality.

Integrity: Wholeness, being entirely and totally, 100 percent yourself.

Concepts

The Guiding Principles of Human Interaction

What is a "guiding principle?"

A guiding principle is something fundamental about the human condition; a statement that a particular behavior or phenomenon typically occurs, a theory that consistently explains the facts. Guiding principles are like living, breathing things that adapt and grow over time as others test and explore them further. The guiding principles of CoachInc.com also describe an essential aspect of coaching: they speak to what coaches do when they coach and also who they are with their coachees.

How the guiding principles originated

The guiding principles grew out of an ongoing conversation among experienced coaches and the faculty of CoachInc.com. The questions they sought to answer were, "What does it mean to be a coach?" and "What needs does coaching fulfill in the world?" In answering these questions, several fundamental truths about people emerged, beliefs about people that all the coaches shared. These truths became the guiding principles.

The guiding principles are simple, and so basic to human interaction that they typically remain invisible, like the air around us that sustains us. Describing them to people is like describing water to fish. Although they are universally true, each individual has a unique experience of each guiding principle based on his or her cultural and personal history. Therefore, staying true to the collective wisdom, the discussion and exploration of the guiding principles will continue to evolve and grow to explain what it means to be a coach and what needs coaching fulfills in the world.

A guiding principle is something fundamental about the human condition; a statement that a particular behavior or phenomenon always occurs, a theory that consistently explains the facts.

The format of the guiding principles module

All nine of the guiding principles are presented in the applications section of this module. For each guiding principle, there is a theoretical discussion, describing what the principle is, its validity and how it appears in human interactions, as well as a description of the relationship between the guiding principle and coaching.

How the guiding principles impact coaching

Each type of coaching has a set of skills associated with it that overlaps with the guiding principles, and all are deeply rooted in love, honoring and valuing one's self and others. Love, honor and valuing one's self and others creates a strong catalyst for change, discovery, and forward movement. These nine types of coaching represent different sides of a prism a coach can look through to see people differently; as such, they also represent nine different frameworks from which a coach can provide value to others.

Guiding Principle		Coaching Base	What It Means
1.	People Have Something in Common	Common-ground-based coaching	Tapping into your own deep love, honor, and value for yourself and others, resulting in a heart-to-heart and respectful connection that invites your coaches to do the same.
2.	People Are Inquisitive	Inquiry-based coaching	Staying in your own wonder and curiosity as long as possible, letting surprising new information appear, rather than jumping quickly to reliable answers and established solutions.
3.	People Contribute	Contribution-based coaching	Acknowledging how those you coach already contribute to others, and assisting them in shaping their contribution to become even better aligned with their purpose and values.
4.	People Grow from Connection	Connection-based coaching	Developing a rich and powerful connection with those you coach that fosters a synergistic flow of creative energy.

5.	People Seek Value	Value-based coaching	Actively listening to those you coach with all of your senses in order to access values that might otherwise remain invisible.
6.	People Act in Their Own Interest	Interest-based coaching	Championing the best interests of those you coach so that they can openly participate in living the life they most want based on their values.
7.	People Live from Their Perception	Perception-based coaching	Creating a larger, more inclusive experience of reality for yourself and those you coach by sharing experiences with each other and living fully in the present.
8.	People Have a Choice	Choice-based coaching	Raising the awareness of choice for those you coach.
9.	People Define Their Own Integrity	Integrity-based coaching	Noticing the level of wholeness and well-being of those you are coaching, and assisting them in gaining an ever-stronger alignment between their calling and their conduct.

Distinctions

Distinctions are subtle, yet important differences in meaning between closely related terms. Understanding distinctions allows you to perceive new layers of meaning and offers you new choices for shifting your thoughts, attitudes and actions.

Guiding Principles versus Human Laws

Guiding principles are fundamental principles or truths about the nature of people. Human laws are guidelines and restrictions designed by society for the collective good.

Mastering versus Gaining Mastery

Mastering implies an endpoint: the game is over—you won. Gaining mastery is a process of continual personal growth and skill development.

Distinctions between commonly used terms are an important part of discovering new opportunities for growth. Each guiding principle examines several such distinctions as they relate directly to that principle. For this reason, these distinctions are presented with the body of information about each guiding principle in the following concepts section of this module. The distinctions listed below are detailed:

The distinctions listed in this table are detailed in the information provided about each guiding principle in the application section.

Guiding Principle	Distinctions
1. People Have Something in Common	Common and same Different and unique Discernment and judgment Inclusion and separation
2. People Are Inquisitive	Wonder and curiosity Curiosity and inquiry Questioning and inquiring Inquiry and inquisition
3. People Contribute	Talent and passion Contributions and life purpose Intention and impact Potential and actualization
4. People Grow from Connection	Artistic and creative Connection and network Creative and productive Authenticity and uniqueness
5. People Seek Value	Value and values Hearing and listening Listening and attention
6. People Act in Their Own Interest	Discernment and judgment Judgment and criticism Selfish and self-interest Selfish and self-care
7. People Live from Their Perception	Living in the present and living in the past Living in the present and living in the future Behavior and conduct Perception and perspective

Guiding Principle		Distinctions
8.	People Have a Choice	Choice and decision
		Awareness and knowledge
		Awareness and analysis
		Reacting and responding
9.	People Define Their Own Integrity	Values and calling
		Calling and role
		Integrity and morality
		Life purpose and career

Application

The Nine Guiding Principles of CoachInc.com

Guiding Principle 1	**People Have Something in Common.** We return to the common ground of being by loving, honoring, and valuing ourselves and others. People are drawn together in companies through a compelling mission and shared vision.

This principle explores the meaning of the common ground of being, and how people frequently lose touch with it. It explores how we can strengthen our connection to it whenever we choose, by loving, honoring, and valuing others and ourselves. Genetically, all human beings are 99.9 percent identical. Sharing the same genetic code means that although we look, think, and act differently, we share many of the same emotions, motivations, impulses, desires, strengths, and weaknesses. We humans also possess a common inner quality: We all need and desire love, respect, and being of value. This is our common ground of being.

Whatever we do is our contribution to the world at large and supports the ground of being from which others draw. When our actions are based in this common ground of love, honor, and respect for ourselves and others, they promote our ability to return more to our families, communities, organizations, and the world. Awareness, choice, and responsibility are the keys to fulfilling contribution. When we are richly connected and contributing to our common ground of being, our interactions with others are smoother, more effective, and enjoyable. This behavior moves us away from competition and judgment to collaboration and acceptance.

Distinctions

There are subtle yet important differences in meaning between the following closely related terms. Understanding these distinctions allows you to perceive new layers of meaning and offers you new choices for shifting your thoughts, attitudes, and actions.

Common versus Same

Common means having something shared; to be the same means being identical—you've seen one, you've seen them all. Each of us is absolutely unique, completely different from everyone else, not the same, yet made of the same stuff, and sharing a common ground of being.

Different versus Unique

Different is an adjective of comparison, pointing to disparities and dissimilarities. Unique is an appreciation of one person or thing, and how this one special case is utterly different from all the rest.

Discernment versus Judgment

Discernment is an act of perception either through the senses or the intellect. It means seeing or noticing something, such as the color of the sky or the expression on a person's face. Judgment follows after discernment, when we fit our observations into a frame of reference, form an opinion, or assign value.

Inclusion versus Separation

Inclusion is bringing together or embracing; separation is to pull apart or divide. One draws together, the other pulls apart. Both have their place.

What This Guiding Principle Means for Your Coaching

Coaching is a catalytic relationship that is designed for the acceleration of development. It is love in action, set in a professional context. The central task of coaching is to assemble knowledge, experience and wisdom into the clearest and most effective framework to support another's growth. The foundational principle of coaching is that it brings people more deeply into the common ground of being, which is the place of unconditional love and abundance.

In a corporate sense, the ground of being is the source of our decisions affecting interactions with family, friends, customers, vendors, employees, etc. Like everything else, the coaching profession ultimately originates from the common ground of being. The coaching relationship honors and values people exactly as they are, in their absolute uniqueness and shared humanity. To do so requires a commitment to explore how this person is different from everyone else, and to develop him or her in the direction of his or her vision for life. At the same time, the coach builds awareness of, and relationship with, the common ground that this person shares with all others. It is a paradox of coaching to support both simultaneously; yet without one or the other, coaching loses its power to transform.

As a coach, living from this principle means experiencing unconditional love, honor, respect, and acceptance for those you coach, and assigning them unique value. When you coach from a place of such unconditional positive regard, you have faith that the success of those around you is ultimately good for you too; there is no need to maneuver for position by judging and criticizing. Instead, there is an enormous space for appreciation and celebration. Their success becomes a catalyst for your own. When you assume a common ground of being with those you coach, it frees you to see and honor everything about them that is magnificently unique, to trust everything that flows through you as part of the coaching process, and to be fully and completely present, telling the whole truth at all times.

Shifts in the Coach's Perspective

A variety of internal shifts occur in the coach's attitude and perspective about the coach/coachee relationship as a result of celebrating the common ground of being. Some examples of these internal shifts are listed below; please add your own based on your TeleClass and personal experience.

Disconnected From Common Ground of Being	Deeply Rooted In Common Ground of Being
Coaching is hard work	Excited about coaching
Need to look good	Focused completely on coachees
Feeling highly responsible	Conversation flows; is generative
Prescriptive	Coachees/coach receiving value
Unconnected	Glad to be with/hear coachees
Draining	Could coach all day; energizing
Worrying	Know they are okay between calls
Merging/codependent	Coachees not needed but chosen

Demonstration of Shifts in Coaching

As the coach shifts to being more truly loving, one result is external changes in behavior and as a result communication occurs in the coaching relationship. Some of these changes are listed below; please add your own based on your TeleClass and personal experience.

Disconnected From Common Ground of Being	Deeply Rooted In Common Ground of Being
Coach doing a lot of talking	More listening than talking
Not connected heart to heart	Warmth in the interaction
Focusing on *what* and *how*	*What* and *how* emerge from *who*
Judgment and evaluation	Real growth and progress
Feeling of not enough, doubt	Abundance and perfection of the moment
Coach and coachee roles rigidly defined	No need to impose will on outcome
Goal-oriented, strong accountability	Exuberant, spontaneous
Serious, strict, dry, formulaic	Great sense of humor, playful, acknowledging

Guiding Principle 2 | **People Are Inquisitive.**
Wonder, curiosity and inquiry are the source of all learning. Organizations that encourage curiosity accelerate learning and creativity.

People have a natural desire to know more, evidenced by the wonder and constant questioning of young children. Early learning begins with wonder, which turns to curiosity, then inquiry, then knowledge, which yields an ever-deeper wonder. A child's innocent inquiries have a kind of lightness and ease, and are generally rewarded by the adults around them. As children grow, however, their natural curiosity often gets shut down, as the adults who provide answers begin to feel annoyed by the constant barrage of questions and challenges. Over time, with the added impact of the focus of traditional education models, children will go from inquisitive wonder to merely seeking the right answer instead of continued questioning and staying open to exploration and all possible answers.

This principle describes the enabling power of not knowing, and finding the new learning in every situation by staying open. The more we wonder and express our curiosity, the more we can learn. It explores how we can recapture our ability to live in the world with a more open, curious perspective, accelerating our own learning by tapping into the vast resources around us. Being more inquisitive affects:

> Your relationship with yourself, as you become more comfortable with the process.
> Your relationship with others, by making you more attractive.
> Your relationship with your circumstances, by being freer to take more risks.
> Your relationship with your company or organization, by embracing collaboration and change.

The point of this principle is not to diminish the value of knowledge in any way. Expert advice is tremendously valuable in the right context, and knowledge creates a platform for effective action and further inquiry. This principle simply emphasizes an important shift in perspective, where the value you have to offer is not solely based on what you know, but also on your ability to not know with confidence—to be inquisitive, and to guide your coachees into the same self-learning behavior. Not knowing is the starting point for inquiring, receiving knowledge, and creating new learning; it is the power you bring to the coaching conversation.

Distinctions

There are subtle yet important differences in meaning between the following closely related terms. Understanding these distinctions allows you to perceive new layers of meaning and offers you new choices for shifting your thoughts, attitudes, and actions.

Wonder versus Curiosity

Wonder is a state of consciousness that is open and receptive to new learning. It is marked by feelings of amazement, marvel, and/or anticipation of unexpected events. Curiosity is the desire to know more about something. Curiosity is characterized by an array of various thoughts, posed as questions.

Curiosity versus Inquiry

Curiosity is the desire to know more about something. It shows up as an array of possible questions. Inquiry is a concrete, directed line of thought, exploring specific possibilities.

Questioning versus Inquiring

Questioning is the skill of finding answers or solutions. Inquiring is more evocative than descriptive, and leads to creative discovery—but not necessarily specific answers or solutions. Questioning is typically linear, leading to prescribed outcomes; inquiry finds its own route to unexpected results.

Inquiry versus Inquisition

Inquiry has a high level of lightness and freedom in its very nature, because it is a venture into the unknown. It is evocative and unattached to specific conclusions. Inquisition means attempting to obtain support for a pre-established theory. It is highly descriptive, precise, and evokes images of glaring lights and hot seats.

What This Guiding Principle Means for Your Coaching

One of the primary objectives in coaching is to assist coachees in recapturing their natural state of wonder and inquiry, in order to accelerate their capacity for learning. Inquisitive coaches are deep and genuine listeners, adept at staying in a place of wonder and openness and creating useful paths of inquiry for their coachees. Curious coaches are able to pose statements and questions in a way that fertilizes the ground of the creative process. By choosing to stay open and inquisitive, coaches build energy in the space that exists between them and their coachees, inviting the coachees to explore several options and positions before choosing a new belief or action.

The cycle of learning and wonder—leading to curiosity and inquiry—leading to knowledge, is the natural path to creating a larger context from which a coach and coachee can explore possibilities and options. An important aspect of coaching is to help coachees develop the ability to access their own sense of wonder and openness, so they can use, enjoy, and learn from it on a regular basis. Many adults have given up this type of thinking, opting instead for finding the right answer or solution to each situation. It is the task of the coach to continually invite the coachee into the cycle of learning by creating the environment and listening for innovation and uniqueness in the coachee's conversation.

Shifts in the Coach's Perspective

A variety of internal shifts occurs in the coach's attitude and perspective about the coach-coachee relationship as a result of becoming more truly inquisitive. Some examples of these internal shifts are listed below; please add your own based on your CoachInc.com training and personal experience.

Non-Inquisitive Coaching Mode	Highly Inquisitive Coaching Mode
Doing coaching	Being a coach
Afraid of not knowing what to say	Truly listening and eliciting
Uncomfortable with silence	Valuing silence
The coach knows	Coachee and/or coach knows
Coach feels driven and anxious	Coach feels calm, at ease
Coachee is a chore, with problems to fix	Seeing coachee as whole and magnificent
Needing to solve coachee's problems	Seeing dilemma as perfect for learning
Worried about being a perfect role model	In the process of struggling and learning
Technique of coaching is focus	Being with people is focus

Demonstration of Shifts in Coaching

As the coach shifts to being more truly inquisitive, external changes in behavior and communication occur in the coaching relationship as a result. Some of these changes are listed below; please add your own based on your CoachInc.com training and personal experience.

Non-Inquisitive Coaching Mode	Highly Inquisitive Coaching Mode
Goal-oriented questioning as main tool	Open-ended path of inquiry
Yes/no questions	Open-ended questions
Talking a lot	Preferring to listen
Effort in questioning	Childlike wonder
Questioning to arrive at a destination	Questioning to go to unknown places
Preoccupied with results	Focused on interacting with coachee
Purposeful, conscious	Fun, open, spontaneous
Striving to apply techniques, bag of tricks	Tapping into coachee's wisdom

---

Guiding Principle 3 | **People Contribute.**
Contribution based on purpose generates true fulfillment. When organizations recognize individual contributions, they grow leaders at every level.

This principle examines the nature of, and relationship between, one's life purpose and the contributions and choices that align the two. A fundamental part of human nature is the desire to be valued for who we are and what we do. When our need for meaningful contribution is met, we experience a sense of flow, and a connection to others and our purpose in the world. When meaningful contribution is missing, we experience a constant search for validation, happiness, and significance. It is important that your coachee recognizes contributions being made on a regular basis. Studies on work satisfaction consistently report that appreciation and being valued for contributions rank higher than paid wages.

The impact of our contributions is directly related to how closely they are aligned with our life purpose, and the degree to which they are consciously chosen. Life purpose is a natural expression of our unique gifts, natural talents, and inherent skills. Living on purpose brings a sense of alignment between purpose and contribution that is energizing and creative, and fosters actions that are rich and rewarding. Realizing the contribution we are already making allows us to make choices that bring our own lives into harmony as well as those of our coachees. Understanding that everyone has the ability to make extraordinary contributions profoundly affects the way we interact with others.

Distinctions

There are subtle yet important differences in meaning between the following closely related terms. Understanding these distinctions allows you to perceive new layers of meaning and offers you new choices for shifting your thoughts, attitudes and actions.

Talent versus Passion
Talent is what you are naturally good at; passion is what you love to do. We are often rewarded for expressing talent, so our innate desire to contribute often leads to doing what we are good at, not what we truly love.

Contribution versus Life Purpose
Contribution refers to what we say or do, and the resulting effect it has on others. Life purpose is what we are uniquely designed to express, the demonstration of deeply held values, interests, and passions.

Intention versus Impact

Intention is the vision or desire of an anticipated action. Impact is the way an action affects others. The intention behind an action can strongly shape the actual impact.

Potential versus Actualization

People have unlimited potential, which is their range of options for choosing their contributions. Actualization is the process of turning potential into something real.

What This Guiding Principle Means for Your Coaching

As a coach, one of your primary objectives is to assist others in becoming aware of their life purpose, so that their contributions can reflect that purpose. The entire coaching conversation can invite a coachee to discover and participate in his or her own magnificent life purpose. People tend to think about their contribution to life in future terms; as a coach, you have the opportunity to focus the conversation on the value of the immediate contribution they are making. Life purpose is often disregarded, as our affinity for comfort and familiarity can dull the edge of our natural curiosity and passion. People easily confuse their life purpose with strengths, skills, credentials, history, marketability, and anything else for which they are acknowledged. The task of a coach is to assist coachees in peeling away these layers and discovering the innate purpose that lies within. Coaches can assist their coachees to develop an internal gauge that helps them determine whether specific actions are purposeful or not. Coaches who are thoroughly grounded in their own ability to choose their contribution and to be on purpose bring power into the coaching relationship. Coaches who are not on purpose risk draining the coaching relationship of its power by attempting to get their needs met through the relationship. By being self-aware and intentional, coaches demonstrate a deeply held belief in the potential of others, and continuously find ways of adding value to the growth and development of their coachees.

Shifts in the Coach's Perspective

A variety of internal shifts occurs in the coach's attitude and perspective about the coach-coachee relationship, as a result of recognizing the coachee's need to contribute. Some examples of these internal shifts are listed below; please add your own based on your CoachInc. com training and personal experience.

Non-Contributory Coaching Mode	Highly Contributory Coaching Mode
Needs acknowledgment from coachees	Confident in own contribution
Looks for something to fix	Looks for things to acknowledge
Invested in outcome of coaching	Trusts outcome to the coachees
Concerned about keeping coachees	Concerned about being supportive
Worried about how you look or sound	Focuses on the coachees
Trying to suck validation from coachees	Self-validating, coachee-validating
Tried and true formulas	Allows creativity, anticipation
Competitive, judging	Warm and inclusive

Demonstration of Shifts in Coaching

As the coach shifts to contributing more, external changes in behavior and communication occur in the coaching relationship as a result. Some of these changes are listed below; please add your own based on your TeleClass and personal experience.

Non-Contributory Coaching Behavior	Highly Contributory Coaching Behavior
Distracted by own issues	More listening than talking
Unprepared, not on purpose	Ready for coachees
Calculating, serious	Spontaneous, playful, light
Formulaic	Eager to learn
Technical	Full of heart
Hurried, pressing	Patient, graceful
Asking for acknowledgment	Acknowledging, championing
Stepping lightly	Challenging boldly
Asking safe questions	Asking tough questions

Guiding Principle 4 | **People Grow from Connection.**
Connection is the wellspring of creativity. Collaboration is the conduit for enhancing people's strengths and generating innovative solutions.

This principle explores the dynamics and benefits of connection and how to create a highly desirable state of flow and creativity, through enhanced connections. Creation does not occur in a vacuum, with a single person or entity creating entirely on its own. Creativity is the capacity to call something into being where nothing existed before; it represents our ability to think about and respond to things in a new way in the present moment. When connection is in place, synergy emerges and creativity happens spontaneously and naturally.

Thus the focus of this principle is more on connection than creativity. Our connection with our self, others, and circumstances has a generative nature that is the source of all new things. It is how we grow. People living or working in isolation simply do not grow or develop as quickly as those having strong connections.

Connecting to one's self provides a sense of confidence and reassurance. Connecting with others generates great growth potential. Connecting to circumstances elevates awareness of everything around us. All connection feeds creativity. The more connection we experience with self, others, and circumstances, the more we feel free to deeply and authentically express our true selves. The "authentic expression of self" means acting without self-editing and being genuinely available.

Distinctions

There are subtle yet important differences in meaning between the following closely related terms. Understanding these distinctions allows you to perceive new layers of meaning and offers you new choices for shifting your thoughts, attitudes, and actions.

Artistic versus Creative
What is commonly meant by artistic is the creation of recognizable, often inspiring or beautiful works of art. Being artistic is one way of participating in the creative process. But creativity has many other manifestations; everyone is creative all the time, continuously creating with every word and deed and bringing new things into the world that never existed before.

Connection versus Network
To connect means to join, fasten, or associate with. We can choose to connect with self, others, and our circumstances. A network is a set of connections we maintain for the sake of social or business activity. The level of connection among individuals in a network directly affects the amount of meaningful creativity generated among them.

Creative versus Productive

To be creative is to make something that has not been before, something imaginative and new. To be productive is to create or make something out of existing ideas or materials. A fruit of the creative process, when combined with intention, is often a productive end.

Authenticity versus Uniqueness

Authenticity refers to being genuine and real. In coaching it refers to the degree to which we fully allow our various sides to be present and fully expressed. Uniqueness refers to our own special blend of personality ingredients, and the ways we are remarkably different from other people.

What This Guiding Principle Means for Your Coaching

Connection and creativity in a coaching relationship means entering into a conversation that is powerful, generative, and focused on the coachee. Energy flows back and forth between the participants, and the coach gains from the experience as well, but only as a by-product of the conversation. As you develop and refine your own capacity for connection with self, others, and circumstances, you support your coachees in doing the same. Building an authentic connection with your coachee opens the flow of an extraordinary exchange of information, ideas, energy, and possibilities.

As a coach, it is important that you are aware of all the roles you play, the connectors that make them up, as well as how these roles affect the energy in the conversation. Two kinds of energy dynamics frequently appear in a coaching conversation: the logjam (being stuck) energy that is blocked, and the high-energy spin (going around in circles) energy that people get caught in that goes nowhere.

Connection stoppers

> Being judgmental
> Having only one viewpoint or perspective
> Holding back the truth

Connection promoters

> Accepting your coachee unconditionally
> Cultivating a high degree of self-acceptance
> Being truly present in every moment
> Trusting your intuition

Ultimately, all parts of you influence the way you connect as a coach, and the better-integrated your parts are, the more you will have available for your coaching.

Shifts in the Coach's Perspective

A variety of internal shifts occur in the coach's attitude and perspective about the coach-coachee relationship as a result of becoming more connected. Some examples of these internal shifts are listed below; please add your own based on your TeleClass and personal experience.

Low Level of Connection/Creativity	High Level of Connection/Creativity
Forced relationship	Energized
Effort, strain in relationship	Looking forward to sessions
Coach performs	High level of enjoyment
Nothing generated	Synergy
Fixing the coachee	More responsibility from coachee
Needing the coachee	Deep appreciation of coachee
In it just for money	Recognition of own humanity

Demonstration of Shifts in Coaching

As the coach shifts to being more truly connected, external changes in behavior and communication occur in the coaching relationship as a result. Some of these changes are listed below; please add your own based on your TeleClass and personal experience

Low Level of Connection/Creativity	High Level of Connection/Creativity
Frustration with practice	Satisfaction with practice
Performing	Partnership, mutual give and take
Looking for "right" way to do it	Using techniques
Giving advice	Speaking from intuition
Labeling or mislabeling coachee	Trying things on, experimenting
Persuading	Synergy, basis for growth
Solving problems	Accomplishments beyond perceived limits

Guiding Principle 5 | **People Seek Value.**
Listening provides an ever-present access to value. Listening beyond words is the currency of valuing human capital.

People are naturally attracted to interactions that provide them with value and opportunity. This principle describes the way that value is around us at all times, and speaks to how we can attract and share it through effective listening. Everyone is listening in a conventional mode all the time. By gathering information through the senses, our attention moves in all directions, inwardly and outwardly, continuously searching for value in any form. We are always looking for something of value, something that gives us energy or adds to our experience of life.

The easiest way to increase our access to value and gain more from our interactions is to develop different types and focal points of listening. Listening to an interaction provides content and information. When we learn to listen beyond what is being said or what is apparently happening, and engage with all of our senses, we dramatically increase the exchange of value. Utilizing different types of listening puts us in a state of flow. When we are in a state of flow, we are able to add value for others and ourselves.

To truly hear another person means devoting your full attention to their communication, so that you catch the richness of it. The highest level of listening involves all your senses, as well as your heart. When interacting with others, there are different kinds of listening techniques you can use:

- Listening to the content
- Listening for underlying causes or relationships
- Listening with all your senses simultaneously

You can also direct your listening toward others, your circumstances or yourself. When you listen with your whole being, you can hear the purpose of someone's communication, and gain a genuine appreciation of who they are and where they are coming from. The more deeply you hear the whole message and incorporate it, the more value you and they receive. The more you develop your ability to gain value from anyone, anywhere, at any time, through listening, the richer your experience of life will become and the more value you can add to others.

Distinctions

There are subtle yet important differences in meaning between the following closely related terms. Understanding these distinctions allows you to perceive new layers of meaning and offers you new choices for shifting your thoughts, attitudes, and actions.

Value versus Values

Value is anything that enhances you; things that increase your ability to express who you are and do more of what you want to do. Values are ideals that are personally important and meaningful for you and direct your actions.

Hearing versus Listening

Hearing is an auditory function. Listening is an active and intentional process. In this principle listening means actively perceiving information, and can be done with the ears, or with any of our other senses.

Listening versus Attention

Listening is an action, a verb, perceiving actively and intentionally. Attention is a noun, something we give when we listen with any or all of our senses. When we add attention to hearing it becomes listening; when perfected it becomes flow.

What This Guiding Principle Means for Your Coaching

It is a coach's duty to use listening skills to serve their coachees, assisting them in gaining as much value as they can, whether it comes from themselves, circumstances, or others. Understanding and incorporating this principle into your coaching will increase your ability to give to, and receive value from, your coachees. By listening to, for, and with your coachees, you will become increasingly aware of the underlying dynamics in the conversation, which will cue you to potential sources of value. The hallmark of a great coach is to be able to do all three well, in a way that benefits the coachee.

Listening to the coachee is a skill that gives him or her the valuable experience of being heard. In addition, a seasoned coach knows that there are literally hundreds of interrelated things a coach can listen for, such as values, strengths, passions, motivators, and gaps (what's missing). And, if you're coaching groups or teams, there are even more things to listen for. Listening with all of your senses during a coaching conversation requires being highly present in everything that is going on. To do this, you cannot be preoccupied or distracted with things in your own life. The key is to develop the skill of listening for clues and indicators, then to practice listening with the coachee and trust that in the flow of the coaching conversation your intuition will signal you when there is something to listen to.

As a coach, you partner with your coachees to access value for them as well as for yourself. To be truly effective, it is extremely valuable for you to be able to move freely and easily between the different types and foci of listening. Effective listening is done in a spirit of genuine partnership—it is sharing that arises out of the mutual growth of both parties. It honors the fact that the coach and coachee are in the process together; the coach is learning and changing, just like the coachee.

Shifts in the Coach's Perspective

A variety of internal shifts occurs in the coach's attitude and perspective about the coach-coachee relationship as a result of listening more effectively for the purpose of adding value. Some examples of these internal shifts are listed below; please add your own based on your TeleClass and personal experience.

Undeveloped Listening	Highly Developed Listening
Not knowing what to do	Lots of suggestions
Rote responses	Challenging, questioning, celebrating
Resolution of problem rests with me	Resolution of problem lies with the coachee
Mechanical	Empathizing, responding to what's there
Propose alternatives	No pat answers
Jumping to solutions	Going in deep, asking for clarification
Coach talking about self	Coaching focused on coachee
Not much silence	Timing and rhythm are natural

Demonstration of Shifts in Coaching

As the coach shifts to effective listening, external changes in behavior and communication occur in the coaching relationship as a result. Some of these changes are listed below; please add your own based on your TeleClass and personal experience.

Undeveloped Listening	Highly Developed Listening
Doing a lot of coaching	Listening, being with the coachee
Giving a lot of advice	Evoking, not knowing, inquiry, wondering
Asking a lot of questions	Dance between two has rhythm
"Coming back to my point ..."	Like ice dancing or ballet, coach supports, coachee is the interesting one
Lack of action, promises broken	Acknowledgment of energy and intention
Coach's words disconnected to what coachee has just said	Focus and purpose to conversation
Technique being practiced	Genuine interest being expressed

Guiding Principle 6 | **People Act in Their Own Interest.**
Discernment reveals the opportunities in every situation. When people link the values of self-interest with self-responsibility, all their interactions improve.

It is important to begin the discussion of this guiding principle with a distinction between acting in your own self-interest, and being selfish. Without this understanding, this guiding principle cannot be fully understood, or its power released. Acting in your own self-interest means behaving and making choices based on a commitment to doing what serves you the best, with a high regard for the interests of others. Selfishness means acting exclusively in your own self-interest, usually in competition with, and sometimes at the cost of, the self-interest of others. This principle explores human motivators like needs-fulfillment and the expression and definition of values and personal payoffs as the basis for negotiating a satisfactory exchange with others.

The two main human motivators are needs and values. We act in our own interest by fulfilling our needs and expressing our values. The most basic needs are survival needs, such as food, water, and shelter. When our basic needs are met, we are more likely to act with regard to our values, like faith or citizenship, honesty, or inspiration. If it comes down to a choice, and we can't find a way to satisfy both at the same time, we may satisfy a need first, though in many cases a need may be to live true to our values. As you assimilate this principle you will gain a heightened awareness of how you have always acted in your own interest, sometimes with mixed results. You will better understand the needs and values that motivate you, and be able to act more quickly and effectively in your own best interest, and ultimately in the best interest of others as well.

When we understand that everyone around us acts from self-interest just like we do (remember the distinction between acting in self-interest and being selfish), it allows us to practice forgiveness on a moment-by-moment basis, releasing us from unproductive conversations laden with criticisms, expectations, blame, and second-guessing. You will deepen your capacity for discernment; extending your ability to stay in a state of openness, even when tempted to make judgments that close you down. As a result, you will feel less entangled in expectations and be able to participate in win-win situations more often.

When we fully understand and accept our own payoff in every situation, and also the payoff for others, we can interact with them in a more accepting way. Personal payoffs are everything that people value and seek to gain from their interactions with others. Payoffs can include enhanced reputation, personal satisfaction, excitement, power, love, and so on. A personal payoff may also be what we give to others, instead of what we gain. When we accept this reality, we see how everything we ever did worked for us, whatever the outcome, and how it continues to work now. We learn to trust that self-care is the basis of positive interactions and by staying in a state of discernment reveals the opportunities in every situation.

Distinctions

There are subtle yet important differences in meaning between the following closely related terms. Understanding these distinctions allows you to perceive new layers of meaning and offers you new choices for shifting your thoughts, attitudes, and actions.

Discernment versus Judgment

Discernment means noticing: the act of perceiving, being aware of the differences between one thing or another, one person or another. Judgment means assigning value or preference to something or someone.

Judgment versus Criticism

Judgment means placing something on a scale: good versus bad, pleasant versus unpleasant, and so on. Criticism is simply negative judgment.

Selfish versus Self-interest

Selfish means acting exclusively in your own self-interest, usually in competition with, and sometimes at the cost of, the self-interest of others. Self-interest means a commitment to doing what serves you the best, with a high regard for the interests of others.

Selfish versus Self-care

Selfish means taking care of one's self without caring about others. Selfish usually refers to the lowest levels of self-care. Self-care is looking after the needs of oneself; that may be selfish or extremely generous, depending on the kind and level of need that is being satisfied.

What This Guiding Principle Means for Your Coaching

Embracing this principle will enhance your ability as a coach to stay in a state of discernment and acceptance, when your immediate impulse might be to react or judge. You will learn the different processes and outcomes of coaching at the level of needs, wants, and integrity, and become more keenly aware of what to do when a coachee is challenged by unmet needs. You will define your own personal payoff as a coach, and use that knowledge to benefit yourself and your coachee.

As you incorporate this principle into your coaching you will be able to create richer coaching interactions based solely on the coachee's definition of self-interest in any situation. You will be able to see the payoffs your coachees are deriving from their choices, and support them in meeting their needs and expressing their values. You will sharpen your instinct to look beyond the obvious, where judgments lie, and better discern the underlying purpose of each situation.

As a coach, it is inevitable that you will have reactions and opinions about what your coachees say and do. To some degree, what your coachees hire you for are your unique judgments and reactions. What you think should happen and what you would do in a similar circumstance enters into the coaching process. It is your responsibility to own these reactions and judgments, and temper the degree to which they determine the direction and effectiveness of the conversation.

Shifts in the Coach's Perspective

A variety of internal shifts occur in the coach's attitude and perspective about the coach-coachee relationship as a result of accepting that others act in their own self-interest. Some examples of these internal shifts are listed below; please add your own based on your TeleClass and personal experience.

Unaware of Acting in Own Self-Interest	Consciously Acting in Own Self-Interest
Judgment about coachee acting in own interest	Expecting and encouraging self-interest
What do I have to learn to know how to work with this coachee?	Drawing agenda from conversation with coachee
There is an end to any process	Coachee's life always flowing, goals change as you get there
Setting up tension between needs and values	Synergistic relationship of needs/values
Focused on what went wrong or future	Learning from past but living in the present
Not honoring coachee's personal payoff	Accepting WIIFM (What's In It For Me?)

Demonstration of Shifts in Coaching

As the coach shifts to the acceptance that all people act in their own self-interest, external changes in behavior and communication occur in the coaching relationship as a result. Some of these changes are listed below; please add your own based on your TeleClass and personal experience.

Unaware of Acting in Own Self-Interest	Consciously Acting in Own Self-Interest
Bring own agenda and ideas to table	Highly developed conversation; full, enticing
Slip into consulting/advising/parenting role	No answer, direction, solution
Judgmental or critical language	Coach confident, enhancing
Challenging coachee to do it your way	Trusting expertise of the coachee
Second guessing coachee's past	Acknowledge what is true about the past and its bearing on present; building foundation from what has occurred
Stepping over coachee's self-criticism	Stop coachee's self-criticism, identify personal payoff

Guiding Principle 7 | **People Live from Their Perception.**
An inclusive, present-based perception of reality is the platform for effective action. Recognizing that people perceive reality through their own filters leads to effective communication and creates a platform for positive action.

People perceive reality through the filters of past experiences and prior learning. Each of us interprets events in a limited way, and the disparity between interpretations can lead to communication and decision-making problems. Understanding this principle will allow you to see how past experience and culture imposes definitions of reality on us, and learn the limiting result of remaining in a historical, personal comfort zone. Central to this principle is the notion that the difference between a past- present- and future orientation to personal reality is the key factor in shaping our perceptions, experiences and ultimately the quality of our actions.

Because we interpret our circumstances through the filter of what we already know, it naturally limits what we understand of ourselves and others. Our limited perception of reality is not always the same as reality, and it is easy to confuse the two. Our perceptions and interpretations are sometimes different than those of others, and this can lead to communication breakdowns, judgment, criticism, and hurt feelings. As we learn to expand our frame of reference, our conduct becomes more accurately based on a broader, more inclusive reality. This principle is about creating a larger frame of reference from which conduct can be chosen. It is about the opportunity to live a larger, more inclusive life by learning to remain in the present moment, where multiple perceptions of reality exist and inform our choices.

The present moment is really the only one that truly exists. The past has become the pages of books and the future is only an idea. The present moment can be a frightening place to dwell, because therein lies the responsibility to choose what we think and feel, and arrange our lives the way we want them to be. Our personal power also lies in the present—the true sense of living a life of value; a way of living that is based on our own infinite worth, as well as the worth of others. The central benefit of incorporating this principle is moving from a highly limited, isolated, self-centered version of reality to a more expansive, highly inclusive one, which creates a powerful present and unlimited possibility for the future.

Distinctions

There are subtle yet important differences in meaning between the following closely related terms. Understanding these distinctions allows you to perceive new layers of meaning and offers you new choices for shifting your thoughts, attitudes, and actions.

Living in the Present versus Living in the Past

Living in the present means being aware of what is happening right now, in yourself, in others, and in your circumstances. Living in the past means dwelling on the way things used to be and making choices based on a perception of what was, rather than what is.

Living in the Present versus Living in the Future

Living in the present means being aware of what is happening right now, in yourself, in others, and in your circumstances. Living in the future means envisioning how things will be different later, and making choices on an ideal—what will be, rather than what is.

Behavior versus Conduct

Behavior is what you do. Conduct is intentional behavior based on awareness, and translates into choices that more accurately represent who you are.

Perception versus Perspective

Perception is how we assimilate all the information that our five senses give us. Perspective can mean either an internal point of view or one's external vantage point.

What This Guiding Principle Means for Your Coaching

The nature of a true coaching relationship can only happen in the present. If a coach is coming from the past or spending too much time in the future, then the energy available in the moment is not being tapped. If your coaching is delving frequently into the past, you are probably doing therapy or healing, for which you are usually not trained. One of the reasons people spend so much time dwelling on the past or anticipating the future is that they are looking for measurements of self-worth. In addition to focusing on the present, we need to be present with our coachees in order to be effective—not preoccupied or distracted with our own thoughts, past or future. Showing up for a session grounded and fully present is one of the most important things a coach does. Your undivided attention is the fuel that makes the coaching engine work. You can't talk to people about their level of present focus and clarity when you are not experiencing it yourself. Everyone's perception of reality contains intrinsic value, and ultimately the environment you provide for others grows out of the way you see them. A coach is someone who has developed the insight that all people have incredible value, just by being, and holds them in unconditional high regard, in the present.

Shifts in the Coach's Perspective

A variety of internal shifts occur in the coach's attitude and perspective about the coach-coachee relationship as a result of becoming more truly present. Some examples of these internal shifts are listed below; please add your own based on your TeleClass and personal experience.

Exclusive, Small Reality	Inclusive, Larger Reality
Answers	Questions
Judgment	Unconditional positive regard
Thinking you have to know it all	Realizing that answers occur in the conversation
Making things nice	Allowing discomfort
Exclusion of ideas	Inclusion of possibilities
Outcome depends on the coach	Power to produce rests within coachee

Demonstration of Shifts in Coaching

As the coach shifts to being more present, external changes in behavior and communication occur in the coaching relationship as a result. Some of these changes are listed below; please add your own based on your TeleClass and personal experience.

Exclusive, Small Reality	Inclusive, Larger Reality
One-way coaching	Coaching is an exchange
Looking for right way to phrase things	Spontaneous conversation
Few choices in conduct	Wide range of choice in conduct
Coachees are scarce	Coachees are abundant
Problem-solving focus	Focus on vision and purpose

Guiding Principle 8 | **People Have a Choice.**
Awareness is the precursor to choice. Shifting perspectives expands awareness and reveals new choices.

Cultivating awareness creates a fuller way of being in the world. The more aware we are, the more options we have. In any given moment, people are aware of many things. Whatever captures our attention is included in our range of awareness. However, the awareness captured in this principle means more than just the focus of our attention or the sum of everything in our field of perception. It also describes a state of mind where you consciously step back and see new options and possibilities. When people are able to see multiple opportunities in a situation, they have access to more resources, greater clarity, and an increased degree of choice. From the platform of broader awareness and expanded choice, we are able to make effective decisions about life.

We all have the ability to consciously expand our range of awareness at any time by stepping into a quiet, open space. Innovation resides in that open space of life. When we step back far enough to see our own habits and patterns, we can construct new perspectives, see fresh options, and make better choices. By noticing and increasing our ability to work with the open space, we gain the kind of awareness that reduces struggle and frustration and increases our potential. By recognizing and utilizing the energy of this dynamic environment, we gain a wiser perspective on what options truly exist in the present. That kind of shift from a limited range of focus to a wider range of attention is what keeps our experiences from becoming circular, tired, and static. It gives us the freedom to rearrange parts of our lives that would otherwise seem fixed and immovable.

Incorporating this principle will allow you to shift your awareness and thus continually operate from a full abundance of choice. When coaches remain in the open place of abundance of awareness and choice, they assist their coachees in generating multiple options for themselves. When we consciously create unstructured space in our coaching, coachees become aware of their limiting beliefs, defeating patterns and choices, and can begin to generate decisions that are self-affirming and powerful. Stepping into the open space of increased awareness and innovation allows people to become unstuck and able to move forward again.

Distinctions

There are subtle yet important differences in meaning between the following closely related terms. Understanding these distinctions allows you to perceive new layers of meaning and offers you new choices for shifting your thoughts, attitudes, and actions.

Choice versus Decision

Choice is a process and a state; decision is an action. Choice is freedom among options. Decision is a commitment to a path.

Awareness versus Knowledge

Awareness is a state or high-order internal process: a precursor to knowledge. It creates the environment for clear choices and learning. Knowledge is the accumulation of what is known or can be learned about a subject. The more awareness you have, the more applicable knowledge can be.

Awareness versus Analysis

Awareness is a non-linear activity involving retreat from preconceptions, fostering openness, receiving. Awareness is about seeing options, but not feeling pressured to decide or do anything. Analysis is a more linear function involving probing and processing; it deals with choices, judgments, right versus wrong, fit or not fit. Awareness is a precursor to choice, and analysis is often a precursor to decision.

Reacting versus Responding

Reacting is making a decision without conscious awareness or analysis: a knee-jerk action that follows a stimulus. Responding is making a decision with the involvement of conscious choice. It is inclusive of alternatives, variety, exploring, abundance, and the possibility of no action at all.

What This Guiding Principle Means for Your Coaching

Coaches who have fully incorporated this principle into their own lives see opportunities for increasing awareness everywhere. As a coach, you speak up in support of your coachee's self-care and self-value, guiding her to the place where she can best make powerful choices that are consistent with her purpose and values. To get there, she must first enter a state of awareness—an open space free of restrictions and limiting perceptions.

Capitalizing on the value of this open place of retreat and re-creation is the coach's gift to the coachee. Inviting the coachee to step back and reflect allows him to discover elements of purpose, vision, and meaning for his life. A coach's perspective and support, from outside a coachee's behavior pattern, provides the coachee with valuable information he can use to enhance his awareness and perception of his options. Most people feel a little trepidation when entering into the open place of their lives because they are accustomed to clinging to familiar patterns and known outcomes. When you help them take the time to quietly look at themselves and their patterns, they may realize they are either stuck or running a maze, and their perspective and awareness of options often change dramatically.

All of us have different levels of awareness in different arenas of life. When you master this principle, you coach from your heart (feelings, intuitions, compassion), not just your head (analysis, logic, planning), and you are able to connect to your coachee's essential purpose and values, not just his or her goals and thoughts. Your own intuition and awareness are essential elements in helping others get unstuck through the coaching process. New insights into behavior, brought to light by your own awareness level, can lessen the struggle and analysis in the decision-making process, and assist your coachees to trust in their own intuition.

Shifts in the Coach's Perspective

A variety of internal shifts occur in the coach's attitude and perspective about the coach-coachee relationship as a result of becoming more aware. Some examples of these internal shifts are listed below; please add your own based on your TeleClass and personal experience.

Unaware Coaching Mode	Highly Aware Coaching Mode
Presuming that you have an answer	Creating opportunity for people to be in their open space
Fixing coachee	No urgency
Similar awareness levels	Expanded awareness
No open space	Lots of places to go
Performance anxiety	Abundance of choices
Focus on you, not coachee	Trusts in intuition, uses it
Holding position of faux strength	Being transparent
Coach's needs drive it	Totally focused on the coachee

Demonstration of Shifts in Coaching

As the coach shifts to a place of full awareness, external changes in behavior and communication occur in the coaching relationship as a result. Some of these changes are listed below; please add your own based on your TeleClass and personal experience.

Unaware Coaching Mode	Highly Aware Coaching Mode
No open space	Pauses, silences
Lots of chatter	Telling potent parables
Performing to fill the space	Allowing expectant pauses
Entertaining coachees	Coach being fully present
Humor as distraction	Playfulness, fun
Focus on coach	Focus completely on coachee
Agree about difficulty of circumstances	See new options

Guiding Principle 9 | **People Define Their Own Integrity.**
The vigilant development of the fit between calling and conduct creates integrity. Integrity for individuals comes from continuous alignment between the organization's mission, vision, and values, and their own.

Maintaining integrity is not a process of attaining perfection, but a dance of continual adjustment between who we are and what we do. This principle describes the increase in personal integrity that results from aligning calling with conduct. This is not a principle of right and wrong or good and bad. Integrity is a state of personal wholeness, well-being, and fulfillment, not something to achieve, but rather a statement of our being. It is a reflection of who you are in any moment and is the dynamic relationship you maintain between purpose and path. It is the vigilant development, or continual adjustment of the fit between our calling and conduct that allows us to sustain a high level of integrity.

Understanding this principle allows you to explore the notion of integrity as expressed through your calling—which is the path you feel compelled to walk in order to express your authentic self. Your life purpose is the collection of values that uniquely represent you and describe who you are here to be. Your calling is the path your values compel you to follow. The better we can define our life purpose the more easily we can align our actions with it, and the more well-being and fulfillment we will experience as a result of defining and living in our own integrity.

Every interaction with others, circumstances, and self, causes us to define and sometimes redefine our integrity. Challenges provide us with an opportunity to restore our integrity by finding different kinds of conduct more congruent with our calling.

Distinctions

There are subtle yet important differences in meaning between the following closely related terms. Understanding these distinctions allows you to perceive new layers of meaning and offers you new choices for shifting your thoughts, attitudes, and actions.

Values versus Calling
Our values are the things that are important to us and uniquely distinguish us from each other. Our calling is what we feel compelled to do, based on our values, and the way our purpose is made visible in the world.

Calling versus Role

Each of us takes on many different roles in life, often simultaneously. Roles are socially recognized functions that we step into. Callings are the unique paths we follow as we attempt to express our values.

Integrity versus Morality

Integrity is a measure of personal wholeness. It describes how well your actions align with your core values and represent your purpose. Integrity is different for every person. Morality refers to standards of conduct upheld by social forces such as culture or religion. These standards are typically considered to be universal.

Life Purpose versus Career

Our life purpose includes everything that we are motivated to do as an expression of our values. It includes elements of career, social life, family life, and private life. Our career is our chosen field of endeavor—not our purpose, just as our job titles do not describe who we really are as human beings.

What This Guiding Principle Means for Your Coaching

It is essential for coaches to maintain a high level of personal integrity and wholeness as a part of their profession. A coach with a lower level of integrity must default to the technique of coaching, instead of the spirit. When a coach's deep sense of purpose is reflected in the relationship and everything the coach says resonates with truth and authenticity, then the entire conversation is founded on strengthening the integrity and ultimately the purpose of both parties. Externally imposed standards can provide a framework for the development of personal standards of conduct and integrity. In the same way, a coaching relationship can support a person in building a meaningful framework for discovering and developing integrity, calling, and mature conduct.

As a coach, it is important to be continuously and vigilantly developing your own alignment between calling and conduct. When you actively develop your own integrity, you naturally stand for the integrity of others around you. This is a stepping-stone from doing coaching to being a coach.

Shifts in the Coach's Perspective

A variety of internal shifts occur in the coach's attitude and perspective about the coach-coachee relationship as a result of developing more integrity. Some examples of these internal shifts are listed below; please add your own based on your TeleClass and personal experience.

Low Coaching Integrity	High Coaching Integrity
Based in theory	Based in experience
Looking good with no substance	Vigilant development of integrity
Focus on the coach	Focus on mutual integrity
Having "arrived" as a coach	Continuously evolving, expanding
Playing the expert	Co-creating ideas

Demonstration of Shifts in Coaching

As the coach shifts to more integrity, external changes in behavior and communication occur in the coaching relationship as a result. Some of these changes are listed below; please add your own based on your TeleClass and personal experience.

Low Level of Coaching Integrity	High Level of Coaching Integrity
Only one explanation	Variety of options and perspectives
Prescribing	Creating or eliciting
Moralizing, imposing values or beliefs	Focusing on alignment of calling and conduct
Judging and evaluating	Finding value in anything
Giving advice	Creating from what's already present

Resources

Attention Readers:

Thank you for participating in the collective wisdom of Coach U. Together, we all continue to learn. Additional resources and forms can be found in *Coach U's Essential Coaching Tools: Your Complete Practice Resource* by CoachInc.com.

Attention CoachInc.com Students and Graduates:

CoachInc.com students and graduates may find additional and/or more recent resources associated with this module in the resource area of the student-only web site. If you are a student or graduate of one of CoachInc.com's ICF-accredited coach training programs, you can access these by searching under the name of the course. When the course description page appears you may find a link to the list of additional resources. Each item is a live link to its actual location on the web site. Click on the item to access the information.

Do remember to take the associated online self-test for this module once you have completed the course in person or by TeleClass. The tests are required for coach certification with the International Coach Federation. Throughout the course or anytime you find valuable resources for a particular course please feel free to add to the value of our curricula by forwarding the resource to revampteam@coachu.com.

Chapter 3

Context for Coaching

Overview

By participating in this module you will learn how to effectively craft a coaching relationship to connect strongly with your coachee. You will be able to clearly distinguish between coaching and other professions and become familiar with the coaching framework and several coaching models.

Relating, valuing, hearing, understanding, reacting, accepting, responding, honoring, intuition, discernment, corporate coaching, coaching models, and *Who/What/How*.

A Coaching Interaction

Coaching is a collaborative partnership between a coach and a willing individual that connects at the deep personal level of beliefs, values, and vision. Coaching is an interdevelopmental relationship that develops both the coach and the individual being coached, although the coach's development is a natural result of the interaction, not the focus of the connection. Coaching is a generative, ever-evolving relationship. Because you begin a coaching conversation where the coachee is at the moment, the coach can never foresee exactly what will emerge from a particular interaction. The Coaching Core Competencies give you a framework from which to work, but the true essence of the conversation is unpredictable. The coach's focus is on connecting with the coachee in a way that provides an environment of motivation and inspiration, where the coachee can be vulnerable without concern.

○ Distinctions

Go to Page > 100

Hearing versus listening, hearing versus understanding, understanding versus accepting, compassion versus empathy, modeling versus performing, typing versus judging, authentic versus truthful, and model versus framework.

○ Application

Go to Page > 103

Framework for the Coaching Interaction

Core Coaching Competency Questions
Core Coaching Competency Assessment
Who/What/How Coaching Model
CoachInc.com's 123! Coach Model
The Five-S Model
The Masterful Coach

○ Resources

Go to Page > 116

Benefits

By participating in this module you will understand the coaching skills and steps involved in relating to your coachees and establishing sustainable relationships with them. You will be able to use the process steps of relating to: value, hear, understand, react to, accept, respond, and honor your coachees effectively. You will learn how to create a safe environment for your coachees.

This course is designed to:

O Teach the framework of relating skills used in a coaching interaction to establish trust and create a safe environment for the coachee's growth

O Show the Seven-Step Relating Cycle and how the steps sequence logically and continuously throughout the coaching process

O Help you understand the choices that a coach must make at every step in the relating process

O Help you prepare to relate successfully to your coachees using self-awareness and self-questioning for wise choices

O Impart tools and methods for successful relating

O Give you important distinctions in various relating behaviors, attitudes, and language

O Inform you of the behaviors that promote relating, and those which become pitfalls, and how to avoid them

Definitions

The following are common words used to gain a better understanding of the coaching process, particularly in regard to language.

Relating: Establishing an association or a connection with a coachee. Relating is the overall term to describe a number of processes by which you connect with a coachee. Relating implies a reciprocal relationship of interaction.

Valuing: To value is to assign relative worth or importance to a coachee. It means placing him or her in high regard, giving him/her significance. It implies that the coachee has excellence and merit, regardless of behavior, attitude, circumstance, or any other influence.

Hearing: Hearing, in a coaching interaction, has two separate meanings and functions. One is the faculty or sense by which you perceive the sound, the words of the coachee—the auditory function. In the second function, hearing is the faculty or sense by which meaning is perceived—going beyond the ears and mind to the heart.

Understanding: To understand is to grasp the significance or the importance of something, to perceive the meaning, have comprehension, knowledge, and familiarity. Understanding a coachee is knowing who he or she is, and the significance of his or her words, actions and attitudes.

Reacting: To react is to act in response to something: a person, an agent, an influence, or any other stimulus. A reaction happens in response to an action, and is a natural part of being, and of coaching, especially as it impacts relating.

Accepting: To accept is to receive with approval or favor. Accepting is a validating action for a person or a thing. Accepting someone or something does not depend upon our opinion or values.

Responding: To respond is to answer or reply to behaviors or signals from an external stimulus. In coaching, responding is the visible, perceivable and processed that expresses our reactions. Valuing, hearing, understanding, reacting, and accepting are usually internal activities, while responding is the external relating the coachee can perceive.

Honoring: This is the process of conferring distinction on someone or something. It means to treat with respect, fairness, and integrity. Literally, it means to be aware, and give credit to something or someone.

Intuition: This is the perception of truth, facts, information, or other input not based on any reasoning process. It is the ability to have insight into something based on our own inner knowledge and truth, and not on external stimulus.

Discernment: This means the ability to perceive and distinguish between things, usually through intuition or other internal knowledge. It means to recognize contrasts such as good and bad, right and wrong, timely and untimely, truth and untruth, real and false.

Corporate Coaching: Corporate coaching is central to a cultural evolutionary process that shifts the landscape of the workplace from one where people receive direction from others to one where people commit to doing things about which they care passionately. Corporate coaches explore the possibilities for learning, advancement, and renewal with coachees and their organizations to realize greater results. As a result of corporate coaching, everyone wins, because organizations achieve competitive advantage when organizational members' creativity and potential are realized. Corporate coaching is centered in workplace settings including small and large businesses, non-profit organizations, human service agencies, and government agencies.

Coaching Models: Coaching is not a formulaic process. However, to uncover and learn the dynamic elements that are present in masterful coaching it is useful to break apart the process and identify the individual elements present in the interaction.

The following definitions refer to CoachInc.com's *Who/What/How* Coaching Model.

Who: The *who* refers to the coachee's inner being. It is easily understood by the coachee as the real you. The *who* often drives the what, but is not always consistent with it. Elements that make up the *who* in personal coaching are things like needs, values, desires, experiences, motivators, education, dreams, passions, and feelings. Elements that make up the *who* in business coaching are things like history, number of employees, years in business, stage of business, industry, culture, position in marketplace, key management, and geographical location.

What: Within the context of the three-step coaching model, the *what* refers to a combination of several different things. The *what* is considered to be the coachee's presenting package. It includes what the coachee wants to work on during the coaching conversation, the presenting circumstances of the situation, and the realities of the coachee's physical world. The *what* is the view from the limited outside reality, including everything that makes up that reality, such as behavior, the public self, and what we show to others. In business coaching, some *what* elements would include vision, desired outcomes, work products, and company or departmental goals.

How: The third component of the model is the set of processes, methods, and values that drive our behavior—in other words, how we do the things we do and how we are who we are. The *how* step of the three-step coaching model is demonstrated by the action and movement the coachees make as a result of the coaching interaction. Typically the how step includes strategizing, planning, goal setting, and identifying purpose and vision.

Concepts

A Coaching Interaction

Coaching is a collaborative partnership between a coach and a willing individual, which connects at the deep personal level of beliefs, values, and vision. Coaching is an interdevelopmental relationship that develops both the coach and the individual being coached although the coach's development is a natural result of the interaction and not the focus of the connection. Coaching is a generative, ever-evolving relationship. Because you begin a coaching conversation where the coachee is at the moment, the coach can never foresee exactly what will emerge from a particular interaction. The Coaching Core Competencies give you a framework from which to work, but the true essence of the conversation is unpredictable. The coach's focus is on connecting with the coachee in a way that provides an environment of motivation and inspiration, where the coachee can be vulnerable without concern.

Coaching is a body of knowledge, a framework, and a style of relating that focuses on the development of human potential.

Coaching is one of the most fascinating and demanding professions that exists; being an effective coach requires much more than just knowledge and techniques. A coach must skillfully create a connection with another human being in a profound manner. Coaching does not happen when the coach tells others what to do or think. Instead, coaching occurs when a person is given an opportunity to think out loud and create possibilities with his or her collaborative partner, the coach.

The Process of Relating

The coaching process requires more than just information, expertise, and support. Sustainable success depends on a strong relationship between you and the coachee, one that can be trusted during times of extraordinary growth or challenge. Connecting well to coachees is at the heart of every coaching interaction. A good relationship between you and the coachee will speed and maximize successful results for the coachee. A stronger connection and a higher degree of relating results in more effective coaching.

Relating is all about communicating. It is about establishing the lines of transmission, clear of static and interference, between you and the coachee. It is the establishment of a connection and understanding, rooted in your desire to serve the coachee effectively. To relate to someone is to share a sense of commonality. The greatest, and perhaps sometimes only, platform of commonality in the coaching relationship is the coachee's success. Relating is only successful when there is unconditional positive regard for the coachee.

Guiding Principle 4 | People Grow From Connection.
Collaboration is a conduit for enhancing people's strengths and generating innovative solutions.

Simply stated, relating is about who and how to be with your coachee in order to establish the connection needed to best support his or her success.

Basic Best Practices of Relating

Basic common-sense practices of relating include the following.

○ Be a model in every way.

○ Show more compassion than you think necessary.

○ Work on developing a model relationship.

○ Be engaged in curiosity, wonder, and excitement about the coachee's agenda.

○ Empathize; don't sympathize just to make them feel better.

○ Understand who the coachee is, beyond what he or she does or says.

○ Give the coachee what he or she needs, not what you need for them.

○ Match the coachee's mood and language.

○ Identify the coachee's condition quickly, if possible, to save time and relate better.

○ Show that you care; don't just talk about it.

○ Want more for this person than he or she wants for him or herself, and share it.

How is Coaching Different?

As a coach, it is important to understand the different dimensions of your role, and to see clearly that which lies outside your realm of professional expertise. For example, some lines of inquiry can lead you into a therapeutic relationship; others can lead you into a consulting or parenting role. Each discipline requires a different skill set; gaining mastery in one does not imply mastery in others. It is just as important to define the conversations you will *not* have as the ones you will. The focus of other professions is typically on the knowledge the professional brings to the conversation. Coaching works best when the focus rests upon the coachee. A coaching conversation is most productive when the coachee, not the coach, does most of the talking.

The coaching profession shares much in common with many other professions. Each profession that is focused on developing human potential and possibility will have crossover with the core competencies of coaching. Also, many professions have adopted a coach approach to their specific delivery by developing coaching skills and utilizing various coaching methods in their work. This obscures the line between coaching and other professions even further. As with many concepts covered in the curriculum, the intention of this discussion is to provide a framework from which to work, not to limit or box in the coaching profession or any other profession.

It could be said that all coaching is personal because the common element is the relationship between the coach and coachee and the intended development of human potential. Business and corporate coaches use different language, methods, and technologies to support the coaching process in organizations, but the result is the further development of the human being. A way to consider the differentiation between personal coaching, and business and corporate coaching, is to look at who benefits from the coaching, as well as the way the value and effectiveness of the coaching is measured or assessed.

Consider the following definitions:

Personal Coaching

Personal coaching is a unique and powerful form of human interaction where the agreed purpose of the interaction is the development of one individual, the coachee. The coach is focused on relating with and developing the coachee while taking positive steps toward realizing the coachee's vision.

Business Coaching

In business coaching, we are referring to the small business with few employees or offices. In this environment, the needs of the business often drive the priority of the coaching. The primary beneficiary of the coaching is the business, although the individual benefits within the context of how his or her development impacts the success of the business. The coaching success is often measured by increased performance and contribution.

Corporate Coaching

Corporate coaching is focused in larger corporations where there can be a matrix of relationships to consider. The ultimate benefactor is the corporation, which gains an increased competitive advantage because of the realized potential of the individuals. The individual may also benefit, but often times the value gained from the coaching relationship is directly related to the corporate initiative.

Executive Coaching

Executive coaching is a subset of corporate coaching, focused specifically on executives and management. The focus is remedial or developmental and includes issues such as effective leadership, empowerment, and delegation. And, just like with corporate coaching, there is benefit to the individual but within the context of the agreed-upon development for the good of the organization.

To add further clarity to the role of the coach, consider the following distinctions:

Coaching versus Consulting

Coaching emphasizes the coachee's responsibility for the results he or she receives from coaching and focuses as much on whom the coachee needs to be or become as what business practices need to be done differently. A consultant is employed to deliver an end result that meets a specific need or goal. The consultant takes responsibility for the project and is a specialist with expertise in a given situation or industry, providing content and expert knowledge. A consultant focuses on what needs to be accomplished to improve the business.

Coaching versus Therapy

Therapy focuses on the life an individual is living as related to past, often childhood issues. Therapy focuses on accompanying feelings and emotions, patterns of behavior and any self-destructive tendencies. A typical outcome of therapy is healing the individual, the creation of more useful and healthy coping skills, and dealing with current issues and challenges. Coaching focuses on what a person wants, beginning in the present and moving forward, developing the person to engage life with new behaviors and ultimately to achieve his or her definition of success. It can be useful for the coachee to access information or knowledge from the past in order to identify past patterns of behavior that do not produce the preferred outcome. A succinct way of identifying the line between coaching and therapy is that if a coachee's past is an issue he or she may benefit from therapy, but if the past is a fact, he or she is coachable.

Coaching versus Mentoring

A mentor is an expert with knowledge in a particular field or within a particular company who can guide others to move forward within the company or field by benefiting from his or her experience. A coach is an expert on the development of people in general, and helps people move forward on their own unique path that may be very different from that of the coach.

Coaching Models

Throughout the CoachInc.com curriculum you will be introduced to many different coaching models. One of the values of studying and applying coaching models is to begin to give depth to your coaching and to unravel some of what creates mastery of the coaching conversation. As we have discussed previously, agreeing and adhering to Coaching Ethics and using the Core Competencies as a framework for your coaching conversations will support you in remaining in a coaching interaction rather than compromising the relationship by combining the responsibilities of others' roles. Utilizing different coaching models will help determine what is included in your actual conversations.

Models are to be used as tools included in your coaching toolbox that you can access during any coaching interaction. All models have identifiable steps, but none are meant to be truly linear in nature. You can start coaching at any entry point in a model. For example, you may begin with a middle step presented in the model and then repeat the first two steps several times before moving on. Coaching models can be viewed as cues from a director, not scripts.

You may be very conscious of a particular model at play through your conversation, but it is not necessary or even valuable for a coachee to be aware of the framework. You never want to force the coachee into a particular coaching model during your conversation, but instead allow the model to evolve from the conversation. You will want to practice the various coaching models until the steps of the model are familiar and you are fluid in using them.

Distinctions

There are subtle yet important differences in meaning between the following closely related terms. Understanding these distinctions allows you to perceive new layers of meaning and offers you new choices for shifting your thoughts, attitudes, and actions.

Hearing versus Listening

In the context of this module, hearing implies two ways of perceiving what a coachee is saying. One is the auditory function of receiving the actual words the coachee is speaking. In the second function, hearing is the faculty or sense by which meaning is perceived—going beyond the ears and mind to the heart. Careful listening is what connects these two functions. We hear with our ears, listen and process with our mind, in order to hear with our heart. Listening is not as comprehensive as hearing with our heart.

Hearing versus Understanding

To hear with the heart is to actually feel what is said, and perceive the meaning behind the words. To understand is to know and acknowledge the importance or significance of what you have perceived through hearing. When you understand a person, a two-way connection is established, which permits a flow of information, empathy, love, feelings, energy, etc., between both parties. Understanding should become effortless for the master coach.

Understanding versus Accepting

Understanding involves grasping the significance of something you have heard through careful listening, and does not necessarily imply acceptance. Accepting something or someone is a choice to allow it and receive it favorably, without judgment or personal bias. Accepting does not always mean agreeing with something or someone, but allowing it to be true for another person, free of your own personal filters. Accepting what you know is true for others is very important in the relating cycle, because you may be the only person to do this in your coachee's life. Accepting frees a coachee to be honest, open and authentic.

Compassion versus Empathy

Compassion is the perceivable expression of concern, kindness, consideration, and even sympathy for someone. When you show compassion, you are giving him or her a gift. Showing honest compassion is free of personal experience or identification with the person and his or her situation. Empathy is your identification with someone and their experiences, their feelings and their thoughts because you have experienced them as well. Empathy is a more passive approach to caring which, while useful, does not give the recipient all that much. Compassion is a mindset and not dependent on your experiences. Compassion is an essential skill in coaching, but only occurs when one has no need whatsoever to be compared to another, or feel threatened or influenced by that person.

Modeling versus Performing

When you have good communication, living, and relating skills, you are naturally a model for others. Modeling involves being authentic. You are just being yourself and others see you as someone worth emulating or aspiring to become more like. If, however, you are trying to be a model, then most likely you are performing, not being natural and authentic. Most people can tell the difference, especially in the long run. Performing is about trying to be someone else. Modeling is being you.

Typing versus Judging

Coaching involves a fair amount of identifying and typing of coachees and their behavior. Typing is a non-judgmental statement of the facts, using a shorthand way of describing a situation or behavior. For example, you may type someone as being controlling, or enterprising. Typing turns into labeling and judging when any kind of negative connotation is placed on the type. You may tend to judge when you have not fully and honestly responded to coachees, or have not related to them without bias.

Authentic versus Truthful

Being authentic is being yourself, who you really are, without performing or trying to be someone else. An authentic person knows whether or not another person is authentic. Being truthful is being honest, telling the truth, living the truth, and living honest to your values.

Model versus Framework

Just as when a house is being built, the frame is the first evidence that a structure is being built. Next the walls are built and the roof is put on. Finally the inside is decorated to the buyer's taste. This analogy can be used for the coaching conversation. The Core Competencies are the framework; the walls and roof are coaching models. The actual conversation you have with a coachee is like decorating the house to the taste of the buyer.

Application

Framework for the Coaching Interaction

As with coaching ethics, the value and meaning of the core coaching competencies are not realized until put into action in an authentic coaching conversation. We have mentioned that coaching is not an intellectual process that can be learned separately from the practice of coaching. You may be able to learn some important definitions and facts about coaching, but the actual practice of coaching is where the true learning occurs. We suggest that you practice coaching using the framework of the coaching competencies as often as possible and in a variety of circumstances to truly develop your skills, and understand and apply the knowledge base.

Core Coaching Competency Questions

Consider the following questions in regard to applying the Core Coaching Competencies:

1. What is important to you about the Core Coaching Competencies?

2. What one competency seems most significant to you and why?

3. What is one responsibility you have as a coach that is new information to you?

4. What will be important for you to consider when you are determining whether a potential coachee is an effective match with your coaching method?

5. Coaches who work with managers and executives seek to further the potential of their coachees by focusing on the person being coached and supporting his or her development and capabilities.
   a. *What is different about the approach in a business relationship?*
   b. *What is important about this?*
   c. *How does a coach do this?*
   d. *What is challenging to you about this?*

6. Establishing trust and intimacy with a coachee.
   a. *Why is this key for the coaching relationship to work well?*
   b. *How do you establish trust?*
   c. *What role does confidentiality play?*
   d. *If the organization pays you as a coach, what significance does that have?*

7. Attends to the client and the coachee's agenda, and not to the coach's agenda for the coachee.
   a. *What is vital about this to a coach?*
   b. *What might get in your way of doing this?*

8. Encourages, accepts, explores and reinforces the coachee's expression of feelings.
   a. *What concerns do you have about this?*
   b. *What are the boundaries of appropriate sharing in a coaching conversation?*

9. List the important characteristics of a coaching relationship.

10. What must you work on to become a more effective coach?

Following is a competency assessment that we intend you to use in a variety of ways. First, you will want to score yourself on the assessment now, with your current understanding of the competencies. After completing more of your course work you will want to revisit the assessment and score yourself again. With more information, you may find that your original score may go down before it goes back up. And finally, your mentor coach may find the assessment useful when reviewing your coaching session. Of course, you will need to get written permission from your coachee for these reviews.

Core Coaching Competency Assessment

On the following assessment of your competencies, honestly score your present state of mastery by circling the appropriate number. Use the following key:

1. Very little mastery.
2. Some mastery.
3. Average mastery.
4. Above-average mastery.
5. Strong mastery.

Competencies					
Setting the Foundation					
1. Meeting ethical guidelines and professional standards.	1	2	3	4	5
2. Establishing the coaching agreement.	1	2	3	4	5
Co-Creating the Relationship					
3. Establishing trust and intimacy with the client.	1	2	3	4	5
4. Coaching Presence.	1	2	3	4	5
Communicating Effectively					
5. Contextual Listening.	1	2	3	4	5
6. Powerful Questioning.	1	2	3	4	5
7. Direct Communication.	1	2	3	4	5
Facilitating Learning and Results					
8. Creating Awareness.	1	2	3	4	5
9. Designing Actions.	1	2	3	4	5
10. Planning and Goal Setting.	1	2	3	4	5
11. Managing Progress and Accountability.	1	2	3	4	5

Who / What / How Coaching Model

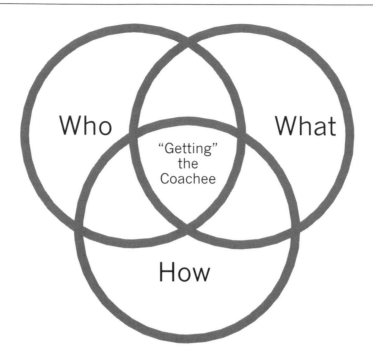

This model represents who the coachee is, what he or she wants or is facing, and how he or she intends to get the desired results.

The *Who*

The *Who* is most easily understood as the real person or organization. It is the inner spirit that truly motivates our lives and the life of an organization. One of the best ways to help a coachee become more successful is to expand who he or she is.

The *What*

In a coaching conversation the *What* is typically comprised of what the coachee says he or she wants. It is the story that is told and where that story leads. The coach helps a coachee clarify what he or she wants.

The *How*

The third component of the model is how the coachee will get what he or she truly wants, once his or her wants are aligned with who he or she is, and what is the clearest, most expeditious path for the coachee to take. The key to the most successful coaching is developing the *How* strategy.

Often in a coaching interaction, the coach is tempted by the two step coaching model. Sometimes, coachees are so convincing in their stories, and justifying why they should have exactly what they say they want, the coach will move to solving the presenting problem, skipping over the discovery of the true who in the scenario. Often, when new in coaching, the *Who* step is overlooked by the focus on providing value. Don't forget the value in reflecting back to the coachee a clearer picture of who he or she truly is rather than being a problem solver. Supporting the coachee in coming to his or her own solutions is clearly a step in the coaching process but it is not the only value step.

Using the *Who/What/How* Model, an initial starting place in a coaching interaction is exploring what the coachee wants. In some cases the story coachees will tell you will reveal rather clearly what they want, or at least, you think they do. Consider the follow scenario:

Emily is a single mother, with one young daughter. She works full-time as a graphic designer for a large corporation and loves what she is doing. She is finding that balancing work and time with her daughter has become quite a challenge. She would love to spend more time at home; however she must also pay for the necessities of life.

Emily starts her coaching session with the following:

"I would really like to focus our session today on trying to figure out how I can balance my life a little better. My daughter is growing up so fast and I feel that I am missing out on it, yet in order to give her the best possible life, I need to work. I love my job; the people I work with are great. Maybe I'm asking for the best of both worlds, time with my daughter and a fulfilling job; I just don't see how I can have both."

What does Emily really want?

List three qualities of who Emily is revealed through this scenario.

Brainstorm three ideas on how Emily might have both. Step out of the box and stretch yourself.

Diane is an accomplished leader. You have been her coach for the past two years, working in the trenches with her on reaching the top of her potential. She has worked very hard, and is beginning to wonder what is next in her life.

In your next session she begins to articulate that she is ready for something else. She says, "You know what? I'm discovering that this isn't as rewarding as I thought it would be. I'm making good money, I'm sought out for my expertise and I've accomplished about as much as I can here. Life is pretty good, but isn't there more to life than this?"

What is your first response based on the CoachInc.com *Who/What/How* Coaching Model?

What are some appropriate *Who* based questions?

What are some appropriate *What* based questions?

CoachInc.com's 123! Coach Model

You can use this particular model in literally any situation—whether you're coaching or sitting at the dinner table with your family. This model focuses on making sure that your coachee feels heard and understood. You have an opportunity to learn more, much more, while giving the other person some space to arrive at his or her own conclusions and strategies.

Listen

When we listen to our coachees, we actively listen to what is being said and what isn't being said. We allow our coachees to fully express themselves.

Learn

A coach can learn about the situation, our coachee's perspective, our coachee's previous experience with the situation, and more when we listen. When we immediately offer solutions, we inadvertently disempower our coachees. Rather than jumping in with advice or a solution we can encourage our coachees to evaluate the situation more closely. Here, you and the coachee both have a great opportunity to learn more so that you can address the source of the problem rather than the symptoms that are present.

Empower

Once you and your coachee have noticeably moved forward in the discussion, it's important to respond to the situation. Now would be a good time to further empower your coachee before aligning on a course of action. Confirm that he or she is on the right path, that you understand where he or she is coming from and, briefly, what your perspective is or what your experience has been with something similar in the past.

Recap

The recap is a necessary step. As you may have covered a lot of ground, or perhaps your coachee has jumped forward as a result of having the space to think aloud, it's crucial that you both know where you are currently before you align on a course of action. You will want to avoid a situation where in the end you discover that you're talking about two different things. The objective of recapping is for both you and the coachee to be clear.

Action

Accountability plays an important role in the coaching relationship. Coachees decide to hire a coach to support them in achieving their goals in the least amount of time and with the least amount of energy. Your coachees will expect you to keep them on track to reach their goals and meet their commitments, as well as to inquire into the status of their progress.

After you have thoroughly explored the current situation or issue, your coachee feels empowered and supported, and you have summarized and confirmed that you are both on the same page; it's time to align on a sound course of action. This can be to identify a short- or long-term strategy with associated action steps and for the coachee to commit to what he or she will do in the short term, by next week.

Listen:

Ways to Demonstrate Listening
- Remain silent.
- Say "okay" or "go on."
- Remain silent even if there is something you could say.
- Share—"hmmm mmmm."

Discussion Questions

1. How long should you listen before saying something?
2. How can you listen quietly yet still have the coachee know that you're there?
3. Why do we talk so much instead of listening?
4. What is a good listen/talk ratio for you to respect?

Learn:

Ways to Facilitate Learning
- Mirror back what the coachee has shared.
- Ask a great question.
- Inquire whether the coachee meant what he or she said.
- Find out if the coachee would handle the situation the same in the future.
- Admit when the coachee has lost you.
- Share what is obvious to you.

Discussion Questions

1. How hard should or can you push?
2. What if the coachee isn't telling the truth?
3. What questions might you ask?

Empower:

Ways to Empower
- Acknowledge the coachee.
- Make your coachees right.
- Share your inklings.
- Give your point of view.
- Draw a conclusion.

Discussion Questions

1. How do you know when a coachee is empowered or disempowered?
2. Why is it so important to make a coachee right, no matter what?
3. When is giving advice all right?

Recap:

What to Include in a Recap
- The symptom of the problem.
- The real problem.
- The source of the problem.
- The real opportunity versus the perceived opportunity.
- The truth of the situation versus just the facts.

- The priority of this problem or opportunity.
- The degree of commitment or readiness to act/resolve.
- The real win or success for the coachee, not just the result produced or problem solved.

Discussion Questions

1. What happens when the coachee gets really clear?
2. What physical, emotional, and intellectual changes result from this?
3. How are these changes beneficial to both you and the coachee?
4. What's wrong with being really positive or helping the coachee to interpret the facts as being positive, when in fact they are not?

Action:

What to Consider

- Why this action is important.
- What this action will accomplish.
- Other commitments or conflicts that may serve as obstacles.
- If the action takes coachee out of his or her comfort zone and how far.
- If these actions and strategies support the coachee's short- and long-term goals.
- If this is indeed the best action and strategy for this specific coachee.
- If the coachee owns and believes in it, or is willing to experiment.
- How this action will benefit the coachee.
- Who the coachee really is, underneath it all.

Discussion Questions

1. Who should determine the action steps and fieldwork, the coach or the coachee?
2. Why is it important that the coachee really owns or believes in the action to which he or she is committing?
3. How might you share the distinction "under-promise versus over-deliver" with a coachee?
4. What do you do when you know the coachee can commit to taking more action in a given week?
5. What if your coachee fails to take a committed action after several weeks?

The Five-S Model

The Five-S Model is helpful in crafting your approach to a coaching interaction. It provides a comprehensive structure within which you can gather information and get to the root cause of the coachee's issues. Learning to listen for these five elements will help dictate where you move the focus in any conversation.

○ Shifts: What is the lasting change the coachee wants to achieve?

○ Solution: What direction do I move the coachee toward?

○ Source: Why is this happening?

○ Situations: What is really happening?

○ Symptoms: What do I see, sense, or hear?

Symptoms

These are the coachee's outward signs, words, or actions that give you a clue as to what the coachee is really feeling, what is motivating him or her, or what is getting in the way of the coachee accomplishing his or her goals. Although it may seem obvious to you what the symptom means, you must always check out your assumption with the coachee for clarity. There are literally hundreds of symptoms you look for during the coaching process. For example:

Symptom	May Indicate
Intense effort	Strong desire to succeed
Forgetting appointments	Emotional upset
Repeated failure at completing items	Unrealistic goals, lack of motivation, or a need for skill building
No progress	Underlying mental health issue
Talking non-stop	Lack of focus, fear of silence, or trying to avoid telling the truth to self or the coach

Although it may seem obvious to you what the coachee means, you must always check out your assumption with the coachee for clarity.

Situations

A coachee's situation is a combination of all the factors impacting his or her current behavior and the results he or she is getting. Learning to use a word or descriptor to identify a situation helps the coachee to own his or her behavior as normal, and therefore something that can be changed. For example:

- By helping the coachee to identify that he or she is overstating their qualifications each time they go for an interview, he or she can bring their resume in line with his or her actual experience.
- By helping the coachee see that he or she continues to tolerate the presence of annoying people in his or her life and are thus wasting precious time, he or she can begin to reevaluate their relationships and decide which ones to keep or to let go.

Sources

Sources are the *why* of the way we do things. There are at least twenty sources, and when you learn how to match symptoms with sources, *why* people do things (or don't do things) can become quite obvious. With this new clarity you can immediately focus the coachee on the source, instead of chasing symptoms. For example:

- A person may be experiencing communication mishaps with others (*what* is happening) because he or she lacks the confidence to speak clearly for themselves (*why* it is happening). By working on building self-confidence you can more quickly address the communication failures.

Coachees are looking for changes—they want the coach to be skillful at directing them in achieving good outcomes.

Solutions

Many things are discussed in a coaching conversation, and coachees rely on your skills to direct the conversation towards assisting them in finding ways to realize their goals. Coachees are looking for change, and want you to be skillful at directing them in achieving good outcomes. When issues come up in a coaching interaction, it is important that you listen for those issues that relate to the coachee's goals and move the conversation toward those topics. For example:

- If a coachee's goal is to achieve more financial freedom, listen for ideas, opportunities, and places where the coachee could put his or her energy to produce more wealth and/or teach him or her to more prudently manage their money.

Shifts

You can use various listening tools to help a coachee shift into a more productive life, in alignment with his or her values. Shifts are internal changes of ways of thinking that support sustainable changes in behavior. For example:

- Coachees might go on a diet to lose weight, a change which may or may not be sustained, or they could embrace a new vision of their own wellness and begin to exercise, modify their eating habits, and rid themselves of addictions, making a permanent shift in lifestyle.
- A coachee might get a new job with more money (a change), or he or she might begin to see him or herself as capable of creating abundance and begin to attract people and opportunities that move them into more prosperous arenas of business and living (a shift).

The Masterful Coach

Think of a leader—perhaps a former or current manager, coach, mentor, or supervisor, who demonstrated outstanding leadership qualities. What qualities made this leader outstanding? Consciously or unconsciously we often model ourselves after great leaders who we have observed in action. As coaches, we can continually observe great leaders in action and develop skills to enhance our own leadership abilities. We may also recognize that while we observe our models of leadership, our coachees may be modeling themselves after our leadership qualities.

The masterful coach is:

- *Highly competent in establishing relationships.* Is able to easily form partnerships of a collaborative nature.
- *A creator of coachable environments.* Is able to quickly set the stage for changes where the coachee is willing to shift from one frame of reference or behavior to another.
- *A quick reader of human context.* Is able to quickly determine the human and/or business context a person brings to the table in order to assist in discovering underlying options. The coach holds great respect for diverse styles.
- *A masterful listener.* Listens with ego and agenda set aside in order to understand both what is and isn't being said.
- *A masterful facilitator of discovery.* Is able to ask questions that assist coachees in drawing options, making choices, and analyzing consequences of their decisions and behaviors.
- *A laser articulator of information.* Conveys messages with the least amount of words in the most respectful way. Always speaks the truth.

- *An efficient and effective gap delineator and bridger.* Can have others see both where they are and where they want to be, then quickly coach them to build their own bridges over the gaps.
- *A stretch requester.* Will ask more of others than they ask of themselves, which sets up possibility thinking and promotes development of one's full potential.
- *A consciously competent celebrator of human accomplishment.* Can genuinely endorse and acknowledge others.
- *Able to apply the best of being a teacher, trainer, facilitator, advisor, consultant, mentor, or leader, depending upon the need of the coachee.*

Resources

Attention Readers:

Thank you for participating in the collective wisdom of Coach U. Together, we all continue to learn. Additional resources and forms can be found in *Coach U's Essential Coaching Tools: Your Complete Practice Resource* by CoachInc.com.

Attention CoachInc.com Students and Graduates:

CoachInc.com students and graduates may find additional and/or more recent resources associated with this module in the resource area of the student-only web site. If you are a student or graduate of one of CoachInc.com's ICF-accredited coach training programs, you can access these by searching under the name of the course. When the course description page appears you may find a link to the list of additional resources. Each item is a live link to its actual location on the web site. Click on the item to access the information.

Do remember to take the associated online self-test for this module once you have completed the course in person or by TeleClass. The tests are required for coach certification with the International Coach Federation. Throughout the course or anytime you find valuable resources for a particular course please feel free to add to the value of our curricula by forwarding the resource to revampteam@coachu.com.

Competency Assessment

On the following assessment of your competencies, honestly score your present state of mastery by circling the appropriate number. Use the following key:

1. Very little mastery.
2. Some mastery.
3. Average mastery.
4. Above-average mastery.
5. Strong mastery.

Competencies					
Setting the Foundation					
1. Meeting ethical guidelines and professional standards.	1	2	3	4	5
2. Establishing the coaching agreement.	1	2	3	4	5
Co-Creating the Relationship					
3. Establishing trust and intimacy with the client.	1	2	3	4	5
4. Coaching Presence.	1	2	3	4	5
Communicating Effectively					
5. Contextual Listening.	1	2	3	4	5
6. Powerful Questioning.	1	2	3	4	5
7. Direct Communication.	1	2	3	4	5
Facilitating Learning and Results					
8. Creating Awareness.	1	2	3	4	5
9. Designing Actions.	1	2	3	4	5
10. Planning and Goal Setting.	1	2	3	4	5
11. Managing Progress and Accountability.	1	2	3	4	5

Part 2
Core Skills

Chapter 4

Listening

Overview

○ Benefits   Go to Page > 125

By participating in this module you will increase your understanding of the common elements of listening effectively to your coachees. You will be able to use various listening skills to know what to listen for, avoid listening pitfalls, and use the skill that is most appropriate at any place in a coaching conversation. By participating in this module you will be able to move freely and easily between the different types and focuses of listening. You will also learn to listen for clues that indicate where a person is on his or her path of development, and whether the issues presented are best referred to another type of professional.

○ Definitions   Go to Page > 126

Symptom, motivation, therapy, context, solution, intuition, discernment, shift, flow, reflecting, legacy, efficacy, tracking, integrity, values, needs, and wants.

○ Concepts   Go to Page > 128

At the heart of good coaching is the exchange of value between you and the coachee, facilitated through the listening process. Solid listening skills are a part of the toolbox of an effective coach. Listening to another person for the purpose of his or her growth involves knowing how and when to listen and respond, what to listen to and for, what the coachee's words mean, and when it's appropriate to move the conversation in another direction. Listening is more of an art than a science; you cannot learn to listen perfectly, but through intentional practice you can greatly improve your skill.

Distinctions

Hearing versus listening, listening versus attention, gist versus literal, shift versus change, values versus needs, wants versus needs, and feeling versus emotional reaction.

Application

Listening as a Coaching Skill
    Listening for Values
    Listening Realities
    Listening Behaviors: Promoters and Pitfalls

Resources

Listening Chart

Benefits

By participating in this module you will be able to move freely and easily between the different types and focuses of listening. You will be able to use the various listening skills to know how to actively listen and what to listen for, avoid listening pitfalls, and use the skill that is most appropriate at any place in a coaching conversation. You will also learn to listen for clues that indicate where a person or team is on their path of development, and whether the issues presented by an individual are best referred to another type of professional.

The material in this chapter is designed to:

O **Teach** the essential listening skills that are used in a coaching interaction to promote clarity and ensure the maximum growth of the coachee

O **Present** an overview of what to listen for in a conversation and how to move the interaction in the direction of optimal value for the coachee

O **Describe** the ways coaches listen—highlighting what a coach really does when they are listening to a coachee

O **Define** the ways in which you can listen for the alignment of the coachee's goals and personal values

O **Increase** awareness of listening realities: the fundamental truths of coachees, coaches, and coaching interactions

O **Inform** of the behaviors that promote listening, and those that become pitfalls, and how to avoid them

Definitions

The following are common words used to gain a better understanding of the coaching process, particularly in regard to listening.

Symptom: The visible expression of a condition or situation; something that indicates the presence of something else. For example, if your coachee is speaking very quickly, he or she may be upset or not sure of what to say.

Motivation: An incentive or inducement to action. For example, a coachee may work hard at improving her communication skills because she wants to be promoted at work.

Therapy: A set of specific actions performed by an educated and licensed professional for the purpose of healing a diagnosable disease or disorder. For example, you may identify that your coachee is struggling with a diagnosable and unresolved issue, like depression or anxiety, that would be better served by obtaining the services of a psychotherapist.

Context: The immediate environment, backdrop, or conditions in which something is taking place.

Solution: The answer to a particular problem, situation, challenge, or dilemma. For example, a common solution to miscommunication is to clarify what you hear the other person saying.

Intuition: The immediate understanding of truths or facts without the benefit of reasoning. For example, you may get a sense that your coachee is upset, even though, when asked, he or she says everything is fine.

Discernment: Keenness in perceiving and understanding; good judgment; shrewdness. For example, in a conversation, you may decide that a certain subject is best left for another session, due to the way your coachee is responding that day.

Shift: A dramatic, observable, permanent change in one's thoughts or behaviors.

Flow: When a person is performing an activity that is so in line with their values and passion that the activity feels effortless and powerful. For example, after you have been coaching for a while you may find that you ease into and out of the interaction with such comfort and confidence that you are not even sure how you do it or what exactly you have said.

Reflecting: In conversation, to reflect means to show back to your coachee the same message that you have received. It can also mean showing your coachee a reaction, a look, or a message that he or she just gave. For example, your coachee sighs with sadness as she tells you about her disappointment with a recent incident with her child. You respond back with a lowered quiet tone, and use soft, understated language.

Legacy: Something that a person or individual becomes known for and can be handed down from an ancestor or predecessor. For example, a coach might leave a legacy of helping by doing pro bono coaching, thereby paving the way for the next generation of coaches to embrace the same heart of generosity. Parents might leave their children a legacy in regards to a charity, social cause, or firmly held religious beliefs.

Efficacy: The power to produce a desired effect or result. For example, you might become very good at eliciting the truth from coachees, saving yourself and your coachees weeks or months of chasing after the wrong goals.

Tracking: To track your coachees in an interaction is to stay so focused on them and what they are saying that you are moving with every move they make. When they get excited, you get excited; when they speak in hushed tones, you drop your volume as well.

Integrity: Integrity is a state of personal wholeness, well-being, and fulfillment. It is not something to achieve, but rather a statement of our being. It is a reflection of who you are in any moment and is the dynamic relationship you maintain between purpose and path. It is the vigilant development, or continual adjustment, of the fit between your calling and conduct that allows you to sustain a high level of integrity.

Values: Values are ideals that are personally important and meaningful for you and draw you forward. Values are inherent in each person's make-up; we all have them. They are specific and individual, but people can share common values. For example, people often value honesty, openness, and respect in a conversation.

Needs: Needs are the emotional aspects that drive individuals. The driving force behind needs is based in human yearning for wholeness. Often, needs direct major life decisions until they are met. Needs can also sit on top of, or get in the way of, a person clearly identifying their values and living life based on those values. The kinds of needs we are discussing here go beyond the basic needs for food, air, water, and shelter to the things that a person feels they must have. For example, coachees may need to be accepted, to accomplish, to be acknowledged, to be loved, to be right or to be cared for.

Wants: To want something is to wish for it or desire it. Wants are flexible and/or optional; if you get it, great; if not, you are still okay. When your needs are met and your life is oriented to your values, your wants tend to proportionately decrease. For example, I may want to succeed in business, to have a great body, or to have a big house.

Concepts

Listening

Effective listening is at the core of good coaching. Many people take listening skills for granted. Although most of us would say that we listen to others all the time, there is a decided difference between hearing, in a conventional sense, and listening in a way that promotes the growth of another. Hearing is a sensory ability. Listening is a skill.

As discussed in Guiding Principle #5 (People Seek Value), listening provides an ever-present access to value for you and the coachee. As you learn to listen more effectively and deeply to your coachees you will become a source of value to them, and they to you. Coachee-centered listening is done in a spirit of genuine partnership; it is sharing that arises out of the mutual growth of both parties. It honors the process that you and coachee are in together.

To truly hear another person means devoting your full attention to his or her communication, so that you catch the richness of it. Truly hearing another person also includes providing questions to the speaker that support the flow of conversation and confirm mutual understanding of the content of the intended message. The highest level of listening involves all your senses, as well as your heart. When you listen with your whole being, you can hear the purpose of someone's communication, and gain a genuine appreciation of who he or she is and where he or she is coming from.

Coaches often spend more than 70 percent of their day listening. How much of that listening time is productive? Consider that all of it is absolutely essential to the successful coaching conversation. You cannot afford to miss critical information in a conversation with a coachee. Like most skills, listening requires practice and active improvement. Undisciplined listeners can lose up to 50 percent of the content of a conversation.

> **"** When people talk, listen completely.
> Most people never listen. **"** | **Ernest Hemingway**

There are many ways in which good coaches listen. Seasoned coaches hear both the words said as well as what is not said. They hear the emotions expressed. They discern the gaps between what a coachee says and the true reality. They recognize the shifts the coachee makes and listen for the developmental space the coachee is in at any given moment.

Experienced coaches have the ability to listen to their coachees in a way that assures they are heard, because coaches know the following:

- There is a distinct difference between hearing and listening.
- There is value in actively listening in a coaching interaction.
- You will not and cannot hear everything in a conversation.
- By knowing what to listen for, you can focus on the important elements of a conversation.
- Effective listening offers you options for navigating the conversation.
- Listening to your coachee frees you from having all the answers.
- Listening intentionally increases the coachee's ability to hear him- or herself.
- Listening will prevent more problems from occurring within a team environment.

It is essential to fully understand and make use of the context in which the coaching interaction takes place.

- Choose among the hundreds of things to listen for in any conversation.
- Learn to quiet the chatter in your own head.
- Value and allow silence in the coaching interaction.
- Choose the listening style that best fits the coachee.
- Listen for what the coachee can or cannot say.
- Listen for what is motivating each coachee.
- Listen to your own reactions to the coachee.
- Listen for what the team or group truly needs to succeed.

As your listening skills improve, you will learn to spot those elements in the interaction that provide you with the information you need to move your coachee forward by listening for:

- The genuineness and accuracy of your coachee's goals.
- Your coachee's true desires and wants.
- When needs, circumstances, and beliefs are blocking your coachee's success.
- What's missing in order for your coachee to succeed.
- When the coachee has had a win or shift that has been unrecognized.
- How you and your coachee are growing in the relationship.

Talented coaches use a variety of listening skills to demonstrate their interest in their coachees and to encourage them to share more in an interaction. This is done by:

- Discerning and identifying certain distinguishing characteristics unique to your coachee.
- Creatively reflecting back what the coachee is saying.
- Revealing your intuition to the advantage of the coachee.
- Clarifying communication to get at the heart or truth of the matter.
- Prompting coachees to share more and thus achieve more focus.

Distinctions

There are subtle yet important differences in meaning between the following closely related terms. Understanding these distinctions allows you to perceive new layers of meaning and offers you new choices for shifting your thoughts, attitudes, and actions.

Hearing versus Listening

Hearing is an auditory function. Listening is an active and intentional process. Listening means actively perceiving information, and can be done with the ears or with any of our other senses.

Listening versus Attention

Listening is an action, something we do all the time. Attention is a noun, something we give when we listen with any or all of our senses. When we add attention to hearing it becomes listening; when perfected it becomes flow.

Gist versus Literal

Gist is the term used to describe the general theme, overview, or idea of a conversation. Literal refers to the exact words, terms, facts, phrases, or tone of a communication. Rather than listening too hard for the facts or details of what the coachee is saying, listen instead for the gist of what he or she says—what they mean. Respond to the spirit of the conversation, not just the individual elements of it. Get, don't acquire, what is being said.

Shift versus Change

Shifts are internal movements at the core of an individual; they represent a deep transformation in a person's way of thinking, approach, understanding, awareness, and beliefs. Change is often environmentally induced and can be fleeting; changing usually involves behavior, focus, or one's responses. Shifts are permanent; changes are often temporary. Listen to see if the coachee is shifting or changing.

Values versus Needs

Values are ideals that are personally important and meaningful for you, and naturally draw you forward. Needs often hold more urgency and are what drives us, whether or not we are aware of it. A coachee's needs may masquerade as values. Values bring joy; needs satiate. For example, a coachee may say he or she values notoriety when what they really value is contribution. Listen for what's motivating your coachee, and coach accordingly.

Wants versus Needs

To want something is to wish for it, or desire it. Wants are flexible and/or optional. Needs tend to come before wants and hold more urgency. For example, a coachee may say he or she wants a new job, bigger house, or fuller bank account, but the compelling need is a greater sense of security or safety.

Feeling versus Emotional Reaction

Feelings are bodily sensations such as fear, anxiety, joy, anger, curiosity, resentment, delight, frustration, and many more. Feelings are a rich part of the human experience. Emotional reaction is a knee-jerk response to a situation that is driven by old conditioning, and generally takes place outside of a person's awareness. As one develops self-awareness and self-regulation, he or she tends to have fewer emotional reactions and more genuine feelings. Listen for the contrast between the genuine feelings of a coachee and an immediate emotional reaction.

Application

Listening as a Coaching Skill

In conversation, individuals often form conclusions quickly through an unconscious process. These conclusions about the speaker, the issues being discussed, the circumstances of the conversation, and so on, are often subjective interpretations based on selective information. Within the context of the conversation the listener selects data that is brought forth through the senses, attaches meaning to it, aligns the conclusions with beliefs and values, and takes action, based on the output of this rapid thought process. During this process, the listener may not hear valuable information that the speaker is sharing because he or she is so preoccupied with the conclusions. The speaker and the listener can quickly develop different interpretations of a common conversation.

Listening is an active job function when performed correctly. Active listeners are completely tuned into the speaker's words, and as a coach, active listening is a prerequisite. How well you pay attention to what people tell you will determine to a great extent the quality of information that you can learn from them. Therefore active listening is essential to a productive work environment and successful professional relationships.

There are many layers to a coaching conversation beyond the spoken words. Often a coach must peel back the layers to help the coachee discover truth and possibilities. Just listening to what the coachee says (the words) is not enough to propel the paradigm shifts in the coachee's life. A coach must listen to the coachee in the context of the particular coaching conversation. In addition to the spoken words, the coach listens for the issues the coachee is facing, the uniqueness of the individual, the barriers, and the gaps that present appropriate coaching opportunities.

[handwritten margin note: authentic vs. chatting]

❝ It was hard to get a conversation going because everyone was talking so much. ❞ | **Yogi Berra**

Active Listening Quiz

Answer Yes or No to the following statements.

	Yes	No
1. I consciously clear my mind of personal worries and other concerns before entering the coaching conversation.		
2. I mentally tune out when the person is overly detailed or verbose.		
3. I remain focused on the other person's conversation even when I do not think it is relevant to the coaching conversation.		
4. I anticipate the coachee's concern before he or she has finished talking.		
5. I am uncomfortable with silence.		
6. If I ask the coachee to repeat or clarify what he or she said, I have revealed that I was not listening well.		
7. I am so in touch with my coachees that I often finish their sentences for them.		
8. I interrupt the conversation if I know what the coachee is saying to keep the conversation moving.		
9. I am able to multitask and remain focused on the coaching conversation.		
10. I can continue to listen even if the coachee presents information that is disagreeable to me.		

Answer Key:

If you selected Yes,

1. Congratulations. You are making an effort to keep your ego out of conversations.
2. Caution! Make an effort to stay tuned in. The crux of the coachee's issue may be embedded in the smallest detail.
3. Congratulations. You recognize that issues may be interrelated. However, remember to focus to keep the conversation on track.
4. Caution! There may be many layers to the conversation. Prejudging the conclusion may cause you and the coachee to focus on the wrong issue.
5. Caution! Silence can be a powerful space for discovery and valuable meaning.

6. Caution! Asking a coachee to repeat or clarify him- or herself is a sign of active listening. When you are listening well, repetition and clarification prevent assumptions and help you and the coachee focus on the real issues.
7. Caution! The coachee needs to discover the answers for him- or herself. The coach supports the process but should not assume he or she knows what the coachee will actually say.
8. Caution! Coaching conversations may seem limited in time, but the coachee is often sorting through some difficult issues. Allow the coachee time and space to gather his or her thoughts. Remember to use silence.
9. Caution! You cannot remain completely focused on the conversation when you are multitasking. Demonstrate to the coachee that he or she is your priority.
10. Congratulations! In spite of disagreeable issues, you can remain egoless in your conversation.

The following behaviors represent those things that you can incorporate into your style of interaction that will demonstrate that you are fully ready to hear, respond, and support the coachee in his or her growth process and can become a discipline in developing your coaching skills.

Attending—To attend to someone in a conversation means to be fully present in a way that demonstrates that you are focused on him or her and what he or she is saying. Some of the attending behaviors may not be possible because of the manner in which you choose to engage in coaching conversations.

Eye Contact—Looking directly into your coachee's eyes shows the invitation to connect, respect for the person you are engaged with, focus on the communication, and respect for the other person in the conversation.

Facial Expressions—The coach's expression should match what is being said. Be cautious even over the phone. For example, if your typical expression is smiling, your coachee can sense your expression even if it cannot be seen, and a smile is not always an appropriate expression.

Voice Tone—Matching the tone of your coachee demonstrates that you are present with your coachee, connected, and listening to him or her completely.

Voice Volume—Voice volume is also important in demonstrating your connection and attentiveness to your coachee. Be certain that if you are coaching over the phone that technology is not affecting the volume or tone of your voice.

Space—The physical space between you and another person can reveal a number of important issues in regard to the relationship. For a typical coaching conversation you want to position yourself close enough to hear the nuances of your coachee's communication, but not so close that you invade his or her personal space. Be attentive to your coachee's response to the distance that you have positioned throughout the coaching conversation to connect to your coachee in the most effective manner.

Position—As with space, your positioning during the coaching conversation can impact the connectedness and attentiveness of the communication. Consider that leaning forward or backward, crossed arms, standing, or sitting all impact what you are communicating to the coachee about what is being said, and perhaps even your general overriding feeling or opinion.

Distracting Gestures—Tapping your fingers, excessive nodding of agreement or disagreement, looking away, or being distracted in any manner from total attentiveness to the coachee will have an impact on the connection with the coachee. Remember also that gestures like head nodding or eye rolling can be sensed even over the phone.

Remove All Distractions—Make certain that you are fully ready for a coaching appointment. This means more than just being on time. Make sure that you have prepared your environment so that there is no interruption. Be fully present with your coachee as if there were no one else on earth but the coachee. If coaching over the phone, a headset is the most important piece of equipment that will allow you to fully hear and be heard by your coachee.

Reflecting

Reflecting is the art of showing your coachee what you are observing in him or her. You can reflect in a conversation whether in person or on the phone. Some things you might reflect back to a coachee are:

- Emotional state: joy, fear, anger, and excitement
- Intensity of their reaction
- Inconsistencies between how they seem and what they are saying
- The match or mismatch between behavior, goals, and commitments
- When something said doesn't fit with the rest of the conversation
- Identifying and bridging gaps

Paraphrasing

To paraphrase in a coaching conversation means to reform and restate the message you heard the coachee give, keeping the original intent, but changing the way in which it is expressed. Paraphrasing can also be a way of focusing the conversation in a particular direction. Sometimes this is done in very similar language, and sometimes the paraphrasing language is quite different from the original message. Example:

Original message:

> "I just don't seem to connect with my staff anymore. They just don't seem to get what I'm saying. I try to be clear, but they're always asking me to explain what I mean."

Paraphrase

> "So, you think your staff isn't really understanding you, even though you are trying to be as clear as you can."
>
> Or
>
> "So, you think your staff isn't understanding you, because they keep asking for clarification."
>
> Or
>
> "So, you don't feel like you're connecting with your staff these days."

Truth Telling

Often the most valuable component of a coaching relationship is for the coachee to have a confidential source of truth. Most people do not have anyone who will tell them the real truth about themselves or how they are affecting those around them. When others do present them with the truth, good or bad, it is often done in a hurtful and/or unhelpful way.

Often the most valuable part of a coaching relationship
is for the coachee to have a confidential source of truth.

As their coach, you can take care to present the truth in a respectful and sensitive way. Some of the truths that coachees may need to hear are:

- How they affect others
- How marvelous they really are
- That they are okay—just as they are
- How their behavior is in line or out of line with their goals
- When others are trying to sabotage their best efforts

Clarifying Distinctions

Clarifying distinctions between words and phrases is essential in the listening process. Helping a coachee see the subtle distinction between two words, phrases, or ideas is a helpful use of language which, when used strategically, can accelerate a coachee's growth.

For example, there is a huge difference between strength and power. Personal strength is a manifestation of who the person is and what he or she can do. Power is dependent on others either granting it to you or you taking it. Both terms are valid, but when a person reorients around strengthening him- or herself versus attempting to control or have power over others, life gets a lot easier.

Referral Issues

Be aware of the types of issues that are best dealt with by other professionals. In conversations with your coachees you can listen for the signs and signals that indicate that a coachee needs other types of assistance and refer him or her to the appropriate professional.

Should such issues present themselves, your responsibility is to facilitate the coachee in addressing these issues, and not try to tackle them in the context of the coaching relationship. A coachee may choose to continue the coaching relationship while he or she is seeing another professional. A timely referral demonstrates your integrity and is most appropriate and ethical in a coaching relationship.

The following are some issues that are better served by mental health professionals (psychiatrists, psychologists, psychotherapists, counselors).

- Depression and other mental health conditions
- Marital difficulties
- Family dynamics
- Emotional instability
- Addictions
- Disabilities
- Suicidal concerns

A timely referral demonstrates your integrity and is most appropriate in a coaching relationship.

The following are some issues that are better served by other professionals (doctors, lawyers, financial counselors, ministers, teachers, human resources).

- Medical
- Financial
- Legal
- Criminal
- Spiritual
- Skill training

- Discrimination
- Job Safety

Listening within the Context

Listening within the context of the conversation moves beyond active listening or just having good listening skills. Listening within the context encompasses more than just the words. A coach that has mastered this level of listening listens for hundreds of contextual pieces of information available from the coachee. As a coach, you approach listening without preconceived agendas, assumptions, or judgments. You hear the spoken words and discern a deeper message by interpreting the coachee's context. You are able to see beyond the social mask to uncover truths of which the coachee may or may not be aware.

The Coach Approach to Listening within the Context

1. Keep your ego in check.
   - Quiet your mind.
   - Put your own agenda aside.
   - Reserve judgment.
   - Become a searcher of truth.
   - Turn down the volume of the narrative in your head.
2. Use the listening chart (see the resource section).
   - Be present and focused on the coachee for context versus content.
3. Ask questions to which you don't know the answers. —
4. Follow your intuition or hunches to explore what might be going on with a coachee.
5. Support the coachee's search for his or her own answers, rather than imposing your answers.

Listening for Values

In the course of a normal coaching conversation a coachee will say many things. The key is to know what to listen for and pay attention to. Often coachees come to the coaching relationship with expectations of achieving what they perceive to be their grandest goals and/or fondest wishes. Often, an initial motivating focus of a coaching relationship is seen by the coachee as a way to "get what I want."

A byproduct of this perspective is that much of the conversation may be centered on the coachee telling you what he or she needs or wants. To be truly helpful to your coachee you must learn to listen past needs and wants and listen intently for his or her values. Being focused on goals that are not in alignment with values is frustrating to the coachee and ultimately unproductive. Only getting what one wants in life can be very disappointing in the end.

Values are inherent in each individual, and although many values are held in common by many people, they are specific to individuals. For example, most people value family, freedom, loyalty, and honesty. Some value independence, spiritual connection, and physical fitness. A coachee's values system is comprised of his or her ideals, morals, ethics, and the standards that are personally important and meaningful.

To be a truly masterful coach, you must not only tune into your coachee's words, but also discern the entire message communicated through delivery, behaviors, circumstances, and other contextual factors.

These are simple questions that can help clarify whether a goal is in alignment with personal values. Ask your coachee:

- Are you enjoying the process of moving toward this goal?
- Would you pursue this goal even if there were no material or recognition pay-offs?
- Would you pursue this goal even if you didn't feel you had to?
- Is this also in alignment with your professional values?
- If you had all of your needs met, all the money and love you ever wanted, would you still want to do this?
- Do you feel at peace, challenged, energized, and excited about the process—and the end result of this pursuit?

If the answer is yes to these questions, it's highly likely that the goal is in alignment with values. The object of coaching is to help coachees achieve the goals they have set for themselves. If a coachee has set a goal that is in conflict with their basic value system, he or she will have difficulty in ethically and energetically working toward that goal. You will notice this disconnect in behaviors, such as difficulty in articulating the goal, lack of enthusiasm for the process, missed action deadlines, and an emptiness or disappointment when the goal is achieved. All of these indicate the possibility that a goal is not in harmony with a coachee's core values and is therefore failing to draw him or her forward the way a value-centered goal will.

(Refer to Coach U's Tru Values program for a complete list of values and instructions on how to help a coachee identify their values and orient their goals around them.)

Listening Realities

1.	Coachees at different stages of development will require different styles of listening.	As people mature, grow, and progress in life, they face an ever-changing set of challenges and concerns. Recognizing which developmental stage a person is in can be helpful in deciding how and what to respond to in a conversation. People in the restorative stage may want to share their frustration and/or effort, and may want encouragement. People at the attraction stage of development may want a sounding board for decision making or strategic thinking, and so on.
2.	There are hundreds of things to listen for and hear, in any conversation.	Most of us hear about 30–40 things—tone of voice, mood, choice of words, pace, pattern, etc. Your task is to listen and to hear all that is communicated—whether it's spoken, inferred, or not even mentioned.
3.	It is easier to listen when you have an appreciation for all the facets of the conversation.	Become a student who appreciates the subtleties and nuances of the spoken word. As you learn to listen and respond to the subtleties, undertones, and inferred meanings, you will enhance not only your appreciation of the language, but you will hear more of what your coachee is trying to tell you.
4.	You'll become a better listener when there is less going on in your head.	It is hard to really hear the coachee when you have concerns of your own. That kind of noise can be deafening and may make you miss what a coachee is trying to say. Simplify your life; get clarity on your own issues, needs, goals, and tolerations. Becoming more centered will increase your ability to hear your coachees in a richer way.
5.	Coachees will repeat what is important to them and tell you everything you need to know.	When you truly listen, coachees feel more at ease and will gladly reveal themselves and their concerns. There are a variety of ways that coachees choose to tell you what's going on with them; they may either mention it directly, indirectly, or as a throwaway. Everything a coachee says to you is important and, over time, they will give you all the information you need to be of service to them.
6.	Listen for what the coachee cannot say or does not understand.	Be a Seeing Eye dog for your coachees; listen for what he or she is having a hard time getting or seeing for him or herself. Through the use of quiet and respectful reflection, silence, and empathy, you can invite your coachee to inquire, recognize, and experiment with new ideas about him or herself, others, their environment, and his or her goals.

7.	Listen for what is motivating the coachee.	Listening for what is driving the coachee's desire to succeed is the most valuable place to put your attention. Listen for what is motivating, challenging, frightening, stimulating, and compelling him or her. When you understand what is behind their goals, actions, accomplishments, challenges, and problems you can help them move more quickly by tapping into their key motivators to achieve.
8.	Choose carefully what you respond to.	Many things will come up in a coaching interaction. Knowing which things to respond to is perhaps even more important than responding. Wait until you hear something you can comment on that will move your coachee toward his or her goals.
9.	Listening is different than asking questions.	Listening should always take precedent over asking questions. It is better to hear, feel, and get who the coachee is rather than gather information. The 90/10 rule applies here: listen 90% and respond and ask questions 10% of the time. The best questions should motivate, clarify, and simplify, and be used strategically and sparingly.
10.	Listen to your reactions to the coachee.	In each coaching interaction, you will have reactions to what your coachee is saying, experiencing, or wanting to achieve. This is normal, and it is important to notice and understand your reactions—positive or negative. They can provide valuable information. If you are reacting, it is likely that others in the coachee's life are responding similarly. The coaching relationship is an environment whereby the coachee can process and grow from learning how he or she affects others.

Listening Behaviors: Promoters and Pitfalls

The DOS are behaviors that promote successful listening. The DON'TS are behaviors that limit the success of listening.

Do—Understand that telling the truth does not always come easily to the coachee. Don't—Assume the coachee will be able to always say the truth.	Most people do not have the awareness or the phrasing to fully express themselves. Few have the skill of telling the truth easily. This does not imply that coachees will knowingly lie or are dishonest, but simply that most people describe the truth as best they are able. If something the coachee says does not match his or her tone of voice, your past experience, or reality, ask for clarification.
Do—Listen to and hear the coachee fully before coaching. Don't—Leap on the first coachable issue.	It can be tempting to go immediately to the first coachable issue and begin. It is more respectful and effective to hear the coachee out before stepping in. Develop the ability to hear and hold information without having to respond to any of it, until you know what the coachee needs. Remember that many coachees solve their own problems when you listen fully to them. Give them this opportunity.
Do—Listen both for what is said and what is not being said. Don't—Just listen to what is being "said."	Every time a coachee is speaking with you, he or she knowingly or unknowingly holds back information. It is your job to hear what is *not* being said, as well as what *is* being said. If you always assume that some things are not being said, you can listen better to what is being said and prompt the coachee to say more.
Do—Respond to what you do hear. Don't—Try to hear it all.	No coach will be able to hear the multitude of things that are said in any conversation. Trying to do so can distract you from the real issues. Respond to what you do hear, and don't wait too long in the hopes of hearing everything. Conversely, don't jump in too quickly in a rushed effort to get going.
Do—Listen with feedback. Don't—Just listen.	Listening is not a passive process. You need not be silent in order to be listening well. In fact, most coachees need and want you to give indications that you are hearing, feeling, experiencing, understanding, and getting them. Even if you are being quiet, or silent, give the coachee frequent feedback. These verbal responses ("uh-hum," "yes," "oh," "can you explain that a bit more," etc.) encourage the coachee to continue speaking. The more the coachee explains the more quickly he or she gets to the truth.
Do—Take an interest in the coachee. Don't—Try to understand the coachee.	Show that you are genuinely interested in your coachees and what they are going through rather than trying to figure them out. If you focus your energy on the coachee, he or she will naturally feel more empowered to work out the problem or situation. Coachees benefit from your energy, not just your investigative skills.
Do—Listen to both yourself and the coachee. Don't—Listen only to the coachee.	Notice your own language, tone, reactions, assumptions, biases, beliefs, intensity, needs, and favorite topics. By monitoring your behaviors as well as your coachee's, you will be better able to respond in appropriate ways.

Resources

Attention Readers:

Thank you for participating in the collective wisdom of Coach U. Together, we all continue to learn. Additional resources and forms can be found in *Coach U's Essential Coaching Tools: Your Complete Practice Resource* by CoachInc.com.

Attention CoachInc.com Students and Graduates:

CoachInc.com students and graduates may find additional and/or more recent resources associated with this module in the resource area of the student-only web site. If you are a student or graduate of one of CoachInc.com's ICF-accredited coach training programs, you can access these by searching under the name of the course. When the course description page appears you may find a link to the list of additional resources. Each item is a live link to its actual location on the web site. Click on the item to access the information.

Do remember to take the associated online self-test for this module once you have completed the course in person or by TeleClass. The tests are required for coach certification with the International Coach Federation. Throughout the course or anytime you find valuable resources for a particular course please feel free to add to the value of our curricula by forwarding the resource to revampteam@coachu.com.

Listening Chart

The following chart may be useful for the coach to visually track what he or she is hearing during interaction with the coachee. It can serve as a hard copy log of your coachee's progress and/or needs and wants. The items listed in CAPS at the bottom of some lists are suggestions for other Coach U programs which you may find helpful for your coachee.

1. VALUES
   - ☐ Adventure
   - ☐ Beauty
   - ☐ To catalyze
   - ☐ To contribute
   - ☐ To create
   - ☐ To discover
   - ☐ To feel
   - ☐ To lead
   - ☐ Mastery
   - ☐ Pleasure or play
   - ☐ To relate
   - ☐ Be sensitive
   - ☐ Be spiritual
   - ☐ To teach
   - ☐ To win
   - ☐ Truth
   - TRU VALUES PROGRAM

2a. STRENGTHS: PROFESSIONAL
   - ☐ Communication
   - ☐ Craft or technical
   - ☐ Intellectual
   - ☐ General knowledge
   - ☐ Good judgment
   - ☐ Experience
   - ☐ Track record
   - ☐ Results-oriented
   - ☐ _____
   - ☐ _____

2b. STRENGTHS: RESOURCES
   - ☐ Cash
   - ☐ Time
   - ☐ Ideas
   - ☐ Opportunities
   - ☐ Professional network
   - ☐ Centers of influence
   - ☐ Colleagues
   - ☐ Large database
   - ☐ Family connections
   - ☐ _____
   - ☐ _____

2c. STRENGTHS: INNER
   - ☐ Courage
   - ☐ Willingness
   - ☐ Awareness
   - ☐ Adultness
   - ☐ Responsibility
   - ☐ Perspective
   - ☐ _____
   - ☐ _____

3. BEHAVIOR CLUES
   - ☐ Fear
   - ☐ Tiredness
   - ☐ Disappointment
   - ☐ Sadness
   - ☐ Business dips
   - ☐ Bad events
   - ☐ Money tight
   - ☐ Compulsive
   - ☐ Constant changes
   - ☐ Illness
   - ☐ Lateness
   - ☐ _____
   - ☐ _____

4. PHRASE CLUES
   - ☐ Over-promises
   - ☐ Lies
   - ☐ Acts
   - ☐ Judging
   - ☐ Flowering
   - ☐ Charge up/down
   - ☐ Digs
   - ☐ Jargon-based
   - ☐ Heavy filters
   - ☐ _____
   - ☐ _____

5. PERSONAL FRICTION OR BAD HABITS
   - ☐ Causes crises
   - ☐ Victim or suffering
   - ☐ Drama
   - ☐ Things left unsaid
   - ☐ Secret actions or inactions
   - ☐ To-do inventory
   - ☐ Self-imposed limits
   - ☐ Too busy, frantic
   - ☐ Procrastination
   - ☐ Diversion-prone
   - ☐ Adrenaline
   - ☐ Lying or denial
   - ☐ Too-positive a spin
   - ☐ _____
   - ☐ _____

6. LACKING
   - ☐ Structure
   - ☐ Cash
   - ☐ Income
   - ☐ Encouragement
   - ☐ Information
   - ☐ Awareness
   - ☐ A vision
   - ☐ People
   - ☐ Time
   - ☐ Space
   - ☐ A plan
   - ☐ Focus
   - ☐ Profitability
   - ☐ Expertise
   - ☐ Language
   - ☐ Skill
   - ☐ Energy
   - ☐ Strategy
   - ☐ Listening
   - ☐ Commitment
   - ☐ Self-esteem
   - ☐ Community
   - ☐ Network
   - ☐ Big enough game
   - ☐ Order or organized
   - ☐ _____
   - ☐ _____

7. NEEDS
   - ☐ Be accepted
   - ☐ To accomplish
   - ☐ Be acknowledged
   - ☐ Be loved
   - ☐ Be right
   - ☐ Be cared for
   - ☐ Certainty
   - ☐ Be comfortable
   - ☐ To communicate
   - ☐ To control
   - ☐ Be needed
   - ☐ Duty
   - ☐ Be free
   - ☐ Honesty
   - ☐ Order
   - ☐ Peace
   - ☐ Power
   - ☐ Recognition
   - ☐ Safety
   - ☐ _____
   - ☐ _____
   NEEDLESS PROGRAM

8. FOUNDATION
   - ☐ Handling of unresolved issues
   - ☐ Integrity restored
   - ☐ Needs met
   - ☐ Strong boundaries
   - ☐ High standards
   - ☐ Tolerating less
   - ☐ Loving family
   - ☐ Community
   - ☐ Values-oriented
   PERSONAL FOUNDATION PROGRAM

9. PERSONAL DEVELOPMENT
   - ☐ Full reserve
   - ☐ 100% grateful
   - ☐ Present is perfect
   - ☐ Few goals or wants
   - ☐ Inner peace
   - ☐ Gentle
   - ☐ Naturally effective
   - ☐ Attractive
   - ☐ Happy
   - ☐ Self-responsible
   - ☐ Satisfied
   - ☐ Fulfilled
   - ☐ Balanced
   - ☐ Present
   - ☐ Light
   - ☐ High self-care
   - ☐ Purpose clear
   - ☐ _____
   - ☐ _____

10. THERAPY
☐ Addictions
☐ Codependency
☐ Suicidal
☐ Self-sabotage
☐ Major denial
☐ Major resistance
☐ Mood swings
☐ Depression
☐ Shame-based
☐ _____
☐ _____
REFER TO THERAPIST

11. COACHEE TYPE
☐ Entrepreneur
☐ Professional
☐ CEO or executive
☐ Creative
☐ Restorative
☐ Career or corp
☐ Manager
☐ _____
☐ _____

12. COACHABLE
☐ Readiness
☐ Trusting
☐ Willing
☐ Openness
☐ Responsive
☐ Self-creating
☐ "Gets" the process
☐ Self-responsible
☐ Committed
☐ Rapid results
☐ _____
☐ _____

13a. MOTIVATED BY: POSITIVES
☐ Goals
☐ Commitment
☐ Money
☐ Success
☐ Wants
☐ Environment
☐ Choice
☐ Contribution
☐ Values
☐ Needs
☐ _____

13b. MOTIVATED BY: NEGATIVES
☐ Personal friction
☐ Unmet needs
☐ Fear, consequence
☐ Addictions
☐ Psychological issues
☐ _____
☐ _____

Chapter 5

Language

Overview

Benefits

Go to Page > 153

By participating in this module you will be able to identify your and your coachee's preferred language and learn to continually choose the language that, in the moment, best conveys meaning, inspires, challenges, or clarifies. You will become aware of how your coachees use language to explain, defend, inform, describe, and ask for what they want, need, and value. In the process of learning about language and its forms and uses, you will expand your everyday skill to express yourself and be able to help others to do the same.

Definitions

Go to Page > 154

Adage, analogy, body language, cadence, cliché, dialect, example, jargon, language, medium, metaphor, parroting, repertoire, and trigger.

Concepts

Go to Page > 156

What Is Powerful Coaching Language?

This module is about language: its beauty, rhythm, and cadence. It is about words, what they mean, and how they are used. It is about the power of language to lift, illuminate, and move ideas forward. It is about language as a core skill for you. Language is the vehicle used to exchange value, and is a skill that can be enhanced through intentional practice. There are three key elements of language: word choices, alignment with the coachee, and delivery.

○ Distinctions Go to Page > 159

Technology of language versus art of language, language versus dialect, language versus the language of, and parroting versus using a coachee's language.

○ Application Go to Page > 161

The Framework of Language
   Language Delivery
   Speaking the Coachee's Language (Alignment)
   Word Choices
   The Coach Approach to Using Language with Shifts and Distinctions
   Becoming a Language Artist: Ways to Develop the Skill of Language
   The Outcomes of Language Becoming Art

○ Resources Go to Page > 176

Benefits

By fully participating in this module, you will learn to communicate more clearly, be understood more often, invite others to share more effectively and have greater choices about how to convey your message. You will be able to identify your and your coachee's preferred language and continually choose the language that, in the moment, best conveys meaning, inspires, challenges or clarifies.

This course is designed to:

O **Widen** both your knowledge of language and your ability to use it in an effective manner

O **Give** you a greater sense of the language tools you have today, how to expand those tools, how to tap into the language of your coachees and help you use your complete language base more potently with your coachees

O **Develop** the ability to make good choices about using different styles and types of language, as well as knowing when each is most effective

O **Allow** you to learn how to match your language with your intended message, and demonstrate and mentor superior language skills to your coachees

O **Inspire** in you a passion for language and a love of words

Definitions

The following are common words used to gain a better understanding of the coaching process, particularly in regard to language.

Adage: An adage is a wise saying that is widely used and well recognized to convey a particular meaning. For example, "The early bird gets the worm," would be an adage used to convey the idea that it is the person who seizes an opportunity first that benefits most.

Analogy: To draw an analogy is to compare two things, and speak of them as being alike, even though they might not be thought of as being similar. For example, riding a horse is like life—when you get thrown off, you should get right back on.

Body language: When in a conversation, we communicate both verbally, with words and phrases, and nonverbally, with gestures, expressions, positions, and so on. The part of the conversation that is nonverbal is referred to as body language. Body language is a powerful part of any conversation. For example, if you do not make good eye contact when talking with your coachee, he or she may think you are not interested.

Cadence: In language, cadence means the rise and fall of your voice while speaking. It can also refer to the rhythm or pace of your speech. For example, speaking too quickly may convey annoyance, frustration, or simply not being in tune with the coachee.

Cliché: A cliché is a timeworn expression or idea. For example, "When the going gets tough, the tough get going."

Dialect: Most languages have several variations or forms of speech that are used in various parts of the land where they originated. A dialect is a legitimate variation on the language of that group and can denote status or position. For example, people often refer to the Queen's English to describe the dialect of English that is spoken among the royals of England.

Example: Giving an example is saying something to illustrate the meaning of something else. For example, when you read the "for example" section in each of these definitions you can get a better idea of what the word means by seeing how it is used.

Jargon: Jargon is language that fails to communicate because it is strange or foreign to the hearer. Jargon is often language that refers to a particular business, industry, or discipline. For example, to speak of downloads, uploads, and bytes of information is to use the jargon of computer communication.

Language: Language is the written or verbal body of words, sentence forms, and patterns of speech of a particular group of people. For example, English is the common language spoken in North America.

Medium: A medium is the substance or agent through which anything acts or passes. For example, language is the medium humans use to communicate feelings, information, intentions, and directions to each other.

Metaphor: A metaphor is a figure of speech in which a word or phrase that ordinarily means one thing is used with another thing in order to suggest a likeness between the two. For example, you might say your coachee has a heart of gold.

Parroting: In language, to parrot is to repeat words or phrases without understanding their meaning. For example, a coachee may talk about upselling in his business, and you repeat the word upselling without knowing what it means.

Repertoire: A group or list of skills and abilities available for use in performing or speaking. For example, a seasoned coach has a large repertoire of language skills, illustrations, examples, metaphors, and so on to use in bringing clarity to the conversation.

Trigger: A trigger is a word, phrase, or idea that when spoken touches a positive or negative memory, feeling, or specific emotional response in the listener. For example, if a coachee is in jeopardy of losing his or her job, to speak of downsizing could trigger a fear response.

Concepts

What Is Powerful Coaching Language?

Each of us is born with the ability to use language; for most of the population speaking is a natural part of living. To be an effective coach, however, excellent language skills must be learned and cultivated. Taking language from a natural skill to an art form also involves learning the language of your coachee and flexing your language to match your coachee's. It also includes choosing powerful coaching language at the appropriate time in the coaching dialog.

Language is a skill that, although in its fundamental form is a natural ability, can be enhanced through intentional practice. Within any language there are infinite options to choose from when conveying an idea, an emotion, or a request, and the choice of language in a coaching conversation will determine the outcome. Coaching language has the potential to help coachees discover possibilities, create shifts, and find success.

The coaching conversation is focused on the coachee, and words within that conversation move a person or group to deeper levels of thinking than words within general conversations. This happens because the coach listens and responds with powerful language. This allows coach and coachee to engage in challenging familiar patterns and exploring new possibilities. The language is sometimes directive and at other times discovery producing. You will know you are in a coaching conversation when the language facilitates this depth of thinking. As you engage with the material in this module, we request you start thinking in terms of "power language."

Each person has the capacity to learn new language skills and when practiced well, the use of language moves from a technical orientation to being an art form. Becoming adept at language gives you the ability to communicate more clearly, with fewer misunderstandings and miscommunications. Learning the language of your coachee and applying powerful coaching language at the appropriate time is key to effective coaching. It helps you enter the world of your coachee, clarify values, promote mutual understanding and rapport, and ultimately assist your coachee in achieving his or her goals.

The Benefits of Using Powerful Coaching Language

Powerful language contains words that create impact and carry positive, motivating energy. When clean and devoid of judgment and assumptions, coaching language may effect dramatic shifts in a person's life. When straightforward, succinct, and honest, words can be life-changing. Fewer words allow more space for coachee processing. Within the coaching context, powerful language denotes great respect and trust that can lead to significant changes in a coachee's life. The coachee makes the final decision about how or if he or she will be affected by powerful language.

Elements of Language

Language skill is comprised of three elements: word selection, alignment, and delivery. When artfully combined, these elements enhance your ability to deliver your intended message with clarity and confidence. As with all coaching communication, the intention is to deliver a message at a time when a coachee can best receive and process that information and support a change or shift in his or her development.

The elements of language are:

1. Word selection or choice
- The choice of when to use known words and phrases or introduce new ones
- The choice between words, phrases, analogies, metaphors, story telling, and so on
- The recognition of words, phrases, or approaches that encourage and/or stop action

2. Alignment with the coachee's language and experience
- The use or avoidance of jargon
- The coachee's definition or use of the word
- Words, phrases, and illustrations common to the coachee's experience
- Matching your choice of language to the coachee's context (e.g., if the coachee has just been promoted—celebratory language; if the coachee has lost a large account—more serious, reflective language is in order)

3. The Delivery
- Pace
- Tone
- Volume
- Expression
- Words
- Rhythm and Cadence
- Timing

Value is exchanged between you and your coachee through language choices. Guiding Principle #5 says that people seek value, meaning that people are naturally attracted to interactions that provide them with energy and opportunity. Identifying your language preferences and that of your coachee's allows you to artfully navigate the coaching interaction through the careful choice of pace, tone, volume, expressions, words that best fit the context, proper rhythm, cadence, and timing.

The definitions of words, phrases, jargon, and slang are unique to each individual. Knowing the unique interpretation of your coachee's language helps you craft your messages, requests, and questions in a more succinct and readily understood way. Masterful coaches take care to explore the meaning of words with their coachees. They know that although two people may be using the same word to describe, identify, or convey an idea, feeling, or circumstance, the actual meaning of that word can be quite different to each of them.

" The difference between the right word and almost the right word is the difference between lightening and a lightening bug ... **"** | **Mark Twain**

Using language skillfully can move conversations from a technical exchange of words to a beautiful interchange of information, feelings, energy, and value. A love of language is truly the springboard to endless possibilities. When you have evolved your ability to use language more creatively with your coachees you will find yourself coaching more quickly to greater results and having more fun in the process.

Distinctions

There are subtle yet important differences in meaning between the following closely related terms. Understanding these distinctions allows you to perceive new layers of meaning and offers you new choices for shifting your thoughts, attitudes, and actions.

The Technology of Language versus the Art of Language

The technology of language encompasses the words and phrases chosen or omitted when in a conversation. To use language artfully is to construct one's speech in such a way that it uses all of the elements of human interaction to promote understanding and clarity.

Language versus Dialect

Language is the written or verbal body of words, sentence forms, and patterns of a particular group of people. For example, English is the common language spoken in North America. A dialect is a legitimate variation on the language of a group and can denote status or position. For example, in Louisiana there is a dialect of French spoken that the European French would consider too common for sophisticated conversation.

Language versus the Language Of

Language is the written or verbal body of words, sentence forms, and patterns of a particular group of people. For example, Spanish is the common language spoken in Mexico. When coaches speak of business or of love, they are referring to the common words, examples, metaphors, jargon, and style that people involved in a particular endeavor use on a regular basis. For example, when a couple uses the language of love they speak in hushed tones and word pictures, they use lots of body indicators, and their examples are often taken from the natural world.

Parroting versus Using a Coachee's Language

To parrot a coachee's language is to repeat their words or phrases without understanding their meaning. This only serves to make the coachee feel uncomfortable and misunderstood. Using a coachee's language effectively is when you understand what the coachee means by a particular word, phrase, or example and use it in your own conversation with the coachee to promote clarity, understanding, and connection.

Application

The Framework of Language

Developing strong language skills is a central part of the growth of an effective coach. This is a skill that we could take for granted or overlook in our development as a coach, since we speak every day using our skill of language. However, as coaches we use language to lift, illuminate, and move ideas forward in coaching conversations. The ability to do this shifts language from the mundane and unconscious to a conscious awareness of the art of language as a tool for learning. Becoming artful with the skill of language takes intentional practice and considerable dedication.

To begin exploring how you can bring your use of language into conscious development, consider some of the following basic concepts.

Language Delivery

Skillful language involves being able to deliver an intended message with the use of words and phrases combined with the seven common delivery elements.

- Pace—how fast or slow the speaker talks or the conversation progresses
- Tone—the pitch or quality of the speaker's voice
- Volume—how loudly or softly a voice is used
- Expression—body language, the degree of animation
- Words—amount, placement, style, emphasis, choice
- Rhythm and cadence—the flow of words, the give and take, the melody of the words
- Timing—the appropriate, maximized timing for the message

By combining the appropriate words and phrases with the common delivery elements one can craft a message, request, question, or challenge in a way that conveys more or less urgency, power, importance, directness, and overall impact.

Speaking the Coachee's Language (Alignment)

Because we are born into a particular geographic area, each of us has a unique language preference. We may use a particular language and/or a dialect common to the area in which we live. Understanding and choosing to use your coachee's language, dialect, style, or set of expressions will help you enter your coachee's world more easily and communicate in ways that your coachee can identify and connect with.

The artful use of language makes good coaches great. Masterful coaches consider the language of their coachee as the preferred language and try to use it as often as they can. In fact, they absorb and use the language of the coachee on a regular basis, choosing the language that has the greatest positive impact on their coachee. Using the coachee's language can have several beneficial effects. These effects include:

1. *The coachee feels heard.* When coachees hear their language mirrored, they feel you have truly listened to them, caught the meaning of what they said, and are paying attention to it. They also understand that you believe what they say and that what they have to offer has value. Therefore, they also begin to know that you believe in them. Using a coachee's language does not mean simply parroting their words back to them. It requires that you actually note and study the coachee's language, and choose which parts of it are useful for the coaching process.

2. *The coachee feels that you are willing to explore their world.* You are a coachee's partner in exploration of his or her own world and how he or she wants that world to be. When you use the coachee's language, you demonstrate a willingness to enter the coachee's world and to find value in that world. The use of the coachee's language exponentially increases the sense of co-creation between you and your coachee, which is critical to the success of the coaching relationship.

3. *The coachee hears more easily.* It is always easier to hear and understand things that are familiar. This is particularly true in a conversation directed at personal growth. When a coachee is spoken to in words that reflect how the coachee thinks and processes, progress will happen faster.

4. *The coachee readily recognizes new additions to their learning.* When you use the coachee's language in order to make ideas and concepts feel familiar, you also create a second opportunity. When there is new learning to be done, you can present the learning in new language. This will immediately clarify the idea or concept as distinct from old thought patterns. The new learning will be more identifiable and memorable simply because it has been presented in language that is not familiar.

5. *The coach can be with the coachee more fully.* Recognizing and using the coachee's language, you naturally create a deep affinity with the coachee. The

coachee's language helps you understand the coachee's world and gain clarity regarding his or her perspectives, assumptions, and beliefs as the conversation progresses. Through using the coachee's language, you forge bridges for yourself to understand better who your coachees are and how they exist in the world.

Guiding Principle 7 | **People Live from Their Perception.**
Recognizing that people perceive reality through their own filters leads to effective communication and creates a platform for positive action.

---

6. *The coach and coachee can have more fun together.* The shared mutuality of language allows both you and the coachee to relax into the relationship and add humor, whimsy, and irreverence to the coaching partnership. The end result is a foundation for work that is focused and serious, but done with a light touch.

Like all aspects of becoming a language artist, accessing coachees' language takes practice. It is, however, joyful work. The resulting alliance with your coachees, and the increased power and newfound pleasure in your coaching, are more than ample rewards for the development time required.

Guiding Principle 1 | **People Have Something in Common.**
We return to the common ground of being by loving, honoring, and valuing self and others.

How To Access Your Coachees' Language

Here are 10 simple rules that, if followed, will allow you to become an artist at accessing and using your coachees' language as a powerful coaching tool. The first three rules are all about language attitude. The last seven rules provide easy structures to access your coachees' language. Please remember that these rules are not about hearing particular coaching clues like emotions or patterns, but are about listening for and learning your coachee's language so that such language can be used as an effective coaching tool.

1. **Accept that your coachees have something to teach you.** Great coaches are master learners, particularly when it comes to language, and master coaches understand that their greatest teachers are their coachees. They are, therefore, open to all their coachees have to give, including the gift of language. Ap-

proach each language relationship with your coachees with the idea that you will be gifted by their experiences and thoughts, as well as by how they express them.

2. **Accept that your coachees' current language is perfect for who they are.** Accepting that a coachee's current language is perfect acknowledges that the coachee is completely whole and does not need you to improve any part of their life. It allows the coachee to enter the coaching relationship as an equal in all aspects, including language. If you think that you are giving your coachees better language to express themselves, you are subtly diminishing the wholeness of the coachee. That attitude will show up somewhere in the view of the coachee and/or the coaching alliance.

3. **Give your coachees credit for their language skills.** The coachee has, just like you, invested time and effort in learning to describe who and how they are. That time, effort, and knowledge should be acknowledged and honored.

4. **Listen for words that describe their world.** When a coachee speaks, listen to the words that describe their daily world, from work to home. If a coachee is a scientist or a stockbroker, listen for language that can be used to clarify coaching concepts. For example, instead of asking a stockbroker what his next action is, ask what his investment in himself will be. Ask what return he wants on that investment. In short, use the coachee's language to coach, so that ideas have an instant connection to concepts that already exist for the coachee.

5. **Listen for words that help them learn.** Each coachee has a way of learning and processing. Some do better with visual descriptions, others prefer linear formulas, while still others will do best with examples. Listen to those moments when learning occurs for the coachee and how the coachee describes them. That language will give you insight into what language you need to use when new learning and lessons need to occur.

6. **Listen for words that describe their emotions.** You will notice that coachees will use certain language to describe various emotions. Certain words and terms will come up frequently when the coachee feels confident or happy. Other words will be used commonly when the coachee experiences negative emotions. If you notice these differences you can then use the appropriate coachee language to create or shift emotion.

7. **Listen for words that describe their values.** Coachees may rarely say, "my values are." They do, however, repeat those descriptions of ideas and concepts that are truly important to them. When attempting to draw a coachee back to their core values, use their descriptive language to help them choose between ideas and concepts.

8. **Use the words you hear frequently.** Honor your coachees, their language, and what they have to teach you by using their words often during the coaching sessions. It does not expand your language ability to learn your coachees' language if you never use it.

9. **Ask your coachees for language that would work for them.** Your coachees have the answers and know what is best for them. Asking your coachees for

the language to describe, explain or identify an idea is the easiest way to expand your language capacity. It also indicates to the coachee that you trust them to be a partner in the coaching adventure.

10. **Note what books, movies, TV shows, and music interests your coachees.** Much of our language comes from our culture. Often, visual images, meaningful descriptions, and useful metaphors for coachees can be found in their media interests. Ask about them and use them. Your coachees will notice that you pay attention to their lives. They will also relate easily to the coaching conversation when you use the language they already know and love.

Word Choices

Although people may use the same words in a conversation, they may have very different meanings to each individual. An important skill of language is to accurately differentiate between *how a word is used* and *how we know the word*. Often words come to have contextually specific meanings that are different to various groups, cohorts, and segments of society, genders, and communities.

Examples of words with different meanings:

- "Bad" means not-good to middle-aged people and very good to some teenagers.
- "Gay" may mean happy to some, and refer to a lifestyle to others.

Remember, your choice of language in a conversation will determine the outcome. What you choose to say or not say, when you speak, the tone you use, the type, pace, and style of your language will significantly affect how the message is received, and ultimately if, and how, it is acted upon by your coachee. The benefits of exploring your own use of language are:

- Building your confidence in your ability to understand and be understood in a coaching interaction
- Knowing how your communication is received by others: being aware of how often your coachee asks for clarification, pauses for reflection, responds with more conversation, or suggests an action
- Expanding your options for making requests, clarifying or demonstrating caring

Clean Language

An internationally known therapist, David Grove, coined this term in his book *Resolving Traumatic Memories*. Since then, many individuals have recognized that general language often carries assumptions, presuppositions, suggestions, judgments, and at times, manipulation. Coaching language uses the clean approach to emphasize the ego-lessness of the coach. The whole idea of clean language is that the conversation is focused on the context of the person being coached.

Characteristics of Clean Language in Coaching

Clean language is the language and words used by the coach that:

- Is free of presuppositions, judgments, and "make wrongs"
- Is non-manipulative
- Is centered on the information, experience, and metaphor of the coachee
- Is a way of allowing the coachee's language to come forward so that clues to a solution come from his or her own experiences
- Is laser, with the idea that less is more
- Is neutral and non-directive

Examples to Distinguish the Clean Language Approach

In the examples below, examine each response to determine the difference. Which one seems to fit the idea of clean language? Which one leads to a deeper ownership of solutions by the coachee?

Clean language is focused on the information and language used by the coachee.

Coachee: "I don't know why that always happens."
Coach: "Do you think it's because you procrastinate?"
Versus
Coach: "What do you believe contributes to that always happening?"

The first question leads to a conversation about procrastination, which may not be the coachee's issue. The more critical issue may be missed.

Clean language is minimal, laser language with the idea that less is more.

Coachee: "There is a real difference in the way I relate to George and the way I relate to Mary."
Coach: "Well, it could be that you don't like George as much as you like Mary, and that causes you problems in all your relationships here at the office."
Versus
Coach: "What real difference do you see?"

Clean language is without presupposition, suggestion or "make wrongs."

> Coachee: "Today I got myself in a mess with my manager."
>
> Coach: "You've done that before. Why does that always happen when you talk to her?"
>
> Versus
>
> Coach: "What happened?"

Clean language fully explores the relative metaphor of the coachee.

> Coachee: "I want to work at a much higher level than I do now."
>
> Coach: "Yes, I believe you are ready for the next step on the career ladder."
>
> Versus
>
> Coach: "Describe the higher level."

Storytelling and Metaphors

Some language is just information. Other language leaves a powerful impression. The use of stories and metaphors creates a pathway for the coach to connect with the head and heart of the coachee.

Storytelling

Ancient cultures believed that the storytellers, gifted by the gods, were able to see a past and a future that others could not. Storytellers had an obligation to guide and enlighten those who sought their counsel.

Today, we often think of stories as children's entertainment. Timeless classics such as *Grimms' Fairy Tales*, Hans Christian Andersen tales, and Mother Goose rhymes spark the imagination of youth, tap emotions such as fear and hope, and leave readers with a lesson to mull over. Stories appeal to all ages and all learning styles. Storytelling creates an environment, which allows visual, audio, and kinesthetic learners to follow along, comprehend, and retain concepts.

As adults, we are still reviving the lessons learned from stories of the Ancient Greeks, American Indians, and Shakespeare. Modern corporate tales such as *Fish!*, *Who Moved My Cheese?*, and *Penguins and Peacocks* spread through organizations quickly. A story that touches us on relevant levels at an appropriate time can impact our way of seeing our surroundings and ourselves.

" Storytelling is strongly dependent on the power of personal presence ... Whether within a traditional community or a contemporary performance context, storytelling tends to be prized precisely for its immediacy. " | **Joseph Sobol, scholar, storyteller, historian**

Consider the following story:

> A Prince came to Lao-tzu for enlightenment. Lao-tzu told him to climb a banyan tree. The Prince couldn't understand what knowledge or enlightenment had to do with climbing a tree, but the Prince obeyed Lao-tzu and climbed the 50-foot-high banyan tree. Then Lao-tzu told him to come down. The Prince started descending. After the Prince had descended 40 feet, Lao-tzu told him to be careful. The Prince was flabbergasted. Lao-tzu didn't ask him to be careful when he was climbing 50 feet up. Lao-tzu didn't ask him to be careful when he started descending from the height of 50 feet. Now, when he was only 10 feet above the ground, Lao-tzu was telling him to be careful?
>
> Lao-tzu explained that the Prince had no climbing experience. When the pursuit of enlightenment is strong enough, then a man will do whatever is required. But in the last phase of the journey, when the land seems so near, one tends to become careless, lose concentration, and commit mistakes.

Message: Maximum concentration is required in the last leg of your journey.

As a coach, you can warn your coachee to stay focused until the end of the project. Or, you can connect with his head and his heart by telling a vivid story. Coaches who can relay information through the medium of stories and metaphors are more likely to make memorable connections.

An example of this powerful connection is one found through a discussion with an executive about the difference between command and control management and collaborative management.

"When I was right out of high school my first job was on a road construction crew where I was directed to use a jackhammer to break up the old pavement. I had no instruction but immediately held tight to the jackhammer, virtually hanging on for dear life. I went through the entire first day of work. Next morning I was still shaking inside and out. I did not know if I could do the job another day. An older worker said to me, 'Don't try to control it. Just use a light touch and balance the tool and let it do its work.'"

When to Tell a Story
Tell a story to make a point. People don't want to be lectured. Telling a story is a great way to plant a seed that will allow the other person to take ownership.

How to Tell a Story
Gather your thoughts.

Make a list of coachable issues for which you would like to have meaningful examples and stories that make the point for you (e.g., integrity, work relationships). Gather relevant and entertaining stories from your own or others' experiences that convey powerful lessons.

Telling Your Story
Ask for permission to share a story.

"I have a story you may find helpful … may I share it?"

Allow discovery. Don't define the story for the listener. If you begin by telling the coachee, "I'd like to tell you a story about a turning point in my life where I learned that risk is a prerequisite for success," you've basically told him or her the point of the story. You've robbed him or her of the opportunity to discover the meaning as the story unfolds.

Make it relevant. Don't waste your coachees' time by telling a story that gets a laugh but has little application. Make the story relevant by connecting with the personal context of the listener. Does your story cause your coachees to think about the value of family? The importance of integrity? The pitfalls of perfectionism? You want them to listen to your story so that they can hear *their* story. If you tell a story about how you failed miserably as a manager, you want them to relate your experiences to their own struggles as a manager.

> " The primary job that any writer faces is to tell you a story out of human experiences. I mean by that, universal mutual experience, the anguish and troubles and griefs of the human heart, which is universal, without regard to race or time or human condition. He wants to tell you something that seemed to him so true, so moving, either comic or tragic, that it is worth preserving. " | **William Faulkner**

Make it real. Too much exaggeration makes the listener doubt your credibility. Many people may stop listening.

Use visual images and details appropriately to create an impression in the listener's head. Descriptions incorporate all the senses. Use words to denote smell (the acrid smell of the overhead projector bulb burning out), hearing (the heavy silence of 100 eyes looking at me), feeling (heart pounding against my chest as I watched my presentation go up in smoke), and so on.

Describe the emotions to connect with the listener's heart. I felt overwhelmed and short of breath. The pressure was affecting me emotionally and physically.

Describe a shift or transformation. The shift could be from failure to success, from nervous to confident, or from lazy to motivated.

Let silence speak. Silence says a lot. In the silence, listeners *feel* rather than think.

Help them apply the story. Storytelling contains truths that can create shifts. Avoid saying, "And so the moral is . . ." Instead, ask a question about the coachee's similar situation or allow the coachee to ask, "What does this have to do with me?"

Enjoy it. Craft entertaining and humorous stories and metaphors that lighten up a situation.

❝ If you add to the truth, you subtract from it. ❞ | The Talmud

---

Metaphors

Metaphors are figures of speech that rely on a likeness between apparently unrelated situations. The comparative objects share an essential feature, such as shape, color, texture, structure, mechanism, principle, or purpose.

Metaphors have the power to make complex concepts more tangible and frightening tasks more friendly.

Metaphors can create shared visions among different people and different departments, in spite of individual ways of seeing, or unique job responsibilities. Metaphors create mental images that connect with our head and our heart.

Metaphors provide coaches with rich openings for coachee breakthroughs.

Think of the technology metaphors we use to make a complex, vast field, such as computers, more humanized and comprehensible: *Web, mouse, bug, virus,* and *information highway.*

We may describe struggles in our careers: climbing the corporate ladder, breaking the glass ceiling.

Consider using a metaphor with your coachee when she is stuck or doesn't see something. Example:

"Kristine, you are swimming in a sea of ideas."

How to Create Metaphors

Metaphors work best if there is an easy connection in the listener's mind. In developing a metaphor, identify the general purpose or feature and relate it to the concept. For example, if your newly promoted coachee is overwhelmed by the speed at which he or she must learn new information, you may offer a metaphor such as "drinking water from a fire hose." When you introduce a metaphor to your coachee, you also create a safe zone to explore a burden, roadblock, or difficult subject more fully. If your coachee affirms your metaphor, you may ask him

"In what ways is this new job like drinking water from a fire hose?" Together, you may discover that there are "a lot of fires to put out," that someone always needs to be rescued, that you have to be on call 24/7 in case a new fire starts. Metaphors are a way to discover new possibilities.

What is a Shift?

Coaching is the process of helping individuals move from the present to the future by accomplishing their goals. This process indicates a shift from one place or position to another. A coach can create an environment through language for a shift to occur. Only the coachee can make the shift.

As coaches, we work toward a shift from competent to masterful. The shift would be:

$$\text{Present state} \rightarrow \text{Future state} \rightarrow \text{Desired outcome}$$
$$\text{Competent} \rightarrow \text{Masterful} \rightarrow \text{Coaching success}$$

Distinctions

Words that illustrate the contrast or distinction between the current and future state can be powerful motivators. A coach can elicit and clarify distinctions, but the coachee must choose words that are personally significant to his or her current and future states.

The specific words chosen to depict both sides of the shift (i.e., the "from" position and the "to" position) are unique and often meaningful only to the person being coached who is making such a shift. They are words that may have only subtle distinctions, and the coachee will want to be clear about the definition of each distinction. Once clarity of the words is established, the phrase can be used as an affirmation to remind a person of his or her goal. The phrase can also be used as a simple evaluation of how much the shift and behavior have progressed.

The Coach Approach to Using Language with Shifts and Distinctions

The following ideas will assist you in developing the language of shifts for your coachee.

Ask your coachee to describe what he or she wants to accomplish in the coaching situation.

Have him or her discuss the particulars of the desired goal and how it will look, feel, and be like when he or she reaches it.

Ask him or her to describe their current situation in relationship to the desired goal. Deepen the clarity of the present and how it looks, feels, and is experienced.

✳ Request that he or she develop distinct and specific words or terms that uniquely express each of the two positions discussed in the first two ideas.

Explain the formulaic expression of these words (e.g., "I want to move from struggle to effortless"). Have him or her repeat the phrase until it belongs to them. The formula may need some polish with new words until he or she gets it just right.

Request that he or she commit to use this as a daily affirmation until the shift is complete and the goal is reached.

Examples:

Client: "I want my life to be easier. Seems like everything is always so hard."
Coach: "What would an easy life be like when you get it?"
Client: "It would be fun, exciting, meaningful, and easy. I will love it and enjoy waking up to it each day."
Coach: "Describe your present hard life."
Client: "It is very difficult for many reasons. It's always an uphill battle on everything. There's always something new to deal with. I feel behind the curve on everything."
Coach: "Pick two meaningful words that describe the two scenarios you just described."
Client: "My present life is a big struggle and the life I want is without so much effort. So I guess it would be struggle and effortless."
Coach: "So you want to move from struggle to effortlessness. How does that sound? Does it fit?"
Client: "From struggle to effortlessness. I love it. I'm ready!"
Coach: "Let's determine the action steps to make it happen."

Becoming a Language Artist: Ways to Develop the Skill of Language

A language artist is a person who understands and capitalizes on the power of language. They have nurtured their language skills to the degree that they are able to express themselves in clear, brief, and effective ways. New mediums of language are moved into on a regular basis. The following are some of the ways to become a language artist.

1. **Always listen carefully.** Language artists expand their repertoire first and foremost by being consummate listeners. They are always conscious of what is being said and how it is being said. The language artist notes the combination of words and phrases, plays with content, and listens for and creates beauty and magic.

2. **Read all kinds of literature.** Much of the existing artistry of language is preserved in literature, so a true language artist reads a wide variety of literature. Style and substance differ from Shakespeare to children's literature, and both have much to teach; language artists know and celebrate this fact through reading. When reading, observe the use of sentence structure, the blending of words and phrases, and the communication of ideas.

3. **Listen to authors in the oral medium.** Just as exposing oneself to literature expands the language repertoire, listening to language in the oral arts develops a person's ability to communicate more effectively. Language artists go to plays, movies, and speeches; they listen to books on tape, and to good radio. They listen to train their ears and their minds in the art of good language and conversation; they listen to expand the quality of their language and thereby gain the ability to skillfully apply it.

4. **Learn from others; spend time with people who are language artists.** Think through the people in your network and choose those who have a strong grasp of language and seem to know how to say the right thing at the right time. Be with these people; talk with them. See what stirs you as they speak, and see when they are stirred by your communication. Note the context of your conversations, the definition of subject matter, the willing give-and-take, and the exchange of ideas. Bring this learning back to your coaching practice.

5. **Take note of language lessons.** Language artists do not go passively through the world absorbing new language and hoping it will come to mind when needed. They create structures to integrate what they have learned and use it in their own lives and work—noting, storing, and revisiting their lessons regularly.

6. **Listen to yourself.** A language artist steps back often to see what he or she is doing well, and uses that knowledge to make conscious choices about what they want to express and how they want to express it.

7. **Check your patterns.** All of us, even the most skilled speaker, fall into language patterns. Unfortunately, old language patterns often replace true listening presence and genuine response with stale habits. Check speaking for habitual phrases, overused terms, and trivialized acknowledgments.

8. **Add new vocabulary.** The addition of new vocabulary adds greatly to your overall effectiveness. Look to add more words, phrases, descriptions, expressions, metaphors, and analogies to your skill set.

9. **Listen to the spoken word without pictures.** Painting pictures with words is a skill that is especially helpful when trying to capture the meaning of a coachee's message or when conveying a specific or difficult message. In order to fully understand and appreciate how the verbal translates into the visual in the mind, try listening to spoken words with your eyes closed. The absence of outside stimulation allows the mind to tune in completely to the structure, meaning, and emotion of language.

10. **Write.** Writing is a particularly fun and wonderful way to practice expanding your language skills because, when writing, words can be reviewed, rearranged, and changed. Whether writing a short, meaningful sentence, a notable paragraph, or a majestic first novel, expressing ideas on paper can test your skill and improve your ability.

" Be as you wish to seem. **"** | **Socrates**

The Outcomes of Language Becoming Art

Language starts to become art when speakers move past the mundane to richness. If you are willing to experiment by combining the best of what comes from your heart with the best of your knowledge, you create great learning opportunities for both yourself and your coachees.

1. **It has rhythm and cadence.** The skill of language is not just the ability to string words together. Language should have a subtle and wonderful rhythm to it. Effective language artists choose words that flow effortlessly together, "landing" with meaning and conviction.

2. **It is beautiful.** Words, like colors, have beauty to them. Language becomes art when words are chosen not only for their meaning but also for the characteristics they embody. Think about the words you enjoy hearing. They probably have charm, conviction, elegance, seriousness, lightness, or humor about them.

3. **It expresses real emotion.** Language began out of a human need to express emotion. When you can change emotion to language and share it, deep understanding can occur. The emotion may be one of many: happiness, sadness,

tranquility, or anger. The plain and powerful act of sharing emotion often helps coachees clarify their intentions, needs, goals, fears, and dreams.

4. **It expresses a person's truth.** Language as art frequently arises out of a courageous act. It usually takes some degree of courage for a person to tell his or her truth. In that moment, the intersection of courage, emotion, and language can produce powerful insights and growth.

5. **It illuminates and inspires.** Language can open doors and open minds; artful language sheds light and inspires. It can add insight and expand horizons. Words combined in simple, yet unique ways, can help others discover new perspectives, possibilities, and perceptions.

6. **It is simple.** To be artful does not mean to be complex; it means being easy to understand. It means words used to clarify rather than confuse. Language is not art when undertaken to impress or mystify. Language is art when it seeks to share with and include the hearer in a sincere and authentic manner.

Resources

Attention Readers:

Thank you for participating in the collective wisdom of Coach U. Together, we all continue to learn. Additional resources and forms can be found in *Coach U's Essential Coaching Tools: Your Complete Practice Resource* by CoachInc.com.

Attention CoachInc.com Students and Graduates:

CoachInc.com students and graduates may find additional and/or more recent resources associated with this module in the resource area of the student-only web site. If you are a student or graduate of one of CoachInc.com's ICF-accredited coach training programs, you can access these by searching under the name of the course. When the course description page appears you may find a link to the list of additional resources. Each item is a live link to its actual location on the web site. Click on the item to access the information.

Do remember to take the associated online self-test for this module once you have completed the course in person or by TeleClass. The tests are required for coach certification with the International Coach Federation. Throughout the course or anytime you find valuable resources for a particular course please feel free to add to the value of our curricula by forwarding the resource to revampteam@coachu.com.

Chapter 6

Questioning

Overview

Benefits Go to Page > 181

Powerful questioning is at the core of effective coaching. By participating in this module, you will learn to craft and deliver great coaching questions. You will learn how the type, timing, and impact of a coach's questioning differs from that of the typical way questions show up in most conversations, and how you can direct the flow of the coaching interaction for optimal benefit to the coachee.

Definitions Go to Page > 182

Empower, integrity, intuition, judgment, question, shifts, and leaps.

Concepts Go to Page > 183

Powerful Questioning
The ability to ask questions that move coachees forward in a coaching interaction is a key to coaching effectively. Although there are many types and kinds of questions available to you, discovery is the foundational intention.

Distinctions Go to Page > 186

Judgment versus judgmental, questioning versus interrogating.

⊙ Application

Go to Page > 187

The Framework of Questioning

Good questioning is an art form—in a coaching interaction, there are key ideas about questioning that will guide you in deciding which questions to ask and how to respond to the coachee's answer.

> Elements of Good Questioning
> Coachee's Learning Style
> Delivery Elements
> Types of Questions
> Questioning Focus
> Results of a Well-Asked Question

Questioning Behaviors: Promoters and Pitfalls

Resources

Go to Page > 197

○

Benefits

By participating in this module, you will learn to craft and deliver great coaching questions. You will learn how the type, timing, and impact of your questioning differ from that of the typical way questions show up in most conversations. You will also learn how you can direct the flow of the coaching interaction, for optimal benefit for the coachee, through the use of powerful questioning. Well-crafted questions create relationships, build rapport, and connect you with your coachee's way of understanding and dealing with information.

This course is designed to allow you to:

O **Define** the components and qualities of a good coaching question

O **Learn** the types and kinds of questions and their intended purposes

O **Identify** how consideration of coachee types and delivery elements can add to the value of questions

O **Understand** the pitfalls and limitations of questioning

Definitions

The following are common words used to gain a better understanding of the coaching process, particularly in regard to questioning.

Empower: To permit, enable, or give power or authority to someone. In a coaching interaction, good questions can empower coachees to take responsibility for actions toward their goals.

Integrity: Integrity is a state of personal wholeness, well-being, and fulfillment, not something to achieve, but rather a statement of our being. It is a reflection of who you are in any moment and is the dynamic relationship you maintain between purpose and path. It is the vigilant development, or continual adjustment, of the fit between our calling and conduct that allows us to sustain a high level of integrity.

Intuition: This is the perception of truth, facts, information, or other input not based on any reasoning process. It is the ability to have insight into something based on our own inner knowledge and truth, and not on external stimulus.

Judgment: The act of making a decision; the ability to form an opinion or choose between two or more things. It is important to be able to make sound judgments about which questions to ask and when.

Question: A sentence in an interrogative form that is addressed to someone to get information or cause reflection. In a coaching interaction, there are several types of questions, all aimed at discovery.

Shifts: Literally, a shift is a transition from one place or position to another, and includes a change, exchange, or substitution of something. It means to put something aside, such as a concept or understanding, and replace it with another. A shift can be systematic, following an established path of growth, or it can happen suddenly. Shifts are observable in resulting behaviors.

Leaps: To leap is to literally spring from one point or position to another. It involves jumping or springing over something to get to another place. In personal development, a leap is sudden and quick, not following a prescribed pattern of growth, and is usually accompanied with dramatic evidence of the leap. Leaps can be made over short or extensive distances. Leaping is the most obvious of all coachee developments observed by a coach.

Concepts

Powerful Questioning

Asking powerful questions for discovery is essential to good coaching. Well-placed questions allow you to direct the flow of the coaching interaction in the direction of optimal benefit for the coachee. In a coaching interaction, the ability to ask questions that move coachees forward is a key to coaching effectively. Although there are many types and kinds of questions available, discovery is the foundational intention.

Asking questions allows you to maintain the focus and direction of the coaching session. Through questioning, you can skillfully guide the conversation to yield the most discovery and prompt the greatest movement forward. Every coach is a researcher, carefully listening in order to always be alert for the next discovery question. Each coaching moment is an experiment without expectation of a specific response or the direction of the conversation.

Like good conversation, each coaching moment holds space for another question. Look beyond pat answers and simple comebacks; often it is the next question that hits the jackpot.

Coaches:
Ask questions that reflect active listening and an understanding of the coachee's perspective.

- Feeling questions
- Situational questions
- Being questions
- Intuitive questions
- Serendipitous questions

Ask questions that evoke discovery, insight, commitment, or action (e.g., those that challenge the coachee's assumptions).

- Inquiry questions
- Thought-provoking questions
- Information questions
- Probing questions
- Option questions
- Why questions

Ask open-ended questions that create greater clarity, possibility or new learning.

- Rhetorical questions
- Reality check questions
- Focusing questions
- Reminding questions
- Integrity questions

Ask questions that move the coachee toward what they desire, not questions that ask for the coachee to justify or look backwards.

- Goal-setting questions
- Prompting questions
- Solution questions
- Challenge questions
- Motivating questions
- Action questions
- Encouraging questions

Questions are asked in a coaching interaction for the benefit of the coachee, not just to gain information for the coach. Coachees may not always realize it, but they have the answers to their own dilemmas, problems, situations, and challenges. An artful question from a seasoned coach can elicit the answers from the coachee. Well-crafted questions, coming from a nonjudgmental place, and posed at the right time, can invite insight and solutions in a way that information telling never can. The intent of good questions is to elicit information, investigate, and discover while a coachee moves toward his or her goals; in that sense, there is rarely one right answer to any question. It is not finding the answer that is most important to the coachee, but rather it is in the process of answering the question that the benefit is gained.

Guiding Principle 2 | People Are Inquisitive.
Wonder, curiosity, and inquiry are the source of all learning.

There are many kinds and types of questions, each with its own rationale and intended result; good questions are:

- Succinct
- Transparent
- Nonjudgmental
- Intentional
- Directive
- Grounding

In addition, well-crafted questions contain seven basic components:

- A source
- Intent
- A subject
- Styling
- Anticipated outcome
- Timing
- Variety

All coaching questions have one intention—to get results for the coachee. Although questions may vary in type, timing, delivery, and wording, they are all designed to elicit information or a response that will ultimately benefit the coachee in his or her journey toward their goals.

Distinctions

There are subtle yet important differences in meaning between the following closely related terms. Understanding these distinctions allows you to perceive new layers of meaning and offers you new choices for shifting your thoughts, attitudes, and actions.

Judgment versus Judgmental

To make a judgment is to choose between two or more things: to decide what you prefer or what is appropriate for yourself. To be judgmental is to place criticism on someone else, using your set of values or preferences as the standard. While good judgment is necessary for you, never resort to being judgmental.

Questioning versus Interrogating

To question is to inquire, ask for information, or pose something for consideration or reflection. To interrogate is to do the same, but with greater intensity, more thoroughness, and generally with authority. Questioning is for discovery, but interrogation is grilling, and carries a negative connotation.

Application

The Framework of Questioning

A central skill of a good coach is to ask powerful questions. There is no coaching skill that is used distinctly and separately from the others. Questioning is not separate from listening or relating; together they make up the whole of a coaching interaction. Active listening, using intuition, and language skills all work together in crafting effective questions in turn can create relationships and build rapport. Every master coach has the ability to ask questions that move coachees forward in a coaching interaction.

Good questioning is an art form and there are key ideas about questioning that will guide you in deciding which questions to ask and how to respond to the coachee's answer.

Listen first, then create the question. To achieve mastery in artful questioning it is important to listen carefully and recognize exactly what is being said. You cannot ask great questions, for real discovery, without truly knowing what the coachee is expressing. Knowing how the coachee uses language allows you to design questions with familiar phrasing, so the coachee can relate more fully to your questioning.

The way a coachee phrases, or asks a question tells you a lot about their inner voice.

Listening to how the coachee asks questions can also reveal a great deal. The way a coachee phrases or asks a question tells you a lot about their inner voice. Does he or she have a negative premise? Is the cup half full or half empty? For example, a coachee might say, "Why can't I do that?" or "Why did I fail?" as opposed to a more constructive and positive self-question, "What blocked me, or got in my way here?" or "How can I move forward now?" Understanding how a coachee asks questions is important for your phrasing of questions back to the coachee.

Elements of Good Questioning

Common Qualities
There are many kinds and types of questions, each with its own rationale and intended result. All of them, however, should share certain qualities.

Strong questions are:

- Succinct—they are clear, direct, and easily understood by the coachee
- Transparent—there are no hidden agendas; coachees know exactly what is being asked
- Nonjudgmental—no attempt is made to veil a criticism or put the coachee down
- Intentional—you have the best interest of the coachee in mind when asking any type of question
- Directive—causes the coachee to stay in a thinking mode
- Grounding—keeps coachees in the here and now

What's In a Question?
The skill of good questioning is composed of several important elements; use these elements in crafting a question to elicit the desired effect. An effective question has:

- A source—You have several different sources from which good questions originate. They may come from:
  - Fully listening—you are attuned to the coachee and are aware of when to ask what questions.
  - An agenda—you may use a question with a specific purpose in mind: to stop conversation, create insight, shift the focus, or ask for action.
  - Intuition—intuitive coaches will often have the right question pop into their awareness, unsolicited, but perfect for the moment.
  - Knowledge—coaches often ask questions that come from their own experience or knowledge base. These questions tend to inform or create new learning for the coachee.
- Intent—your intent should be to ask a question that provides the coachee with a process to use in order to bring forward the information, idea, action, or solution he or she most needs at that moment.
- A subject—there are several types and kinds of questions. They can involve choices, decisions, options, action steps, reflection, creating insight, or planning, all of which relate to the coachee's goals.
- Styling—questions are sentences that involve the careful choice of words and phrases combined with artful delivery, tone, pace, volume, and expression, to create an atmosphere of understanding and ease of delivery.

- Anticipated outcome—questioning is a way to direct, not drive, the coachee to a desired outcome. The answers given may not be the ones you anticipate, but they are always the right ones.
- Timing—coaching questions are asked when the coachee is ready to hear them, not when you are ready to ask.
- Variety—there is an infinite variety of questions. You need to have a full repertoire from which to draw.

Coachee's Learning Style

People have different learning styles. Some learn by hearing, some by smelling, tasting, or feeling, and still others by being able to mentally visualize an idea or concept. Coachees will phrase their own questions and responses in the style that reflects how they prefer to receive information. Knowing how a coachee learns or hears information can be helpful to you in crafting questions for that particular coachee. For example:

Learning Style	Primary Input	Coachee Language	Coach Language
Emotional	Feelings	I feel drained. It touched my heart.	How do you feel about this? How does this strike you?
Auditory	Hearing	I hear myself getting grumpier.	What did you hear in this?
Tactile or kinesthetic	Feeling, sensory, movement, physical	It smells fishy to me.	What doesn't smell right to you?
Visual	Seeing, inward and outward	Can you see what I mean?	What do you see happening here?

Guiding Principle 8 | **People Have a Choice.**
Shifting perspectives expands awareness and reveals new choices.

Delivery Elements

Regardless of questioning style or type, discovery is the common foundational purpose. By crafting a question through careful consideration of the delivery elements you can offer more opportunity for the coachee to receive the question with the appropriate intent, thereby increasing the possibility of discovery. The delivery elements of a question can determine its overall impact and will greatly affect its power, urgency, importance, and directness to the coachee. You should consider the following when designing a question for discovery:

- Pace—how fast or slow the speaker talks or the conversation progresses
- Tone—the pitch or quality of the speaker's voice
- Volume—how loud or soft a voice is used
- Expressions—body language and/or the degree of animation in the voice
- Words—amount, placement, style, emphasis, choice

Common Types of Questions

Although questions may vary in type, they are all designed to elicit information or trigger a response that will ultimately benefit the coachee in his or her journey toward his or her goals.

Purpose: To reflect active listening and understanding of the coachee's perspective.

Feeling Questions
To find out how the coachee's situation, symptoms, and wants relate to his or her emotional state or feelings.

- How is it affecting you?
- What keeps you up at night?

Situational Questions
To discover what is present or true now; what is clear for the coachee and what is not. This is the first step in discovering the present situation.

- What is presently consuming your time that you wish you could eliminate?

Being Questions
Designed to find out how the coachee perceives him or herself in the world.

- Who is in charge of your life, you or other people?

Intuitive Questions

Designed to reflect your natural knowing about what needs to be asked at that moment, based on a hunch, intuition, or sense.

- Should you be in therapy and be resolving something?

Serendipity Questions

Not designed, but occurring by chance or intuition. The question comes as a result of the moment and your intuition.

- Are you talking about what really matters right now?

Purpose: To reflect active listening and understanding of the coachee's perspective.

Inquiry Questions

To discover what the coachee wants. What is his or her objective and what is the motivation (source) of the want?

- What are some opportunities you are currently not taking advantage of?

Thought-provoking Questions

To make a coachee think or re-think a perspective.

- Are you seeing this situation in a way that may be holding you back?

Informative Questions

To help the coachee gather more linear information, facts, or knowledge needed to make a decision or clarify a goal.

- How will you know how effective our coaching has been?

Probing Questions

Multilayered inquiries. Second questions that go deeper. These are in order when information has been brought out, but there still seems to be something missing.

- Where are you most irresponsible?

Option Questions

To find out what is to be done and what is possible, from the coachee's perspective.

- If you knew you would not fail and time and money were not issues, what three things would you most like to have, accomplish, or work toward?

Why Questions

To peel away layers of resistance or illusion in the way something is viewed or perceived, to get to the source of a block (should not be over-used).

- Why have you hired me as your coach?

Purpose: To reflect active listening and understanding of the coachee's perspective.

Rhetorical Questions

To state an observation as a question to assist in further clarifying a situation, response, idea, or block. A truly effective rhetorical question has no answer to it.

- I wonder if all coaches enjoy coaching as much as I do?

Reality-checking Questions

To clarify major distortions caused by opinions, judgments, and perceptions.

- Are we on track with what you want to talk about this session?

Focusing Questions

To prioritize and bring greater attention to the conversation, an issue, or goal.

- May I suggest we come back to the first issue before moving on to this new idea?

Reminding Questions

To bring attention to unmet deadlines, forgotten values, or goals.

- When will you need to complete that goal in order to keep on track with your plan?

Integrity Questions

To help the coachee connect his or her goals, actions, and behaviors to his or her value system (personal foundation).

- How does what you are thinking of doing fit with your value of honesty?

Goal-setting Questions

To help the coachee clarify and choose between alternative goals and actions.

- What specifically would you like to achieve over the next two years?

Prompting Questions

To get the coachee to tell you more about a particular idea, emotion, or action.

- Will you tell me more about that?

Purpose: To move the coachee toward what he or she desire, not to justify looking backward.

Solution Questions

To quickly facilitate an answer to a particular dilemma, challenge, or problem.

- What's the first thing you need to do now?

Challenge Questions

To evoke a strong response and a move toward shifting perspective or taking action.

- Can you hold yourself to a higher standard?

Motivating Questions

To initiate a forward movement to draw the coachee to benefits.

- How will you benefit when you have completed this goal?

Action Questions

To get the coachee to act on decisions, or shift attitudes and perspectives in order to create desired results.

- When will that be completed? What do you need to do next?

Encouraging Questions

To draw the coachee forward, to celebrate and renew his or her commitment to his or her goals.

- How will you celebrate when you are successful?

Questioning Focus

All questions will elicit a response somewhere on the *What* and *Who* scale. Certain questions are designed to yield information only. These are at the far end of the focus scale, and deal primarily with *What*. Questions designed to cause the coachee to be introspective and to look inside are at the other end of the focus scale, primarily concerned with *Who*.

What	Questioning Focus	Who
Informational	Reflective	Discovery	Introspective

Every question asked will be categorized somewhere on this focus scale. They may be reflective, designed to yield personal discovery, introspection, encouragement, or challenges, or merely to provide information to benefit further growth. In general, those questions which fall at the Who end of the focus scale will yield the most discovery and prompt the most growth as the coachee learns to be, rather than merely act in a certain way or direction. While What questions are important, and vital to the information or fact gathering process for both you and the coachee, the Who questions will go further to promote shifts, leaps, and overall personal development.

> **“** The question for each man to settle is not what he would do if he had the means, time, influence and educational advantages, but what he will do with the things he has. **”** | **Hamilton Wright Mabee**

Results of a Well-Asked Question

Coaches seek certain results when crafting and asking a question. Often the result you anticipate is the one you get, but sometimes the response is quite different than what you expected or are prepared for. Either way, if handled properly, the result can be positive.

- Coachee feels empowered—all good questioning should empower.
- Coachee feels competent and has his or her own answers to his or her challenges.
- Coachee slows down automatic thinking and reactive moves.
- Coachee thinks creatively—out of the box.
- Coachee stops to re-think—awareness is raised, which reveals more options.
- Coachee's current perceptions and patterns of behavior are broken.
- Coachee is illuminated to clarify and examine an issue.
- Coachee moves from seeing what's true to taking action.

Questioning Behaviors: Promoters and Pitfalls

The DOS are behaviors that promote successful questioning. The DON'TS are behaviors that limit the success of questioning.

Do—Question the coachee. / **Don't**—Grill the coachee.	Questioning, in a coaching relationship, is a very powerful tool, with the purpose of discovery. It is not intended to interrogate or grill the coachee and place him or her on the hot seat, under glaring lights. Don't badger or threaten a coachee with the kind of questions or tone that is intimidating. Carefully craft questions so that they hold no threat.
Do—Allow the coachee to answer the questions. / **Don't**—Provide answers to the questions for the coachee.	The purpose of questioning is to allow the coachee to discover the answers. It does not serve the coaching relationship well if you both ask and answer the question. Questioning is not about you, your answers, or your ideas. It is all about the coachee. The coachee will gain much more from his or her own answers than from yours.
Do—Stay in the present. / **Don't**—Allow questions to drift into the past or the unknown.	The coachee can only answer questions from his or her current perspective. Yesterday is history, tomorrow is not known. Be sure your questions are phrased so that discovery of the here and now is determined.
Do—Know that only the coachee has the right answer. / **Don't**—Assume the coach has the only right answer.	You will often have an answer or an outcome in mind when questioning, but should not place those in front of the coachee's answer and outcome. Remember that the coachee always holds the truth. Allow the coachee to answer the question, and allow his or her answer to be correct.
Do—Ask only thoughtful, necessary questions. / **Don't**—Question to be questioning only.	Yes, questioning is one of the key competencies of good coaching, but there is a time and place for all questions. Don't get caught in the trap of thinking you must keep asking questions, just for the sake of asking them. Questioning, like all other coaching skills, has a right and natural place and time.
Do—Use the coachee's natural curiosity and need for discovery. / **Don't**—Forget the coachee's natural curiosity.	We are all curious; it is part of our natural state. A good coach understands that people want to be questioned, and want to know the answers. They desire to find the answers when questioned. Questioning and answering is a natural and normal way for people to learn and grow.

Do—Know there are no right or wrong answers.	There are no right and wrong answers to coaching questions. All of them yield a truth of sorts, and sometimes a perceived wrong answer is a blessing in disguise. When coachees respond to a question with an unexpected answer (perhaps only unexpected by you!), it opens new avenues to explore, such as readiness for action, clarity of issues, and commitment levels. Always look for the "second" question and possible paths open to the coachee.
Don't—Berate so-called wrong answers.	
Do—Ask the right questions before the right time.	Timing is critical in artful questioning. Quite often you will have crafted precisely the right question, but the coachee will not be ready to hear it in a given moment. Listen carefully for the right, perhaps spontaneous (and always intuitively), appropriate moment to ask any question.
Don't—Blurt a question in an inappropriate or premature moment.	

Resources

Attention Readers:

Thank you for participating in the collective wisdom of Coach U. Together, we all continue to learn. Additional resources and forms can be found in *Coach U's Essential Coaching Tools: Your Complete Practice Resource* by CoachInc.com.

Attention CoachInc.com Students and Graduates:

CoachInc.com students and graduates may find additional and/or more recent resources associated with this module in the resource area of the student-only web site. If you are a student or graduate of one of CoachInc.com's ICF-accredited coach training programs, you can access these by searching under the name of the course. When the course description page appears you may find a link to the list of additional resources. Each item is a live link to its actual location on the web site. Click on the item to access the information.

Do remember to take the associated online self-test for this module once you have completed the course in person or by TeleClass. The tests are required for coach certification with the International Coach Federation. Throughout the course or anytime you find valuable resources for a particular course please feel free to add to the value of our curriculum by forwarding the resource to revampteam@coachu.com.

Chapter 7

Strategizing

Overview

Strategizing is a comprehensive coaching practice. By participating in this module you will learn the tools to help your coachees develop effective strategies to accomplish their goals. This module will give you an understanding of the framework of strategizing, as well as practical tools and information about the discernment and attitude involved in being an effective strategist.

Strategy, strategize, priorities, vision, simplification, charting, integrity, values, needs, wants, focus, and flow.

Strategizing for Success

There is a methodology to strategizing. Strategizing is not a single tool, but the combination of all coaching tools and skills, used in a masterful way to assist coachees in creating the strongest plan possible for reaching their goals. CoachInc.com has developed the Strategizing for Success model to facilitate a successful approach for both you and the coachee.

Direction versus control, prioritize versus schedule, simplify versus strip or reduce, focus versus obsess, and vision versus goal.

○ Application Go to Page > 212

The Framework of Strategizing

The framework of strategizing is captured in the Strategizing for Success model. The model contains guidelines, tools, and information that you and your coachees can use to develop your own strategies.

Strategizing for Success Model

      Evaluating and Strengthening the Foundation
      The Here and Now
      Designing the New Wall: The There and Then
      Identifying the Gap
      The Roof (Bridging the Gap)

Strategizing Behaviors: Promoters and Pitfalls

○ Resources Go to Page > 225

Benefits

By participating in this module you will understand the coaching skills and steps involved in helping your coachees develop a strategy for success. You will be able to use the four strategizing steps to set priorities, identify and explore vision, simplify, chart, and monitor goal pursuit. Using these steps has personal and professional applications for both coach and coachee. The purpose of this module is to give you the tools to help your coachees become excellent strategists for their own success.

This course is designed to allow you to:

O **Define** what strategizing means in the context of a coaching interaction

O **Learn** a strategizing model that can be tailored to any goal

O **Identify** specific strategizing steps to help your coachees meet their goals and desired outcomes

O **Help** you create an environment where coachees can fashion their own effective strategy for achieving goals

O **Use** effective strategizing tools for coaching

O **Understand** the pitfalls and limitations of strategizing

Definitions

The following are common words used to gain a better understanding of the coaching process, particularly in regard to strategizing.

Strategy: A strategy is simply a plan or a method for achieving a specific goal. A strategy can be anything from how to accomplish a simple task to how to live life more fully. Strategies generally have several ways they identify and track the goal-seeking process. A good strategy is one that makes use of all available resources.

Strategize: To develop a strategy, plan, or method for achieving goals. A goal is the objective of a strategy, and can be very simple or extremely complex. It is the result or achievement toward which effort is directed: the aim or end of something. A goal implies that work (or effort) is involved to achieve it.

Priorities: A priority is something that takes precedence over something else and something given special attention. In general, priorities are a set of ideals (physical, spiritual, or emotional) that when grouped together compose the items most important to an individual. They are considered to be at the top of any list of things to achieve in any area of life.

Vision: A vision is simply something seen internally. A personal vision is something seen for the future. It is a scene about the way a person wants things to be in the future. It involves anticipation, foresight, perception, conception, and desire. A personal vision is based on wants, needs, values, and goals. A vision may be singular in nature, or involve many facets.

Simplification: To simplify is to make things less complex, less complicated, plainer, and easier. Simplification is the process of simplifying. Simplification can be applied to anything in life from tasks and goals to vision and values—or life in general.

Charting: To chart something is to plan a course of action generally in graphic chart form or a similar format that can be easily conceptualized. A chart is often visually depictive of special conditions, facts, and other important information. Charting, in this module, is also the progressive following of a plan for the purpose of accountability.

Integrity: Integrity is a state of personal wholeness, well-being, and fulfillment: not something to achieve, but rather a statement of our being. It is a reflection of who you are in any moment and is the dynamic relationship you maintain between purpose and path. It is the vigilant development, or continual adjustment, of the fit between calling and conduct that allows us to sustain a high level of integrity.

Values: Values are ideals that are personally important and meaningful for you and draw you forward. Values are inherent in each person's makeup; we all have them. They are specific and individual, but people can share common values.

Needs: Needs are the emotional aspects that drive individuals. The driving force behind needs is based in human yearning for wholeness. Often, needs direct major life decisions until they are met. Needs can also get in the way of a person clearly identifying his or her values and living life based on those values. The kinds of needs we are discussing here go beyond the basic needs for food, air, water, and shelter to the things that a person feels he or she must have. For example, coachees may need to be accepted, to accomplish, be acknowledged, be loved, be right, or be cared for.

Wants: To want something is to wish for it or desire it. Wants are flexible and/or optional; if you get it, great; if not, you are still okay. When your needs are met and your life is oriented to your values, your wants tend to proportionately decrease. For example, I may want to succeed in business or have a great body or a big house.

Focus: As a noun, a focus is the central point of attraction, attention, or activity. As a verb, to focus means to concentrate on something as the central point, freeing self of distractions or other outside influences that would confuse whatever is the point of attraction.

Flow: To flow is to move along continuously and easily, like a stream. When something is flowing, it is moving forward unimpeded, unencumbered, and naturally. You work to improve the overall flow in every area of a coachee's life. In this module, strategizing should have a certain flow to it, as well as the strategy itself.

Concepts

Strategizing for Success

The dictionary defines strategizing as the science and art of using all the available resources and forces to execute a plan as effectively as possible. Efficiency is a consideration, but effectiveness is the primary objective of any strategy. The ultimate objective is reaching a goal or set of goals.

Strategizing is one of the primary activities in any coaching relationship. The coachee comes to you generally to achieve certain goals, and you work with the coachee to develop a strategy (to strategize) to accomplish those goals. Strategizing is how the "gap" is bridged between where the coachee is, and where the coachee wants to be. There may be many goals involved on many levels, or merely a single "problem" or target goal, which requires strategy in order to successfully reach a satisfactory conclusion.

A strategy is a way of describing how you are going to produce an outcome. There may be many possible strategies for any given goal. The best strategy is the one that considers all available resources to achieve this goal, in the easiest, least confusing, least costly (time, money, energy, etc.) manner, while aligning with the priorities, values, and vision of the person seeking the outcome.

Strategies can also have beneficial side effects when developed properly. When the coachee creates a strategy, it gives him or her something to orient around—a way to filter out "good ideas" that may just be distractions. A good strategy both foci and simplifies efforts.

Strategies are based on many factors. These factors include what is good or right to you (personal choice), what has worked for others (emulating), what makes the most sense (logical), what costs the least (low-risk), and so on. There are no rights and wrongs in strategizing (except if the strategy does not align with the coachee's values, vision, and integrity—personal foundation), but it is vital for the coachee to understand why certain strategies are developed, and potential consequences or rewards that may come of them.

> 66 First say to yourself what you would be; and then do what you have to do. 99 | **Epictetus**

Strategizing for Success Model

CoachInc.com has developed a model that is a simplification of the strategizing process, and a way to visually identify the components of good strategizing with coachees. It is a comprehensive model which addresses all the basic needs of strategizing for success. When followed, this model can help a coachee create simple yet highly effective strategies for any goal or desired outcome in life. Individuals, couples, small teams, and large groups can use this model with success.

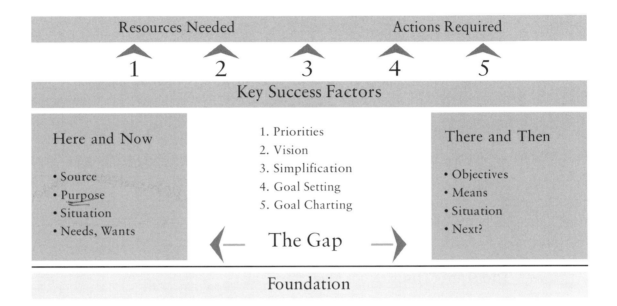

The Components of the Model

The model above is built on the concept of a house, and the structural elements necessary to support it.

Evaluating and Strengthening the Foundation

Essentially, all strategy begins with the foundation—the personal foundation of the coachee or the business foundation of the organization. The foundation is the structural basis that supports living an exceptional life and building a successful business. Just as a house must be built on a strong foundation to avoid collapsing under stress, so must one's strategy for success. No strategy will succeed, no matter how brilliant or well-conceived, if it is not grounded with a strong foundation.

The Here and Now

The one existing wall of the house above is the "Here and Now": what is known to be true at this moment. This wall reveals the objective or the goal. It also contains information about the purpose of the strategy, the current situation, and the needs and wants that relate to the goal.

Designing the New Wall: The There and Then

The second important structure is the other wall of the house: the "There and Then," or "what will be when the goal is met" wall. We know what it will look like, but it isn't built yet. This new wall consists of information about the objective(s), the future situation when the goal is met, what fulfillment looks like, and any next steps beyond this goal.

Identifying the Gap

Between these two walls of Here and Now and There and Then exists the Gap. This Gap can be the size of a football stadium or a simple doghouse. In other words, it can be huge or very small. The Gap is the empty space between where the person is right now (the Here and Now wall) and where they want to be (the There and Then wall).

The Roof (The Bridge Over the Gap)

Over the Gap we construct a roof truss to span the two walls. The materials used to construct the bridge (truss) are the five steps and processes that make up a successful strategy:

1. Priorities

This is a critical first step. Prioritizing helps establish what is most important (and most urgent) in the development of a successful strategy. The identification of practical (from daily life), personal (from the heart), and professional (from the profession) priorities will determine direction and provide an accountability tool as the strategy is utilized. Priorities can also determine the order and consequences for actions.

2. Vision

Vision can only be clearly articulated after priorities are set. Vision is the factor that gives life, perception, and direction to the priorities. A strategy without a vision is merely a goal, and does not include all aspects of an individual or organization. A long-term vision will be created based on priorities and objectives, as well as smaller, more specific visions for intermediate goals. The long-term larger vision should be part of every strategy, whatever the size or scope.

3. Simplification

Simplification is the cleanup step after priorities are established and vision is in place. It takes all the components of both and neatly compartmentalizes and pairs them into a neatly organized package. During this step, all extraneous, complicating, encumbering, and unnecessary parts are eliminated, and those left are streamlined. Simplification gets rid of the impractical and the unrealistic.

4. Goal Setting

This is the step where actual goals are set and determined, taking into consideration all of the steps before it. Priorities determine which goals fit and which are first on the list. Vision helps set the goal, especially if more than one goal is involved. Vision also gives emotional ownership and personal inspiration to the goal. Simplification makes the goal easier to clearly identify, and easier to achieve.

5. Goal Charting

This is the final step in building the bridge between the two walls of the Here and Now and the There and Then. It involves two processes: first, to determine and plot a course of action that is a distinct and clear path consisting of smaller steps to the goal; and finally, to use this chart to follow the progress of the actions as they are executed, realigning, reidentifying, and making course corrections as necessary. This charting process establishes the action plan and also provides a method of accountability, which incorporates all the other components of the model.

The other members of this roof system are the two joists labeled "Resources Needed" and "Actions Required." This is the clear identification of all necessary and available resources that will assist in meeting the goal, as well as the actions required to get there. They are vital to the whole strategizing process, and are especially important in step five above, goal charting.

Together, these five steps and two joists comprise the "Key Success Factors" to strong strategizing.

Distinctions

There are subtle yet important differences in meaning between the following closely related terms. Understanding these distinctions allows you to perceive new layers of meaning and offers you new choices for shifting your thoughts, attitudes, and actions.

Direction versus Control

Direction is pointing toward something with instruction and guidance; it can also be management and supervision. To control is to exercise restraint over something, to dominate and regulate or command. Control can also literally mean to prevent the flourishing or spread of something. You are hired to offer direction, not just facilitate discovery, understanding, or awareness. In fact, the coachee has been attracted to you because of your background, life experience, and direction. It is an accepted part of the coaching relationship that the coachee asks for direction, that you offer it when appropriate, and that the coachee weaves your ideas into his or her own decisions. You do not lead sheep or ask the coachee to blindly follow. Your coachees are thoughtful adults, not impressionable children. You direct, but not control.

Prioritize versus Schedule

Prioritizing establishes the importance or order in which things are done. To schedule means to plan for a thing or series of things to be done at a certain time. When something is a priority for you, you usually don't have to schedule it; you just do it. If you have a coachee who is trying to fit everything in or super-schedule him- or herself, ask them to review their priorities and stop the over-scheduling.

Simplify versus Strip or Reduce

To simplify something (you, your life, a business, a lifestyle, a series of goals) clearly implies a reduction. Most coachees will be reducing activities, goals, shoulds, coulds, appointments, and so on in order to simplify their lives. Simplification can, however, be a creative process. Creativity in the simplification process includes reducing, eliminating, and removing, which can also evoke a sense of loss. A balanced approach of building and reducing is best. Simplification does not mean to arbitrarily strip things away from one's life. It is the careful choosing of what is important now.

Focus versus Obsess

To focus is to see clearly what is most important and concentrate on it; to obsess is to let focus become an end in itself to the extent that the order of integrity, needs, and wants is disturbed.

Vision versus Goal

A vision is what you see as being possible for the future. A personal vision creates excitement and ownership, and even inspires toward accomplishing goals. A goal is what you want to accomplish, and is generally only part of the vision. A vision is something that pulls you towards the goal and helps determine other goals. The coachee needs to understand the distinction when setting goals, and should be encouraged to explore his or her vision (for personal and professional life) first.

Application

The Framework of Strategizing

Strategizing is a common and natural part of life. Throughout both our personal and professional lives we will be developing strategies, whether we are conscious of it or not. When we know and understand the steps and tools available for planning excellent strategies, we can engage in this behavior with more confidence, purpose, and direction, and realize more of what we want. This is a highly valuable practice for achieving satisfaction in one's life, and one that you can facilitate in your coachees. Why strategize? When coachees come to you they will be ready to set goals, if they haven't done so already, so the need for strategy will present itself immediately in the coaching relationship. Setting goals means strategizing. There are an infinite number of reasons for setting strategies. The coachee will most likely fall into one (or more) of these categories or reasons for strategizing. The coachee:

- Is in personal or financial trouble
- Is ready to go for a big opportunity and/or project
- Is making big changes and/or decisions
- Is stuck, frustrated, or blocked
- Wants to make more money
- Wants to be able to do something better
- Wants to start or improve their business
- Wants to know him or herself better—to do better
- Is ready to move to the next level
- Wants a greater challenge
- Is experiencing professional challenges
- Is experiencing personal challenges

Your role in strategizing is to support the development of a strategy. You can do this by first introducing the notion of strategy if the coachee isn't familiar with the concept. Sharing the model, educating coachees on the steps involved in strategizing, and encouraging them to create their own strategy is a strong way to begin. Remember, a strategy is how the coachee will reach his or her goals in the smartest possible way—it is more than just an action plan or time line, and it requires thinking, discussion, refining, and creativity.

There are logical and practical steps involved in strategizing. The model presented in the Concepts section is explored further here, with emphasis on teaching you to train and develop your coachees in using this model for reaching goals and achieving success.

Strategizing for Success Model

The Strategizing for Success model provides a structure for developing strategies to ensure excellence for both you and the coachee.

Evaluating and Strengthening the Foundation

The coachee's personal foundation, or the organization's business foundation, is the structure upon which strategizing for success rests. For the personal foundation, those are *What, Who,* and *How.* For the business foundation, the parts are *Purpose, Values,* and *Future Description.*

An Individual's Foundation
What. We have called this part *What,* as it aptly labels the presenting package of a person. It is *What* the world sees when it looks at us. This element is also composed of several sub-elements, or parts, as well. We can include such things as behavior, the public self, and what we show others.

Who. The *Who* part of you is easily understood as the real you, the core of who you really are, not in presentation of the *What.* The *Who* often drives the *What,* but is not always consistent with it. The *Who* focus of personal foundation begins to look at the alignment between who we are and the behavior we engage in. We often tend to operate more from an automatic pilot, reactive state of decision making, as opposed to a well thought out and explored plan based on what really creates our uniqueness in the world and serves us the best.

How. The third component of personal foundation is the set of processes, methods, and values that drive our behavior—*How* we do the things we do, and *How* we are *Who* we are. The fuel for the *How* of us is the *Who,* which essentially yields the *What.* If you put this into an equation it would look like this: *Who* + *What* = *How.* This aspect of personal foundation helps an individual explore and discover the most articulate and authentic manner to express all the best of *Who*—the real self—in the world. This includes identifying core values, investing in life, choosing work, simplifying life, and attracting what is desired most.

A Business or Organization's Foundation

Purpose. The purpose of a business is the reason the business exists. It can be for simple reasons, such as "to sell chicken soup" or elaborate purposes such as "to sell the best chicken soup on the market today made only from all-organic meats and vegetables, whole wheat pastas and the finest herbs and spices." Every business can benefit from examining the overall purpose of the enterprise. Spending time developing a standard business purpose, fully explored and completely defined, will greatly enhance the overall strategizing process, and help ensure that all future goals are aligned with this underlying purpose. Without a fully defined purpose, known by all stakeholders, future planning and strategizing can be fruitless, or at least, derailed.

Values. Business values are similar to individual values. They indicate how the business operates. Business values include how the business interacts with itself, with others, and with circumstances, both internally and externally. Values cover everything from the quality of the ingredients in the above chicken soup example, to the ethics of the business and the way the business treats employees and customers. Values guide the "how" of daily operations and should be communicated throughout the organization.

Future Description. The future description of a business includes the desires and dreams of the stakeholders for the ultimate destination of the business. The chicken soup business may begin selling only to local supermarkets, but may desire to ultimately sell worldwide through wholesale Internet sales. The future description captures not just one or two goals, but the end result of many steps to achieve it. It may be based on a desired or projected timeline, and in some cases may even seem completely unrealistic or undoable on the surface.

Often, organizational mission or vision statements seek to capture all three of the above components. These should be reviewed, checked for accuracy and completeness, and used as templates to measure all goals, strategies, and work done to achieve them.

An individual's personal foundation is his or her basis for living a meaningful, fulfilling life. A business or organization's foundation is its basis for doing business in a meaningful, successful way. Unless all goals and reasons are founded on and aligned with this, no amount of strategizing will be successful.

Spending ample time here can keep the structure from tumbling down completely. During this step, it is highly possible that the coachee's goals will change, and so will his or her priorities. Be sure to go back to the existing wall and re-evaluate it in light of new growth or information about personal and business foundation. The building process of successful strategizing cannot continue until the Here and Now and the foundation of the structure are aligned, and can stand alone and are strong. The foundation must be able to support all further building activities.

The Here and Now

The existing wall of the structure, which we are calling the "Here and Now," will be the place where strategy begins.

Most often the nonexisting wall, the "There and Then," will be in the design process before honest evaluation of the Here and Now begins. That is fine, but to identify the breadth of the gap existing between the two, it is important to fully explore and identify exactly what is, in order to get to what can be. The There and Then may also undergo a redesign process after truly knowing what exists now.

You will automatically be doing a background evaluation of the coachee's Here and Now. That is a vital coaching function. Just as critical, you are helping coachees understand where they are now. This will require laser questioning, and the honest responses of the coachee.

The Source
Here and Now contains the source for the There and Then. It reveals what has prompted the need to build that other wall, the There and Then. You help your coachees find the reasons behind the goals they wish to achieve.

Exploring the source of an intended or desired goal points out the reasons behind it, and may bring other issues to the forefront that will need to be addressed.

The Purpose
Once the reasons for goals are known and stated, their purpose should be investigated. Reasons are different than purposes. A coachee can have very solid purpose behind a goal, but the reasons can be all wrong. For example, a coachee may wish to double his or her business in one year, the purpose being to be bigger, make more money, be (or appear) more successful. The reasons they have set this goal, however, may not be in keeping with their integrity or values, and may be the result of outside influences, such as "shoulds" or unreasonable expectations. The person may actually be happier being smaller, not bigger. Help the coachee ensure that their reasons and goals match.

To assist the coachee in making the distinction between reasons and purposes, you can ask questions such as:

- Explain why you really want to do or have this.
- Do you really want this goal, or is there something else in the background we haven't discussed yet?
- What is driving your need?
- I know you have told me the purpose, but what are the real reasons you want this?
- Is this an honest goal, or one developed out of a sense of responsibility or other influence?

The Situation

The Here and Now contains a set of information that describes the present situation, what is true now. Knowing what is now also helps identify what can be, and the gap between them. It is a vital part of strategizing. We cannot know how to get somewhere without knowing exactly where we are. This is the starting point on the blueprint or map. Identifying what can be is the end point. Strategizing is drawing the line between them.

The coachee should be helped to explore where he or she is now, and how that really relates to his or her desired goal(s). This process demands honest self-evaluation and will require gentle guidance on your part. Part of this process may be to help the coachee understand that what exists now can be perfect. The need to achieve a goal must come from the heart and vision, not from expectations for self-improvement. Sometimes this step may crumble preset goals, and the coachee will find new ones more in keeping with who he or she is now and who they really want to be. It is much better to discover this at this stage, than halfway to a goal that the person never really wanted.

Needs and Wants

Needs and wants reside in the Here and Now. Help the coachee identify them, express them, and own them. At this point in the strategizing journey, it is not so important to figure out if they are the right needs and wants, or the right goals. That will happen further into the process. Right now they must be completely out on the table, open to look at, and able to be described. What exactly do they look like?

Spending time first in the Here and Now can save valuable time later in the strategizing process. Again, we can't know where we are going until we know fully where we are right now.

Designing the New Wall: The There and Then

After identifying the Here and Now and examining the foundation, the new wall—the There and Then—can be designed. It does not exist yet, but planning is underway. How will it look? How will it be built? What is it made of? How will it be supported?

Objectives

What objectives will be met with this new place, this goal? What does the coachee hope this new goal will do for him or her? How will the goal fulfill him or her? How will he or she feel when they reach this goal? How will the There and Then be different from the Here and Now?

Means

What are the means to achieve this goal? Does the coachee know how this goal will be achieved? Are the team members given authority to use the means to achieve this goal? Is there any vision for it? This is not really the moment when the steps will be outlined for achieving the goal, but it is good to explore whether the coachee has ideas about it.

Situation

Once the goal is achieved what will the situation and the conditions surrounding it look like? Is there a structure in place, or can it be built, to support this new situation? You can help the coachee visualize just what the conditions surrounding this goal, once realized, will look like, and what may be required in addition to the known goals. This step may bring to light a whole new set of goals that may need to be achieved either before or immediately after the original goal(s) have been met.

Next?

Where does the coachee go from here? What does life hold after this goal is realized? Will he or she be fulfilled, happy, content—or ready to jump into the next something? Are there logical next steps? Beware of the "If I could only. . . . I'd be happy" syndrome. Help the coachee to understand that the present can be perfect, but continue to encourage their growth and personal and professional development. This can be a balancing act.

Identifying the Gap

Now that the existing structure is well defined and strengthened, and the new addition is designed, the gap which exists between them can be easily seen, and will make the next phase of strategizing easier and more efficient and effective. Ask the coachee to feel this gap, get into it, and explore it. What exactly is the difference between Here and Now and There and Then? What must fill this gap and how will it be filled?

You must be watching for the size and consistency of the gap. Is it too big to be spanned? Encourage the coachee to place the two walls at a distance that provides the greatest amount of achievable growth. The key word here is achievable. Is it too small, not allowing for the greatest shifts, leaps, and dynamic growth? You may know better than the coachee what the coachee is capable of doing. He or she should be encouraged to make great shifts and leaps, but make sure the leap does not fall short. Incremental goals may need to take the place of giant ones. Have the coachee run periodic reality checks on this gap distance, fully exploring its void before attempting to jump from Now to Then.

The Roof (Bridging the Gap)

Now the construction begins. All other stages have been preparatory to this one. But even before the actual plan can be devised, there is still more work to be done. The five-step process of building the truss to span the gap between the two walls requires the following materials:

Step 1: Priorities

Priorities may have been addressed at earlier stages, especially during the strengthening of personal foundation. However, this is the time to really get honest and thoroughly look at personal priorities in light of the work done to this point.

Ask the coachee to break priorities into at least three groups:

- Practical—what is most important about their physical, daily life?
- Personal—what is most important to them in terms of their hearts' desires?
- Professional—what is most important to them about their work and their needs on a professional level? What have they been hired to do by the organization?

Then, ask him or her to align these priorities with what has been identified as their personal foundation. Do these priorities meet the needs of self, integrity, and values? Once the coachee has done this you must be alert to trends, imbalances, unnecessary burdens and expectations, "shoulds," misalignment with personal foundation, and other signs that might indicate a coachee needs to reevaluate and reidentify priorities.

Once the greater priorities of life are known, the priorities found in specific tasks or goals must be explored. Setting priorities is all about ranking the importance of and setting up the conditions for actual goal planning.

Step 2: Vision

Vision is what gives life, inspiration, perception, and direction to the priorities established. Vision belongs solely to the coachee, not to you. You may (should) have a vision for that coachee, but the coachee must own his or her own vision for achieving those goals. Vision is generally not something you work on—that is planning and strategizing. Vision happens on its own. As hard as you try, you cannot create vision. You can create purpose, mission, and plans, but not vision. Vision is picturing what is possible for the future. It does not always contain the plan, but usually contains the heart and soul of potential. Great vision is clear and inspiring—motivating in itself. Vision requires that the person have complete knowledge and information about the intended actions, goals, and objectives, has aligned them with his or her personal foundation, has established priorities, and genuinely desires to see the outcome realized.

If a coachee insists he or she has no vision, there are ways to help him or her to achieve a vision for life in general, and for specific parts of life. Encourage the coachee to think about this and try to articulate that overriding vision. A vision should be fun, inspiring, and motivating. Vision inspires growth.

Identifying vision involves the following:

- Knowing strengths and weaknesses
- Knowing likes and dislikes
- Knowing wants and needs
- Knowing self in general
- Having a strong personal foundation
- Making full use of life experiences
- Being able to derive inspiration from all sources and resources
- Having true, meaningful goals
- Willingness to bring whole self to achieving vision

Step 3: Simplification

All the information that has been gathered up to this point needs to be on the table for sorting and identification. This step is akin to cleaning closets. Everything needs to be taken out, analyzed, and then put back in—or thrown out. The piles for sorting will include:

- What is known for sure
- Definitive priorities
- Appropriate vision
- Personal foundation
- Complete knowledge of the Here and Now
- The designed There and Then

This is the simplifying, unburdening, and organizing process. You help the coachee through this process by careful listening, laser questioning, and constructive feedback.

Step 4: Goal Setting

What has been done so far in the strategizing process has been to make sure that any goals the coachee brings to the coaching relationship are realistic and worthy of his or her effort. By this step, both coach and coachee know exactly what those goals should be, and their order of importance. This is the certification process for setting the goals.

All About Goals
Types of Goals

Internal: Changing on the inside; being different or better; growing up, attitude changes; raising standards, clarifying values (these goals involve personal foundation, specifically values and integrity).

External: Goals involving the physical self. These can be both wants and needs; new car, better job, more business, savings, clothes, house, and so on.

Skills: Goals that help you do something better; communication, relating, managing, decision-making, problem-solving, and so on.

Goal Base

Integrity-based: Goal is set because the coachee needs to restore integrity, balance, honesty, and/or order. Self or Needs-based: Goal is set because the coachee cannot operate fully without these needs being met.

Values-based: Goal is set in order to express and align with what is most important to the coachee.

Vision-based: Goal is set because the coachee has solid vision about what is to be achieved and a general sense of how. It is important to the coachee, and a source of inspiration for development.

Reaction-based: This is setting goals because the coachee doesn't like what they have, is generally done out of frustration, tolerances, and other outside influences, and can tend to be reactionary. These goals need honest evaluating.

Shift-based: Many times in the development of a coachee he or she will make radical shifts and leaps—this is a good thing! However, it will often cause goals to change.

Questionable Goals or Shoulds: Externally prompted goals are an effort to accomplish, are expensive, and may not be necessary.

Have-tos: Goals should be from coachee's choice, not from shoulds or have-tos. Help the coachee develop enough to make his or her own choices.

Consequence Avoiders: Setting goals to avoid the consequences of not doing something else. This is avoidance, and is immature. The coachee needs personal foundation work.

Fantasies: Fantasies can be part of vision, but these kinds of goals are usually unattainable and a waste of valuable resources.

Too Big: Big is fun, and necessary for great leaps in growth, but goals that are too big invite disaster. Some coachees thrive on this, but are sure they can endure, learn from, and enjoy the failures that will result.

Ego: Goals that puff up the coachee's ego are a wasteful use of time. Help coachees gain their worth from within, not from accolades.

If–then: If I do this, then I can do this. These can succeed, but sometimes are wasteful. Set the goal as the only goal. At this point in the strategizing process it should be fairly clear what goals are to be set, how they are identified, and exactly what they look like. In order to assure that goals are only those which will advance the coachee, keep him or her in integrity and inspire them to further growth, the following suggestions and guidelines are helpful.

1. Find out if the coachee can answer Yes (honestly) to all of the following questions:
    *   Does this goal align with my personal and/or business foundation?
    *   Am I setting this goal for the right reasons?
    *   Does this goal meet existing wants and/or needs adequately?
    *   Is this goal attainable?
    *   Is this goal big enough, or too big?
    *   Do I have a vision for this goal?
    *   Is this goal a priority?
2. Determine if the coachee understands that the present can be perfect, and that no goal achievement will make it perfect.
3. Life can dish up hard lessons through poor choices. If you instinctively know that a certain goal may not be right for the coachee you are obliged to point this out, explain the reasons, and then support the coachee if he or she insists on pursuing that goal. You can help make this learning experience (the pursuit of wrong goals) meaningful, if necessary.
4. Ask the coachee to state this goal or series of goals in writing, as succinctly as possible. Both you and the coachee should retain copies.
5. Take a look at the predesigned wall of There and Then. Do the established goals hold true to the original design? If not, help the coachee or team to redesign a more workable plan.

" By failing to prepare, you are preparing to fail. **"** | **Unknown**

Step 5: Goal Charting

When the personal foundation is strong, the Here and Now is fully known, the There and Then is designed (and perhaps redesigned several times), the Gap is known, priorities are established, vision is explored, everything is simplified, and goals are set and owned, it is time for the strategic plan.

A strategy, or strategic plan, includes several key things. A complete strategic plan would include the following:

*   An outcome or objective
*   List of resources needed and those available
*   Action plans and/or timeline
*   A chart of the various stages

- Alternative plans built in case of change or problems
- Budget with return on investment computed, costs defined (personal, professional, business)
- Analysis of the market or focus of the goal (or other necessary research)

A summary or briefing on the situation and/or opportunity. This is also where the two supporting joists of the roof truss needed to span the gap—Resources Needed and Actions Required—are fully investigated and incorporated into the plan. Planning is relatively easy at this stage of the strategizing process, and does not require a great deal of explanation, especially when time has been given to fully exploring the other steps. Encourage the coachee to develop his or her own plan, while contributing your wisdom, insights, and observations.

Accountability: After the goal has been charted and the plan is established, the next step is to follow the progress. The map or chart created helps to keep the coachee focused and allows both of you to track the strategy. This is a very important part of strategizing—the objective is to reach the goal. Here are several things you can do to help a coachee progress:

- Check progress frequently
- Assist the coachee in reorienting his or her life and growth program to support and integrate the goal
- Help the coachee make adjustments as necessary
- Check timing, follow-through, availability of resources, back-up plans, and the supporting structure
- Assign homework to advance the plan and hold the coachee accountable

Strategizing Behaviors: Promoters and Pitfalls

The DOS are behaviors that promote success of strategizing. The DON'TS are behaviors that limit the success of strategizing.

Do—Understand that a strategy is different than the goal.	Goals, outcomes, and objectives are what you want to accomplish or reach. A strategy is the path, the tools, the approach you will use to get there, and hopefully make it a faster, better, and more profitable journey. Strategies require creative thinking and discussion.
Don't—Confuse strategies with goals.	
Do—Know that strategies sometimes need to change.	Even a highly successful strategy can become less effective over time. The world, marketplace, tastes, times, and individuals change, and so most likely a strategy will need to be adjusted due to these changes. If a strategy is failing, it may be more effective to start over, rather than continually tweaking it.
Don't—Be too attached or wedded to a specific strategy.	
Do—Test strategies.	Strategies can be time-consuming and expensive to develop and manage, and even more expensive if they fail. Continue testing and adjusting as necessary before investing heavily (time, money, etc.), in any strategy.
Don't—Count on a strategy without knowing it will work.	
Do—Be sure goals are worth achieving and realistic.	The best, most proven strategy in the world will not make up for a bad product or an unrealistic goal. A goal can be achieved only to find out that it wasn't worth having, or that the end product was not highly valued.
Don't—Expect a good strategy to make up for a bad product or goal.	
Do—Create simple, uncomplicated strategies.	Strategies work better when they are simple, uncluttered, and uncomplicated. It is helpful to condense the strategy so that it can be expressed in a single sentence or two.
Don't—Try to be overly detailed and complicated in strategizing.	
Do—Encourage emotional and inspirational aspects of strategy.	An effective strategy should make the person(s) executing it feel good, proud, and inspired. Boring strategies and goals seldom work well.
Don't—Create a boring, nonmotivating, and uninspiring strategy.	
Do—Create wide enough gaps for exciting leaps.	If the goal is boring, not big enough, or the vision for it is weak and limited, you will not create a wide enough gap between the now and then to achieve an inspiring strategy, or to make great shifts and leaps.
Don't—Have boring goals or weak, limited vision.	

Do—Remember the vision.	Vision is what gives strategy and goal accomplishment the life it requires for long-term success. Have big visions, big goals, and always keep the vision in the forefront.
Don't—Forget the vision.	
Do—Ask the right questions before creating the right strategy.	Be sure the goal is right first, and then determine which steps will actually succeed in achieving it.
Don't—Leap blindly into strategizing without proper research.	
Do—Allow ample time for strategizing with your coachee.	Strategizing is vital for your coachee to achieve his or her desired goals. Give it plenty of time during the coaching interaction. Give it a high priority, and don't skip the steps.
Don't—Forget to allow ample time for strategizing.	

Resources

Attention Readers:

Thank you for participating in the collective wisdom of Coach U. Together, we all continue to learn. Additional resources and forms can be found in *Coach U's Essential Coaching Tools: Your Complete Practice Resource* by CoachInc.com.

Attention CoachInc.com Students and Graduates:

CoachInc.com students and graduates may find additional and/or more recent resources associated with this module in the resource area of the student-only web site. If you are a student or graduate of one of CoachInc.com's ICF-accredited coach training programs, you can access these by searching under the name of the course. When the course description page appears you may find a link to the list of additional resources. Each item is a live link to its actual location on the web site. Click on the item to access the information.

Do remember to take the associated online self-test for this module once you have completed the course in person or by TeleClass. The tests are required for coach certification with the International Coach Federation. Throughout the course or anytime you find valuable resources for a particular course please feel free to add to the value of our curriculum by forwarding the resource to revampteam@coachu.com.

Chapter 8

Messaging

Overview

○ Benefits   Go to Page > 231

By participating in this module you will learn what to say and how to say it, so that your use of messaging is effective and valuable to the coachee. Messaging is a powerful coaching tool that opens the possibility for a shift to occur. You will become familiar with the mechanics of messaging, including the two main methods used at various times with a coaching interaction, as well as the limitations and pitfalls.

○ Definitions   Go to Page > 232

Advise, tell, inform, consulting/consultant, coaching/coach, challenge, intuition, discern, compassion, edge, expectation, permission, request, huge request, accountability, and evidence.

○ Concepts   Go to Page > 235

What is Messaging?

Messaging is a form of communication with language that is succinct, neutral, and timely. Messages inform, notify, and sometimes request. The message must be delivered carefully and intentionally with the coachee's interest at heart. The intention of your message is to move the coachee toward his or her goal(s)—not expose their weaknesses. Messaging is packaged by the coach into two main delivery styles or formats to enhance coachee acceptance: advising and challenging.

○ Distinctions   Go to Page > 240

Advise versus tell, consulting advice versus coaching advice, perspective versus fully informed, formula versus solution, formula versus analogy, information versus point of view, facts versus ideas, request versus suggestion, request versus question, challenge versus threat, and compassion versus empathy.

⭘ Application

Go to Page > 244

What is Messaging?
The guidelines for messaging, what works and what does not; the how and what of the two delivery formats.

Advising
    Guidelines
    Success Formulas
    Information
    Personal Experience
    Segues

The Components of Challenging
    Compassion
    The Edge
    Expectation
    Requests
    Respect
    Evidence

Messaging Behaviors: Promoters and Pitfalls

Resources

Go to Page > 263

Benefits

By fully participating in the material offered in this module, you will gain a broad overview of the coaching method known as messaging. Messaging is an effective and rewarding technique used in the coaching process, and is most productive when a coach and coachee have established a strong foundation of trust so that the coachee can be open to the intended message.

This course is designed to allow participants to:

O **Define** what messaging means in the context of a coaching interaction

O **Identify** when advising methods can be used to advance the individual growth of the coachee

O **Be** able to identify common situations where advising is a powerful tool for the coachee's success

O **Develop** an empowering perspective on the role of life challenges in personal and professional development and learn to support coachees to proactively engage with life challenges

O **Gain** tools and skills to customize challenges so that each challenge is responsive to your coachee's situation and needs

O **Be** responsible and effective as a coach to fearlessly and compassionately tell the truth, as you perceive it, without attachment to the coachee's response

O **Develop** familiarity and competence with a wide variety of challenging methods, including styles uniquely your own

O **Learn** the behaviors that promote effective advising and challenging, and those that are limiting, and how to avoid them

Definitions

The following are common words used to gain a better understanding of the coaching process, particularly in regard to messaging.

Advise: To advise is to provide information, recommendations, opinions, and counsel in order to guide someone to action; to provide for a trusted basis of thought and conduct. In its best form, advising is done with careful deliberation by someone with relevant knowledge or experience, and can be formatted and packaged in a number of ways. Pure advising does not require or expect the advisee to do anything.

Tell: To tell is to make something known, to communicate, announce, or proclaim something, and often requires the one being told to act or be in accordance with what is told.

Inform: To give or impart knowledge or facts regarding circumstances, people, or things. It implies teaching, training, and instructing, but is usually free of any kind of personal bias or requirement for action. It is an exchange of information only.

Consulting/consultant: The process of advising, telling, and informing a coachee or organization, relative to a specific need, in order to deliver an end result. An expert in the relevant field of expertise does the consulting. A consultant takes responsibility for the project outcomes and focuses on the What of the results.

Coaching/coach: The process of guiding a coachee to achieve desired success, using a number of techniques, including advising, telling the truth, and challenging. The coaching is done by a coach trained in successful coaching skills (who may or may not also be an expert in any given field). A coach allows the coachee to take responsibility for the coaching outcomes, and focuses on the Who of the results.

Challenge: A challenge is an official summons, or a request, to engage in some activity, behavior, or undertaking. A challenge contains the inherent assumption of a test of some sort. The person being challenged can accept or refuse the challenge. In coaching, a challenge is always made to promote the coachee's best interest, encourage the coachee's growth and development, and prompt him or her into forward movement. *Challenging* is the coaching term for the method you will use to present a challenge to the coachee.

Intuition: This is the perception of truth, facts, information, or other input not based on any reasoning process. It is the ability to have insight into something based on our own inner knowledge and truth, and not on external stimuli.

Discern: This is the ability to perceive and distinguish between things, usually through intuition or other internal knowledge. It means to recognize contrasts such as good and bad, right and wrong, timely and untimely, truth and untruth, real and false.

Compassion: Compassion is a heartfelt awareness and understanding of another person's experience, accompanied by a desire to alleviate any hardship. When used in messaging, it is your deeply felt concern, caring, and desire for a coachee to achieve his or her best, especially in the face of current difficulties.

Edge: The edge is a strong quality of messaging, requesting, and genuinely being with a coachee that demonstrates your belief in his or her potential for authenticity, learning, and action toward their dreams. Using the edge typically gets your coachee's attention and is used for that purpose.

Expectation: An expectation is the anticipation of a particular outcome and the prospect of the benefits of that outcome. In the context of messaging, an expectation occurs when you hold the coachee accountable to a higher standard for results or actions than the coachee would otherwise accept for him- or herself. It is the coach wanting better things for the coachee, advocating for those behaviors and outcomes, and holding a space for the coachee to move into. The coach believes the new standard is possible for the coachee and consistently speaks to that possibility.

Permission: Permission is the authorization by someone for someone else to do something, or formally consent to it. It is the agreement between you and your coachee that you may make any request, message, or challenge you deem useful for the coachee and that the coachee may accept, decline, or counter-offer any of these communications.

Request: A request is the act of asking for something to be done. In coaching, requesting is the specific coaching tool of asking the coachee to take an action, stop an action, make an inner shift, or move toward his or her goal in some other way. A request is defined further by its limited response parameters: A request must, within a reasonable time frame, be accepted, declined, or counter-offered. In a counter-offer, the coachee agrees to a different action or shift that he or she deems more appropriate.

Huge Request: The act of asking for something big to be done. These coaching requests stretch the coachee beyond his or her current idea of what is doable, facilitate out-of-the-box thinking, provide the opportunity for a shift or leap to happen, and give focus on what is possible. Huge requests often put words to what the coachee wants, but is reluctant to say or do without the request.

Accountability: Being subject to the obligation to report or justify something. It is being responsible and answerable for actions. In coaching, you hold the coachee accountable for producing evidence that shows a change. It is holding the coachee accountable to measurable targets and timeframes that add clarity and motivation.

Evidence: In the context of challenging, evidence indicates that change is occurring. Therefore, evidence is an indication or a sign that proves or disproves something. Evidence of change is required for successful challenging. It is what tells you whether the coaching is working. Evidence is a tangible, observable sign that a coachee has or has not completed a challenge.

Guiding Principle 2 | **People Are Inquisitive.**
Organizations that encourage curiosity
accelerate learning and creativity.

Concepts

What is Messaging?

Messaging is a powerful tool to keep the coachee on track; it is a series of markers on the coaching path to enhance and encourage the coachee's forward motion. A message is an idea, concept, suggestion, or truth that has a motivating spin on it. The coach makes a very succinct, focused statement to awaken the coachee to a behavior or action and create possibilities for a shift to occur. It is imperative to create a strong basis of trust before using this skill. Be aware that a shift may occur for a coachee immediately or it may take some time for the message to be validated.

There are two main processes or delivery formats of messages that are most useful in a coaching conversation: advising and challenging.

Messaging is a powerful tool to keep the coachee on track. It is a series of directional markers on the coaching path to encourage forward motion.

Advising

Advising is the practice of offering advice and counsel, recommendations and suggestions. Advice informs, notifies, and sometimes requests. It is always given and phrased with the coachee's needs and best interests in mind. Advising is not about you; it is all about the coachee. Advising happens in a coaching interaction when a coachee is exploring options and is open to new information, and you have appropriate advice to offer. When implemented correctly, advising is a very useful and significant shaping and directing instrument.

Advising is purposely packaged by the coach in a number of attractive formats during the coaching interaction. The main categories of advising are information, formulas, personal experiences, and segues. As you experiment with and practice advising, you will find your advice neatly falling into one of these four areas. Advising is a very valuable tool for your coaching toolkit, worth your efforts to develop and use masterfully.

Information

Most coaches are knowledgeable in other fields, and this information (intelligence, data, facts, wisdom, tips, truths, expertise) may be a primary reason this particular coach was hired. In its purest sense, information advising is devoid of personal opinion. The challenge for you is presenting this information in a way that makes the biggest impact for the coachee, and is delivered and heard with a coach approach, so it is not interpreted that the coachee is being told what to do. It is not merely an exchange of facts. There is a very important distinction you must make between the Who and the What of information advising.

Formulas

A success formula is advice packaged in a simple equation such as Focus + Action = Results. Formulas are easy to create, and often provide the kind of visual, memorable representation of a problem and the best path to a solution.

Personal Experience

You routinely give advice—an educated opinion, based on personal experience. It can focus on the person or a situation, and can be professional or personal. Advising from personal experience differs from informational advising, because it contains the element of human experience, and lends more credibility to the information. You need to package this counsel without stepping over the boundaries of what is legally appropriate in any given profession. There are things you can and cannot advise about. Your personal and professional experiences are a good part of why you have been hired. Advising from personal experience, however, means that you tailor this information to the coachee's needs and that you share this information briefly.

Segues

Segues are constructed phrases that help you link together the elements of what is being said during a coaching interaction. Because there are often so many different things being discussed or considered, a segue can provide a clear connectedness that pulls everything together. In music, note segues make a transition directly from one section or theme to another. In coaching, phrasing segues help the conversation move smoothly and without hesitation from one state, situation, or element to another. Segues connect the coaching interaction conversations and add grace and order.

Examples of Advising

This is a brief sample list of potential moments, and methods, of advising:

- Clarifying the facts, not the reactions
- Clarifying the person's values first, then create planning aligned with those values
- Modifying or fixing false or outdated assumptions and replacing with current thinking
- Creating a model (with words or visuals), to help the coachee "get" faster what you're talking about
- Giving direct answers to coachee questions

- Giving perspective by informing the person where they are and where they're heading
- Sharing an opinion simply and without personal bias
- Helping the coachee identify goals, and providing what he or she needs for easy success
- Illustrating your points with similes, metaphors, and analogies
- Sharing your creative thoughts or intuitions (sometimes before giving advice)
- Making your points hit home by phrasing them in the message format
- Painting a descriptive verbal picture of what you want the coachee to have, be, or do
- Putting the person in touch with the key people in your network who might help him or her
- Sharing today's principles, concepts, and models (not yesterday's)
- Sharing formulas that make success simple
- Point out things that might slip by, no matter how small
- Telling the coachee, on occasion, what to do
- Using segues to link your coaching with the coachee's situation

Challenging

You challenge coachees so they may learn and grow. It is a supportive push that entices the coachee to explore, question, or revalidate established beliefs in a relatively risk-free and safe environment. There is no failure around a coaching challenge. A coaching challenge is always useful because learning occurs through the process.

Developing mastery in challenging means hearing what challenges life is offering the coachee, sensing what challenge he or she needs from you to support his or her best internal and external changes in light of these challenges, and using the optimal language to offer the challenge or request. Masterful challengers see numerous ways a coachee might embrace any situation, and enjoy supporting each coachee with a compassionate edge, even when the coachee is facing a difficult circumstance.

Challenging may take the form of either one or a combination of the following types:

Direct Challenge
A direct challenge is a straightforward question or request that can be answered by a yes, no, or counter-offer. This kind of challenge is used to crystallize thoughts and ideas into actionable choices. Would you like to___? Will you___? Are you ready to___?

Underlying Challenge

You use the underlying challenge to explore possibilities for change at the source of a coachee's thoughts and feelings rather than at the level of results initially desired. This type of challenge assists the coachee to address and then eliminate or avoid unwanted future problems. What is underneath that? Why is this important? What don't you want me to ask?

Challenging a Problem

When a problem has been going on too long, you can challenge a coachee to resolve it. You might say: "Enough already—it's time to do something! I request that you solve it or forget about it by next week."

Non-Doing Challenge

The non-doing challenge is a request to stop or abstain from doing something or being in a way that is not working. It is essentially a "stop-doing" or "stop-being" challenge. Are you willing to stop doing that? I ask that you stop thinking that way.

Doing Challenge

A doing challenge is usually task based and time specific. It is used to clarify the coachee's commitment to do what he or she says they are going to do. What are you committing to do? When will you have it done?

Internal Challenge

An internally based challenge is an invitation to be true to self—to live authentically.

Being Challenge

A being challenge is an invitation to try on a different way of being. It's an inside-out approach to show up differently in the world. You may ask the coachee to try being open, honest, intimate, or vulnerable, and observe the results.

Being-While-Doing Challenge

What we are doing and how we are being while doing it can often blend together to create rich and fulfilling experiences, and can also cause tremendous growth. For example, have you ever tried "romancing" the housework?

Environmental Challenge

Shifting things on the surface is an outside-in approach to deep transformational change that can often be effective by itself, or paired with an internal challenge. These challenges can include subtle or major environmental changes as well as breaking certain patterns and habits in life. If you usually drive a certain way to work, try a different route. If you usually sleep late, get up early, or vice versa. Give your office, hairstyle, or routine a total makeover.

" We aim above the mark to hit the mark. " | **Ralph Waldo Emerson**

Coachees come to you for both support and to be challenged—that is, to be asked to do or be more than they were doing or being before coaching. Coaching is all about challenging the coachee to be his or her best. Mastering the methodology of challenging is essential to the development of the masterful coach.

The Components of Challenging

A challenge must include six basic elements to ensure its success. Every challenge must be delivered with, and include:

- Compassion
- Edge
- Expectation
- Respect
- Requests (huge or otherwise)
- Evidence

There is a process, and there are elements of challenging, that when combined yield a coaching skill that will become one of the most effective and trusted tools used by a master coach during every coaching interaction. Effective challenging must be built with these processes and components, and done with confidence and consistency, to ensure the best environment for the coachee to achieve long-lasting success.

Distinctions

There are subtle yet important differences in meaning between the following closely related terms. Understanding these distinctions allows you to perceive new layers of meaning and offers you new choices for shifting your thoughts, attitudes, and actions.

Advise versus Tell

To advise is to offer counsel, to recommend something as being prudent or advisable. To advise is to offer your opinion as a guide to action or conduct for someone or something. Advising allows choice on the part of the advisee. To tell is to announce or proclaim something; in the coaching relationship, it can be seen as a command. Telling does not involve choice.

Consulting Advice versus Coaching Advice

The consultant provides advice in forms of counsel, opinions, and direction with the sole purpose of fixing or resolving the issue (what) for the coachee. The coach advises in forms of messages, personal experience, formulas, and segues with the sole purpose to develop the coachee (who), so the coachee will be able to resolve the issue (what) for him- or herself.

Perspective versus Fully Informed

Perspective is the interpretation of facts and ideas and their interrelationships; it is the ability to see all the relevant information in meaningful relationship. Being fully informed means we have all the information (the facts and ideas) we need to gain perspective. Having information does not automatically assume perspective. Perspective comes through processing information.

Formula versus Solution

A formula is a simple, symbolic expression of the parts of a whole, or the recipe or prescription for something. A formula implies a method or approach to achieve something, and is generally a universal truth that can be applicable most, if not all, of the time. A solution is a process for solving a problem and most often implies a one-time use and limited application. A formula lasts longer and has broader application.

Formula versus Analogy

A formula is a symbolic expression of a method to achieve something, and is generally true most of the time. An analogy is a comparison of, or the similarity between, two things; it does not imply a path or method for achievement and may not hold true for more than one specific application.

Information versus Point of View

Information is knowledge based on facts, which is communicated or perceived. Information, in its purest sense, is devoid of human interpretation, opinion, or bias. A point of view is your opinion about a set of information. A point of view personalizes information or events and is completely based on interpretation and personal bias.

Facts versus Ideas

A fact is something that is true and actually exists. It is a truth or reality that can be proven by actual experience or observation. An idea is an impression of the facts, a thought, a conception, or a notion about something, or even an intention. An idea may also be an opinion, view, or belief. An idea is not always based on reality. An idea may be a groundless supposition or even a fantasy.

Request versus Suggestion

A suggestion is an idea the provider thinks might be helpful. The recipient of a suggestion need not do anything with the suggestion. A request is more formal, implying the need for response. In a coaching relationship a request is a specific tool that you and the coachee agree to use. When you agree, you have permission to make specific requests that the coachee will consider, even if he or she does not immediately see the value of following through on the request. The agreement around coaching requests also grants the coachee permission to accept the request, decline it, or come back with a counter-offer. Once a request has been accepted, the coachee agrees to be accountable for following through with the action.

Request versus Question

A question invites the delivery of information or invites reflection. A request is a specific call to action or reflection. "Are you going to make those phone calls this week?" is a question. A request along the same lines might look more like: "I ask that you make the phone calls we discussed, by Friday, then let me know you have done it." Friends, colleagues, and family members routinely ask questions and make suggestions. Generally, friends and family do not use challenging to make specific requests of the coachee. For this reason the request is a powerful tool that distinguishes coaching from other professions and from friendship or mentoring.

Challenge versus Threat

A challenge is a strong request to embrace a difficult shift through action, attitude, or way of being. A threat is a declaration of the intention to inflict punishment for some action or nonaction. Some coachees will perceive challenges as threats, that is, a challenge that carries a potential consequence. You deliver requests as opportunities for coachees to experiment with new ways of being and doing, not chances for them to disappoint others or themselves or to fail. Effective motivation stirs a person's inner desire to take action for themselves, not to avoid a perceived threat.

Compassion versus Empathy

Compassion is the perceivable expression of concern, kindness, consideration, and even sympathy for someone. When you show compassion for someone, you are giving him or her a gift. Showing honest compassion is free of personal experience or identification with the person and his or her situation. Empathy is your identification with someone and his or her experiences, feelings, and thoughts because you have experienced them as well. Empathy is more of a passive approach to caring which, while useful, does not give the recipient all that much. Compassion is a mindset and not dependent on your experiences. Compassion is an essential skill in coaching, but only occurs when one has no need whatsoever to compare or feel threatened or influenced by the other person.

Application

What is Messaging?

Coaches package a lot of what they say into a format we call messages. Basically, a message is a motivating truth, principle, or point of view you want to share with the coachee. It is a statement that helps the person to see, feel, and understand something quickly and easily. The message's intention is to allow the coachee to grow, shift, or leap immediately because of the accuracy, truth, and simplicity of the message shared.

Messages can be stated in one of three formats, which allow the coachee to process this information quickly. Messaging is more than just a coaching tool; it is an advanced communication tool. When you use messages, you are making your point simply and sharply and the coachee feels motivated to act.

The three types of message formats are:

Type	Why Useful	Examples
The You Message	• Starts with the word "You" • Informs coachee about himself or herself ~acknowledges • Gives them perspective • Helps them to prioritize	• You … • You are someone who … • You are now here (versus there) … • You now need to focus on …
The I Message	• Starts with the word "I" • Shares your opinion • Tells them how you feel about them • Helps you share a (brief) story • Helps you be personal • (Helps you bond)	• I … • I feel that X, Y, Z … • I think you're … • I would give you an example … • I am so sorry that happened … • I know exactly what you mean …
The It Message	• Starts with neither "You" nor "I" • Helps you identify with coachee • Helps you be colleagues	• Life is … Isn't it … It's funny how … • Isn't it great when that happens … • Isn't it the worst when that happens …

A message is NOT a cliché or platitude. A cliché is a universal saying that may be helpful, but is not necessarily personal to the coachee's current needs. A message is always tailored to the person; a cliché is shared as is, not customized to the exact situation. A cliché comes from memory; a message comes from the soul.

Messaging and Questioning

Both are good coaching techniques. But as you get better at messaging, you'll find that you need to ask fewer questions because chances are you will already have heard the answer without even having to ask the question, and your message will speak to that answer.

Messaging and Requesting

Requesting is also another very important coaching technique. When you're really skilled at messaging, however, you will need to make very few requests of your coachees. You will use messages to make your point and the coachee will be inspired to act on his or her own, instead of you having to press your point with a request.

Benefits of Messages	
Messages accelerate the coachee's natural growth	• Messages remove and replace myths and false assumptions that may have slowed the coachee down. • Messages give new truths that lead the coachee forward. • Messages reach behind the coachee's usual doors of learning and don't get diluted as they enter.
Messages help you make your point quickly, deeply, and easily	• Rather than ramble or attempt to convince, speaking in messages helps you touch the coachee fast. • Messages give you the format to say what you really want to say, without the preambles. • Messages force you to crystallize your thoughts before you speak.
Messages are universal, yet customizable (laser) phrases	• Messages are universal yet they can be adjusted to fit the immediate needs of the coachee. • Messages help to articulate truth in a form that is "gettable" by the other person.
Your job is done after delivering a message	• Using messages is like planting seeds; some take and some don't. • Eventually your messages will be heard and responded to. Don't expect immediate responses. • Stop talking and wait for a response. Remember that silence creates room for creative thinking.

Benefits of Messages	
"You" are heard when you use messages	• Your opinion, point of view, and personality are known when you use messages. • Using the message format forces you to be more direct, from the heart, and right on. • People can start to count on you to be a straight shooter with an edge and an angle.
You become more attractive	• People know you stand up for something they believe in or want ... this always makes one more attractive. • When you say what you feel to be true you'll feel better about yourself.

Advising

While it is impossible to detail every kind of behavior, every pitfall, or every nuance of advising, there are general guidelines that you should learn and follow to remain ethically clean in your coaching relationships. Many coach training organizations do not consider advising to be a coaching skill and do not think that it should be used in a coaching relationship. We believe that there are certain conditions where the use of advising is a valuable asset to the coachee and that it can be very supportive in moving a coachee in the direction of his or her goals.

Guidelines for the Use of Advising

- Caution should be used in advising too soon or at an inappropriate time—when the coachee may be inclined to take the advice as THE answer, not one option among many.
- Advice should be simple, clear, and pertinent to the needs of the coachee.
- Consideration should be given to the amount and frequency of advice given during a coaching conversation. As a rule of thumb, if the coach is only speaking 20 percent of the time, only 10 percent of his or her speaking should consist of advice.
- Advice should only be given if you have real experience in the situation and have achieved a recognized level of expertise. Your opinion is not advising.
- Many coachees will beg for you to continually tell them what to do. It is your job as a coach to educate them to the benefits of great coaching that may only be peppered with advising.
- Remember that unsolicited advice is criticism.

When to Use Message Advising

These are examples only. There will be many other occasions and opportunities to use advising formulas.

- To tell (advise) the coachee who they are
- To endorse what they have accomplished
- To provide perspective on where they are now
- To advise them what is next
- To advise them how you feel about them
- To advise them you are with them
- To advise them what you want for them
- To advise them that you understand (empathize)
- To advise them that you agree with them about life
- To advise them of principles and concepts
- Any other time you want to make a motivating statement

" A leader is a dealer in hope. **"** | **Napoleon Bonaparte**

Success Formulas

The best advice is most often the simplest. One of the simpler ways to give advice is to package it into a formula, like an equation or a recipe.

Focus + Action = Results
Personal Foundation + Vision = Contribution
Value-added + Relationship = A Job Promotion

With formulas you can help the coachee instantly see what he or she needs and provide a simple and memorable guideline for achieving goals. Is life as simple as a success potion? No. Can you get a great life just by using a formula? No. Does every formula work every time? No. Formulas are not the answer; they are a simple means at arriving at the answer. Formulas are a place to start looking. They are very effective and leave the coachee with a simple, memorable focus after your coaching session.

Recipe + Simplicity = Formula for Success

How do you create a success formula? You make it up. Just like with all forms of advising, you want to make certain that you have listened very closely to your coachee and are clear on the context he or she is presenting. Do not work on formulating the success formula while the coachee is speaking, as you will become disconnected. When the person completes his or her thought, you may deliver the formula.

There are several examples listed in the table below. Keep in mind that formulas are not limited to only two or three components. They may consist of several, but the simpler the better. Try creating your own in the spaces provided.

When to use formula advising

These are examples only. There will be many other occasions and opportunities to use advising formulas.

- To clarify the path from one point to another
- To provide an easily remembered equation for success
- To help your coachee visualize the steps involved to solve a problem
- To provide a simple focusing tool to guide conversation
- To help the coachee simplify his or her own success

Sample Success Formula

Gratitude	+ Grace	= Compassion
Subtle difference	+ Words	= Articulation
New truth	+ Motivation	= Message
Awareness	+ Shift	= Clarity
Experience	+ Awareness	= Understanding
Holding vision	+ Possibility	= Focus
Efficiency	+ Effectiveness	= Productivity
Desire	+ Evidence	= Dedication
Discipline	+ Structure	= Sustainability
Result	+ Growth	= Accomplishment
Belief	+ Endorsement	= Management
Consistent action	+ Results	= Momentum
Revenue	+ Low expenses	= Profit
Added value	+ Service	= Referrals
Capital	+ Opportunities	= Wealth
High-touch	+ Meet needs	= Sale
Investment	+ Wisdom	= High return

Consistent savings	+ Time	= Retirement fund
CPA	+ Tax planning	= Tax savings
Self-respect	+ Self-care	= Self-esteem
	+	=
	+	=

Information

You possess knowledge about many things, and this information (intelligence, data, facts, wisdom, tips, truths, expertise) is of great value to the coachee. The challenge for you is how to present this information for maximum impact to the coachee. This calls for a *Who* focus, not just a *What* focus. It is not necessarily about the information, but about the person receiving it. You need to personalize, simplify, and package the information so that it can be heard, accepted, assimilated, and appreciated by the coachee.

You must step into the shoes of the coachee and speak from there. This is the *Who* approach, which is the realization that information (the *What*) is a mere commodity and replaceable, but that the coachee (the *Who*) is unique, and his or her development is more important than the information. You must be more concerned about the person receiving the information (the *Who*) than the information itself (the *What*). There is a great difference between receiving information and understanding it. Remember also the distinction between consulting and coaching.

You offer information with detachment, without expectation that the coachee will use or immediately see the value of the information. It is an offer to educate or pass wisdom along with no strings attached. Information is to be offered for the value of the information to the person, not as a way to lead the coachee to your way of thinking. An example of this is a comparison of these two statements:

> Leading or Telling
> "I need you to read the latest Steven Covey book."

> Providing information
> "Steven Covey's latest book was on that very topic."

Information is best when it is *Who*-specific, can be used to grow the individual, and the choice for incorporating the information is the coachee's.

Information advising requires the coach to consider the *What* and *Who* of the information.

When to Use Information Advising
These are examples only. There will be many other occasions and opportunities to use information advising.

- To fill gaps of missing information in coachee's knowledge base
- To provide the coachee knowledge from the coach's area of expertise
- To shed light on the coachee's "in the dark" areas
- To gently guide coachee into making wiser choices, fully informed
- To provide more options for coachee choices

Personal Experience

Personal experience differs from information. Information is generally free of any experiential flavor. Personal experience gives information credibility. It is not just a piece of information, but information that has been lived and therefore verified. You must always remember and realize the power and influence personal advice can have on a coachee. Once we have lived, or have experience in something, our personal set of values and individual uniqueness will automatically give any information a bias. While we should be sharing our experiences and our thoughts about them (our opinions), it is wise to always remember the focus is the coachee—not you.

The sharing of personal experience needs to be relevant to the topic and add value to the coachee's thinking. Advising with personal experience is not about you, and is not a license to tell your stories or offer unsolicited, unhelpful, and biased opinions. Personal experience advising is all about what the coachee needs to hear at that moment. Unlike therapy, you can be and are directive and reflective. Most coaches are hired because of their professional experience and the body of knowledge they have. This is meant to be shared with the coachee, but with great care for the coachee's well-being. There are also legal ramifications about this kind of advising based on personal experience, and it must be clear that the choice to use the advice belongs to the coachee alone.

Personal experience advising is all about what the coachee needs to hear at that moment.

Personal experience advice is not the same as having a good idea. An idea may certainly be good, but it is often not based on any experiential evidence. When ideas are shared, they must be labeled as such—an idea, not personal experience. Personal experience advising is allowing the coachee the benefit of your accumulated knowledge (professional and personal), tailored in a way for easy assimilation and incorporation by your coachee, for his or her own improvement and well-being. Once again, the *Who* and the *What* distinctions are critical.

It is also important for you to understand the limitations of your personal or professional experience, and to know when you may not be the best person to advise on a particular subject. In these times you must defer to other experts and assist the coachee in finding the kind of personal experience advice they need from others.

When to Use Personal Experience Advising

These are examples only. There will be many other occasions and opportunities to use advising through personal experience.

- To provide your coachee the benefit of information which you have personally observed to be true and valuable for him or her in either your personal or professional life
- To gently correct and/or guide your coachee's options for choice by providing another perspective
- To correct your coachee's misinformed assumptions
- To offer advice from your personal experience that you know will be helpful to the coachee
- To offer possible new avenues of exploration

Segues

Segues are the links and constant connectors that pull the coaching interaction together into a logical flow, keeping it focused and relative. During a coaching session many avenues of discussion tend to fragment the conversation, opening the door to confusion and loss of focus. Segues are well-crafted and gentle reminders and supporters of the relevance of any topic to the overall purpose of the conversation.

A segue can be a statement or a question, designed to draw the coachee back to intentional and directional conversation toward his or her goals. Segues are the glue of the coaching interaction, bonding the pieces into an easily understood whole. Segues are included as a form of advising because they also keep the coachee on track and act as markers on the coaching path to enhance and encourage the coachee's forward motion.

Segues are the links and the connectors of any coaching interaction.

When to Use Segues

These are examples only. There will be many other occasions and opportunities to use advising through segue.

- To bring the coachee back to the original intent of a conversation and to establish the relevance of any particular point to another ("That's an interesting point. How does it relate to your goal?")
- To move the conversation in continuing forward momentum ("We've been focusing on X for awhile, and I would like to move on to Y and then relate it back to X. Okay?")
- To alert the coachee to connections embedded within their conversation of which they may have been previously unaware ("Do you see the connection between what is happening and the goal you have set for yourself?")
- To clarify the purpose in any particular avenue of discussion
- To reveal and clarify the connections or significance of apparently unrelated topics
- To dispel clutter and confusion in any conversation and bring order

The Components of Challenging

Challenging is composed of a number of elements critical to its success. To ensure success and sustainability, challenges must include all of the following:

- Compassion
- Edge
- Expectation
- Requests (Huge or otherwise)
- Respect
- Evidence

Compassion

Challenging a coachee without a large measure of compassion runs the risk of an adrenaline-based, production-at-any-cost power trip. This is not coaching. Compassion is both a learned skill as well as natural and developed caring for the well being of others. By showing compassion while challenging coachees, you are endorsing them and letting them know that you understand what they face. Whether you have been there or you understand fully what they are going through does not matter. You are giving them an empowering gift of understanding, acceptance, and endorsement. Real compassion is made of genuine understanding, not false humility. Compassion keeps you from falling into reacting to coachees, which is always about you. Compassion gives you the reserve to handle the weaknesses, concerns, and frailties of yourself and others. The greater your reserve, the easier it is to have compassion. It is something you give freely, not just the absence of reaction.

The Edge

You are helping the coachee to change, grow, and excel, and this process is not without resistance from the coachee. A master coach, while compassionate and accepting, is simply not interested in anything less than the coachee's best efforts. This unwillingness to tolerate mediocrity, yet still be empowering, is calling "having the edge." Every successful coach has it.

The edge is a strong quality of messaging, requesting and genuinely being with a coachee that demonstrates your belief in his or her potential for authenticity, learning, and action toward his or her dreams. Using the edge typically gets your coachee's attention and is used for that purpose. The edge is not the edge of a sharp sword, strong language to hurt your coachee or bully them into taking action. The edge never inflicts deep pain, although it often may strike a touchy chord when it is thoughtful and targeted. A sword is ruthless and inappropriate and leaves the coachee wounded, rather than moved to resolve the issue. Truly effective coaches have the edge, rarely need to use it, and never wield the sword. The edge comes from experience and can take several years to master. Some coaches have a natural edge, others will need to develop and master it.

The edge is also not a club, cattle prod, threat, parenting finger, ultimatum, or weapon. It is simply that something special an adult, strong, powerful, and experienced coach has. Though it shouldn't happen, the coachee often tests you to see how serious you are about his or her success. The successful coach preempts this behavior from the very beginning by making clear the nature of the relationship: It is the coachee's job to perform, not yours. Then, you step over nothing, if something does come up. Compassion is essential with the edge; it is not an excuse to whip your coachees or vent your anger. Experienced coaches are gracious, smooth, sensitive, and respectful, yet have full confidence in the edge.

Even if you never use the edge, you must be willing to do so. The coaching relationship is always threatened by diversions. By using the edge, you command the coachee's attention, return the focus, and let both parties know that the relationship, goals, and coachee's development are not to be taken lightly.

Phrasing Examples

- That's a good effort, but it's not your best.
- Tell me how to coach you so you'll stop this.
- When are you going to stop that?
- Do you really mean that?
- Say it again, in English.
- Sorry, I don't understand. Help me out.
- That's an excellent start. What can we do to increase the momentum?
- Keep going; stopping is not an option.
- Listen, I want you to make some big changes, pronto.
- I want to see a whole different life by next week.
- Don't say you will unless you are going to do it.

" I have the simplest of tastes.
I am always satisfied with the best. " | **Oscar Wilde**

Expectation

A coachee often hires you primarily because you will ask the coachee to do more or be more than the coachee would usually ask of him- or herself. The coachee wants and needs you to ask a lot. The successful coach expects coachees to apply themselves and assumes they are adults. The master coach expects the best for his or her coachees, and is constantly working to achieve it. Fueling every challenge made by you is the expectation that it will bring long-lasting results that stimulate forward progress and impressive growth in the coachee. These expectations are healthy. However, you may need to educate the coachee on how to meet these expectations, and how to anticipate changes for personal development.

You foster change, and coachees generally want change, yet humans naturally resist change. A certain investment in time and energy is required to facilitate and accelerate the change that we naturally resist. This process is called conditioning change. You can make requests, demands, or insist that the coachee change, but it is far more effective if we plant seeds and are up front as soon as we sense a need for change in the coachee. It is right to ask for all that you want for the coachee, but ask for it as soon as you sense it rather than waiting. Conditioning for change may take time. If you delay, the opportunity may disappear, or the coachee may resist in stronger ways.

You will often hold expectations for coachees that are larger than the coachee's own. The language used to express this must be specific and intentionally designed to reveal those expectations. The challenging process must reveal your expectations, at least to the degree that the coachee needs to know in that moment, and in that challenge.

Requests

Every challenging opportunity is really a request you make of the coachee. Some requests will be very small, and some will be huge. It is generally true that coachees are capable of a lot more than is usually asked or expected of them. You sometimes hold back from requesting what you would really like to ask them to start, stop, increase, or change, due to a desire to not offend them or put undue pressure on them. Expect more for and from coachees than you initially intend. Asking more of them will stretch them to achieve their best.

Request More
Request more things, larger shifts, and smarter actions. Request huge shifts, growth steps in which the coachee changes his or her attitude, perspective, approach, or paradigm. Encourage them to share these with you and offer the evidence of these shifts, not just insights. On the

grand scale, focus coachees on results, not just the actions to achieve the results, though these will require specific, targeted focus for a time. Have the coachee simplify his or her actions and begin to be laser directed rather than scattered in their approach.

The Authentic Request

One of the most powerful challenges is to request that a coachee be themselves—his or her real self. Most people are generally "not themselves" most of the time. We are either what our parents or others expect us to be. Point out the qualities, strengths, style, gifts, and other qualities of the coachee in order to point out who he or she really is. Using very succinct, laser-like phrases can be a nonconfrontational form of challenging a coachee to live authentically.

Urgent Requests

There will be moments when you must stand for the coachee on issues that require big shifts and giant leaps, without which the coachee will not achieve lasting successful results, or may possibly be harmed. These requests require the edge and an urgent request from you. This approach is appropriate when you hear that the coachee is putting him- or herself in grave danger, damaging him- or herself physically or mentally, or has not committed wholly to the coaching process or his or her own success. Utilize warnings and conditioning for change if possible, and try to avoid ultimatums, while still advocating for the coachee's best. By not boldly requesting healthy and imminently needed changes in a coachee's life, you are enabling and endorsing potentially harmful behavior. Requesting in these situations requires intuition, discernment, very careful listening, and a great deal of balance.

Nike is Right: Just Do It

Requesting works best when the big changes are handled immediately. It can be tempting for coachees to take long periods of time before getting around to the huge requests. Remember, coachees are adults and need to be treated as such. They don't require you to make their success easy, or to take them by the hand and lead them. They require you to be honest, bold, and always advocating for them. Consider working with the coachee to handle the huge requests without delay. Suggest that needed phone calls be made now. Request that actions begin immediately.

Phrasing Examples

- I ask that you do a 180-degree attitude adjustment by next week.
- I ask that you take the first step toward handling your financial problems by this time tomorrow.
- What drastic changes can you make that make sense?
- What's the one thing you don't want me to ask you to do, but you know you need to do?
- What's really at the source of your problems? Are you willing to handle that?
- It's time you double your goals. Please fax me a new list by this afternoon.
- I want you to have 10 new coachees by the next session and I don't care if you have to pay them.
- Call Y now, and then call me back in 10 minutes.

Coaching is always a collaborative relationship. When a coach makes a request of a coachee there are three appropriate responses. The coachee can accept the request, reject it entirely, or provide a counter-offer. This process of response keeps the decisions in the hands of the coachee, and he or she takes more ownership of their actions and in some cases nonactions. You will want to remind your coachees of this process, especially if you find them taking on your requests and then not successfully completing what they agreed to do. This is typically a sign that the request is off base for the coachee.

Respect

Respect is about esteem, admiration, acceptance, and courtesy. It is the grounding point of reference for all coaching interactions. Everything you do is rooted in respect for your coachees—holding them in esteem, admiring them, accepting them unconditionally, and showing them courtesy. This is no different for challenging. All challenges must be performed with great respect for the coachee. Without this critical element challenging will fail. Respect is a two-way street. In order for coachees to move forward more rapidly than they would without a coach, they need to also respect you as the coach in several ways. The coachee must respect your commitment to him or her, your track record, and your expertise, approach, and standards. Without this, you deteriorate into a best friend or other status, and the goals are not reached.

Evidence

In order for the coaching relationship to work long-term, the coachee must make significant progress. This usually calls for evidence, something indicative—an outward sign, proof, something plainly seen by all rather than something just experienced in the coachee's mind. Evidence helps you ensure that your work is producing results in the coachee's life and that goals are being reached.

Within the context of challenging, you will also expect evidence to show that the coachee has received and has acted upon the challenge. You may have a preconceived set of evidences in mind that may or may not be shared with the coachee. It is best not to box the coachee into your expectations. The actual evidence of progress may be quite different from what you imagine. It is helpful, however, if you have specific evidences in mind that you would like to see as a result of the challenge. Evidence is considered part of the challenge because it is the desired end result, the anchor of the challenge itself.

It is sometimes necessary to explore the possible evidences beyond the obvious, or beyond those which you have already conceived. This confirms your work with the coachee, can alert to potential problem areas and lack of success, and can encourage the coachee to keep growing. During each call, have the coachee relate how he or she is growing and how the coaching has helped. Have the coachee relate the permanent benefits of the coaching. Enable the coachee to emotionally share credit for the accomplishments.

Phrasing Examples

- Tell me how your life has actually changed because of last week's insight.
- How many people have told you that you are noticeably coming across better?
- How much more money are you saving now?
- How many more coachees have signed on over the last two weeks?
- How much have sales increased in your department?
- How many fewer problems have you experienced?
- How do you feel about the changes you've made?

Guiding Principle 6 | **People Act in Their Own Best Interest.**
Discernment reveals the opportunities
in every situation.

Messaging Behaviors: Promoters and Pitfalls

The DOS are behaviors that promote success of advising. The DON'TS are behaviors that limit the success of advising.

Do—Provide more than one option. **Don't**—Advise with no options or choices.	Advise by educating the coachee of various options. Even if you feel one hundred percent certain that the coachee should do X, make sure that you point out options Y and Z, for balance. There will be times when the coachee needs to know your opinions about certain options; just make sure you give them other ideas, too. Sometimes a combination of all options is the best solution.
Do—Format your advising in language the coachee can understand. **Don't**— Use jargon or language unfamiliar to the coachee, or language that is a put-off and not inviting.	Once you know the advice you want to give to a coachee, take a couple of moments and package or phrase it so that they will be as excited to hear it as you are to share it. This will most likely involve using phrasing and terms familiar to your coachee instead of jargon or industry-specific language.
Do—Give what is needed when it is needed. **Don't**—Use bad timing or inappropriate advising. Forget to listen for what is really needed.	Advising is just one of many coaching methods. The point here is to make sure that you are giving the coachee the right thing at the right time. Sometimes advice is good to give, sometimes not. If in doubt, ask the coachee what type of information or support he or she would prefer at this moment. It may be advice, or it may be support, challenging, or something else.
Do—Remember who and what is important. **Don't**—Forget to honor the coachee or be righteous.	Giving advice doesn't give you a license to be righteous. You are being righteous when you feel slighted, or feel badly that the coachee did not accept your advice and thank you profusely. Using the coachee to make your point and prove yourself right or smart dishonors your coachee.
Do—Keep advice simple. **Don't**—Offer complicated, difficult to follow, or unclear advice.	Be sure all the advising you do is so simple anyone can understand it. Develop the art of giving advice in a single sentence.
Do—Ask what they would do. **Don't**—Deny the coachee the opportunity for input.	Most coachees assume they should ask you for advice because they are paying you. In reality, the most valuable coaching is developing the coachee's self-reliance and what he or she internally know is great for them. Give them this opportunity, every time. Explore their responses and compare them to your own.

Do—Advise bigger than the situation. Don't—Limit advice to singular or small solutions rather than global advantage.	Think big. Ask yourself, "What options can I share that will solve this current problem and also propel this coachee forward in other areas, too?" You can then give better advice that has a longer shelf life, like an advice "annuity," because it keeps paying off for the coachee.
Do—Consider in advance how advice may be misheard or misunderstood. Don't—Forget to consider the possibility of misinterpreted advice.	Take a moment, or many moments, to stand in the coachee's shoes and imagine how what he or she is going through will affect their ability to clearly hear your advice and to hear it as advice versus something else. Do this before giving the advice. Don't assume the coachee hears you clearly. Verify what he or she heard you say.
Do—Prepare the coachee with suitable language. Don't—Scare or warn the coachee.	There is a difference between preparing the coachee for a big request and warning or scaring them about the request. Suitable preparation and language will gain the coachee's interest. Warnings will scare them.
Do—Give unbiased, unpushed advice. Don't—Lay your trip on the coachee.	If you have an emotional reaction to the coachee's ignoring or rejecting your advice, it's likely that you are laying your trip on the coachee. When you push your advice, and take it personally when they don't accept it or follow it, your ego is too involved and you are possibly stepping into more of a consulting role.
Do—Hear and understand all the facts before advising. Don't—Leap into advising before knowing the facts.	Sometimes coachees can unwittingly set you up to give them advice too soon—before you fully understand the facts of the coachee's situation. Wait to give advice until you feel certain you understand what is really happening. If the coachee can't or won't tell you clearly, then it probably means that your advice won't be heard anyway. Press for truth and clarity before giving advice. Also, when the truth is eventually clear, the coachee will not need the advice anymore.
Do—Aim advice perfectly. Don't—Shoot random advice bullets at the coachee.	Advice is more effective when you link it to something that is already important to the coachee, like his or her goals, values, priorities, or needs. Customize and contextualize your advice to something that is already known and clear to the coachee.
Do—Think through the consequences of your advice. Don't—Forget to consider ramifications or consequences to the coachee.	Don't give advice until you've thought through the consequences to, or the effect on, the coachee's life if they followed your advice exactly. If you're not sure of the possible consequences ask the coachee to share these with you—they need to be discussed before the coachee accepts the advice.

Do—Utilize prime opportunities.	You don't have to perfect your wording before giving advice. Even if you're not quite sure what to say, preface it with, "Well, I'm not sure how to say this, but ..." While considering language and phrasing is important, especially the Who and the What of your advice, it is important not to allow prime opportunities to slip by because you are still formulating. Trust your intuition.
Don't—Stall or wait until you have it perfect.	
Do—Not assume you have not been heard the first time.	Don't assume that your coachee heard your advice the first time; he or she probably didn't. Everyone learns and adapts at different rates; some coachees need to hear advice two three, four, or five times (sometimes 100) before they finally understand it and incorporate it. Just keep rephrasing or reframing your advice until you see the coachee's light go on.
Don't—Get annoyed because the coachee didn't act immediately.	
Do—Prepare to wait.	Some of the advice you give will be like pruning shears; other advice will be like fertilizer. One kind has immediate results, the other takes considerable time before harvesting the results. Be prepared to wait for the coachee to utilize your advice in the best way for them, in their own time, and through their own methods and adaptation.
Don't—Think your advice should be acted on NOW.	
Do—Prepare the coachee for change.	Coaches foster change, yet people resist change. An investment in time and energy is required to facilitate and accelerate the change that we naturally resist. We can make requests or demands, or we can insist that the coachee change, but it is better if we plant seeds as soon as we sense a need for change. Act early, with continual follow-through and follow-up.
Don't—Try to force the change.	

The DOS are behaviors that promote success of challenging. The DON'TS are behaviors that limit the success of challenging.

| Do—Understand your motivation for challenging a coachee. | It is vital that you remember that you are challenging the coachee for his or her growth and not to live vicariously through them. You can sometimes be tempted to feel that a coachee's failure or slow progress after a challenge is a personal reflection upon you. Remember that this is a reflection on the coachee, and perhaps on the coaching, not on the coach. If a coachee is resistant, find out why, instead of increasing your pace, your edge, or your decibels. Keep in mind that every reaction you have is about you. Carefully evaluate your reactions. |
| Don't—Bully a coachee. | |

Do—Know that challenging will not be right for every coachee. Don't—Think that every coachee will respond positively to challenging.	Not every coachee will receive challenging positively. Just because your Little League coach challenged you in a particular way does not mean that you should be challenging your coachees in the same way—or even at all. The coachee's growth and progress is an optional choice that they make, not one you make for them. Consider also that not every coachee should be challenged.
Do—Challenge a coachee with the edge. Don't—Confront a coachee.	Confrontation generally is a toe-to-toe face-off with lines drawn in the sand. This is not what challenging is all about. Challenging a coachee with the edge means telling the truth and asking for more from him or her. You can use the edge when challenging, advising, supporting, listening, and every other coaching situation. Coachees may not respond to the pressure of a confrontation. You may push the truth to the point of turning off the coachee. It is always better when coachees can discover their own truth. This may be enhanced through masterful coaching, but it is best to empower self-discovery. A challenge is a request, not a mandate. Challenging, in some cases, may be best used as a last resort when nothing else has worked. It should not be the first method employed for a coachee's growth.
Do—"Do no harm." Don't—Cause a coachee pain.	It may be tempting for you to feel like you need to be giving "tough love" to a coachee in order to "get" him or her to change. This is not your role. You are not in the repair or remedial business. If a coachee needs tough love, he or she has needs greater than you should be supplying. Part of a physician's oath is to "do no harm." For you, it should be "cause no pain," even if you think that would be beneficial. Thinking through the consequences of your challenges for the coachee is very important.
Do—Share freely, but cleanly. Don't—Hold back.	You will lose coachees if you hold back ideas, reactions, and thoughts. However, this is not license to beat the coachee up with them, or to be dogmatic in your approach. Your personal agenda cannot enter into the challenging process, but you must be free to share all ideas and thoughts (and yes, even reactions) as long as they are free of personal subjective responses and knee-jerk reactions rooted in your own foundation.
Do—Accept only the coachee's best efforts. Don't—Settle for less than the coachee's best.	Your coachees will relate more readily to you if they know that you expect the best from them, and think them capable of it. There is a gap, which they can then fill, and this can be very empowering. Challenges can be given and expectations shared which ensure their best without being pushy, confrontational, or bullying. Your language and phrasing and charge-neutral tone will go a long way in helping you ask for their best.

Do—Sense when a coachee is only pleasing the coach instead of sincerely wanting the outcome for himself or herself.	Most coachees naturally (and sometimes unconsciously) want to please you. Right or wrong, this is merely a fact of life. It is very important that you discern when the coachee is only acting on a challenge in order to please you, instead of sincerely wanting the outcome for him- or herself. A master coach will be able to know the difference. If it appears that the coachee is only responding out of this need to please, you must question and inform, giving appropriate feedback.
Don't—Confuse your expectations with the coachee's desire to please.	
Do—Have realistic expectations.	When you see a coachee grow as a result of challenges and other developing methods, it is tempting to keep challenging and keep raising the bar of behavior and being just to keep seeing this growth. It is exciting, and can be self-perpetuating. You naturally desire the coachee to grow as much as possible, and rapid growth is sustainable, but rest periods and plateaus are also important, in order to give the coachee time to adjust and be comfortable with what they have done. Resist the temptation to treat the coachee like a hamster on a wheel. Allow the coachee to decide when and how to raise the bar, and discern when he or she is ready to proceed. Continue addressing these areas, but as questions and not as requests, until you sense the moment is right for a shift or leap—another challenge.
Don't—Continually raise the bar just to raise the bar.	
Do—Detect and investigate outcomes to challenges.	It is possible that the coachee's perception of his or her own success, especially in behavior following a challenge, may not be accurate. What they perceive as fulfillment may be partial, and it may not even be what the challenge was about. To support their thinking, have the coachee articulate the actual evidence of the change. Ask for specific outcomes and evidence. Discuss it until both you and the coachee are satisfied that the challenge has been fully and truthfully received and fulfilled.
Don't—Assume that a coachee's perception of their success is accurate.	
Do—Be bold enough to be truthful and to challenge appropriately.	Being afraid to say something out of fear of the coachee's response can paralyze a coaching relationship. Be prepared to accept a "no" to your request, without personal feelings attached. It is your job to ask for more (or less) from the coachee, while being respectful and sensitive to the coachee's situation and needs. If you are getting a lot of "no's" take time to investigate why. Your job is to stretch a coachee in a healthy way, not necessarily to be a nice, compliant friend.
Don't—Be fearful of coachee's response.	

Resources

Attention Readers:

Thank you for participating in the collective wisdom of Coach U. Together, we all continue to learn. Additional resources and forms can be found in *Coach U's Essential Coaching Tools: Your Complete Practice Resource* by CoachInc.com.

Attention CoachInc.com Students and Graduates:

CoachInc.com students and graduates may find additional and/or more recent resources associated with this module in the resource area of the student-only web site. If you are a student or graduate of one of CoachInc.com's ICF-accredited coach training programs, you can access these by searching under the name of the course. When the course description page appears you may find a link to the list of additional resources. Each item is a live link to its actual location on the web site. Click on the item to access the information.

Do remember to take the associated online self-test for this module once you have completed the course in person or by TeleClass. The tests are required for coach certification with the International Coach Federation. Throughout the course or anytime you find valuable resources for a particular course please feel free to add to the value of our curricula by forwarding the resource to revampteam@coachu.com.

Chapter 9

Acknowledging

Overview

By participating in this module you will learn how to effectively use the motivating tools of acknowledgment to help your coachees achieve their vision. You will understand the framework of acknowledging, including the methods and stages, and even the perils. You will be given practical tools and information about skills, discernment of, and attitudes regarding acknowledging, and you will know the pitfalls and promoters of effective acknowledging.

Acknowledging, empowering, disempowerment, strengths, vision, and tolerations.

Acknowledgment: The Process of Acknowledging

Acknowledgment, or the process of acknowledging, is not a goal in itself as much as the action that results from it. Acknowledgment is a catalyst for action—or inaction if not done well. The dictionary defines acknowledging as the process of investing in another with appreciation. The coaching version defines acknowledging as the process of bringing out the coachee's best by reminding him or her of what he or she already knows. There are basic steps and methods to the acknowledging process.

Acknowledge versus endorse, strength versus power, unconditionally constructive versus polite, goals versus shoulds, endorse versus compliment, reframe versus reinterpret, structure versus parenting, compassionate versus patronizing, and toleration versus acceptance.

○ Application

Go to Page > 279

The Framework of Acknowledging

The framework of acknowledgment is composed of stages, methods, skills, and the knowledge of promoters and pitfalls of effective acknowledging. The information here is presented to assist the coach in applying the concepts of acknowledging within the structured framework of this powerful tool.

Methods of Acknowledgment

Endorsement
Focus on Strengths
Wanting For
Removing Barriers: Identifying and Eliminating Tolerations
Holding the Vision
Directness
Silence
Celebrating

Potential Perils of Acknowledgment

Acknowledgment Behaviors: Promoters and Pitfalls

○ Resources

Go to Page > 290

Benefits

By participating in this module you will understand the concept of acknowledging, and the coaching skills involved in acknowledging your coachees to find the sources of their own unlimited power. You will be able to use the various acknowledging skills to: endorse your coachees, focus on strengths, "want" for your coachees, remove barriers, hold the vision, and use directness and silence effectively. You will learn how to create an environment in which the coachee can access his or her own power.

This course is designed to:

O **Teach** the framework of acknowledging skills used in a coaching interaction to promote a coachee's ability to achieve his or her vision

O **Help** you enable your coachees to be self-acknowledging on a continuing, permanent basis

O **Describe** the ways coaches acknowledge—highlighting what a coach really does, or does not do, to acknowledge their coachees

O **Impart** tools and methods for effective acknowledging

O **Give** you important distinctions in various acknowledging skills, behaviors, attitudes and language

O **Inform** you of the behaviors that promote acknowledging, and those which become pitfalls, and how to avoid them

Definitions

The following are common words used to gain a better understanding of the coaching process, particularly in regard to acknowledging.

Acknowledging: The act or process of recognizing the full truth of the best in your coachee. It is the act of expressing full appreciation for who the person is and for what he or she does.

Empowering: The simple definition of this word is to endow with ability, or to enable. When you empower, you enable coachees to acknowledge themselves, giving them the ability to act.

Disempowerment: This is the direct opposite of empowerment. It means to disable, or to remove the ability to do something. Coachees can regularly disempower themselves, or allow other influences to disempower them. There are also a number of ways that you can unintentionally disempower a coachee.

Strengths: Literally, strength is the quality or state of being strong, an intellectual or moral force, a source of power, an attribute, or something with great value. Strengths are a collection of attributes, those things that a person excels at doing, or has natural ability for. Strengths can be physical, emotional, or spiritual. They are values, skills, talents, attitudes, relationships, resources, and other sources of power, sustenance, encouragement, and satisfaction.

Vision: A vision is simply something seen. A personal vision is something seen for the future. It involves anticipation, foresight, perception, conception, and desire. It is a scene of being for the future. A personal vision is based on wants, needs, values, and goals. A vision may be singular in nature, or involve many facets.

Tolerations: To tolerate means to allow the existence of something, to permit or to endure something, to put up with something. This implies that something (or someone) is less than desirable, less than the ideal, and tends to drain a person's energy. A toleration is a situation, a condition, or an influence of any kind, that is allowed to exist, is put up with, or that is less than ideal. A toleration is often a hindering influence.

Concepts

Acknowledgment: The Process of Acknowledging

Acknowledgment, or the process of acknowledging, is not a goal in itself as much as the coachee's actions that results from it. Acknowledgment is a catalyst for action—or inaction, if not done. The dictionary defines acknowledging as to recognize as a fact, to admit the truth of. The coaching version defines acknowledging as the process of bringing out the coachee's best by connecting him or her with their own source of unlimited energy and power by reminding them of what they already know.

Professional athletes know that ongoing acknowledgment and celebration improves on-the-job performance. Fans don't wait until the end of the game to acknowledge a good play—they cheer for each good play. The fans continue to cheer for their favorite players and celebrate the team's wins, even in a tough season. Rather than quietly observing the games from the stands, fans provide feedback and enthusiasm throughout the match.

Most workplaces do not encourage wild cheering from teammates in other cubicles. However, the need for acknowledgment and celebration is as strong for the office worker as it is for the athlete. Unfortunately, in today's fast-paced and measured business world, as well as in life in general, we focus on how much still needs to be accomplished today, this week, this quarter, by the end of the fiscal year or end of the year, and don't take time to recognize how much or what has already been accomplished.

“ I can live for two months on a good compliment. ” | Mark Twain

---

Part of your role as a coach is to acknowledge—literally, it is sharing your observation of the actions the individual or team took and the impact of those actions. Acknowledging is a statement about what the coachee did, the risk he or she took, and the result it created. You can only be a temporary source of acknowledgment for a coachee, not a long-term source. In order to sustain the coachee's self-acknowledgment, it is first necessary for the coachee to develop a solid foundation and the self-esteem necessary to hold onto the value of acknowledgment.

Acknowledgment is stimulated through many different sources, both from within and without. Help coachees explore these sources and assist them to become familiar with how our senses, our values, our experiences, and any number of other inputs can be sources of acknowledgment. Perhaps the ultimate is to be acknowledged by everyone and everything in our lives. Every piece of information, every event—whether perceived initially as good or bad—every person and every situation can be a source of acknowledgment. You can give a coachee the tools he or she will need to take every opportunity to become more self-acknowledged. You can be of great assistance when helping the coachee to connect to a personal power grid—a connection and network of acknowledging sources from which he or she can draw, whether from people or other resources.

" ... those who can most truly be accounted brave are those who best know the meaning of what is sweet in life and what is terrible, and then go out, undeterred, to meet what is to come. " | **Pericles**

Acknowledgment does not happen with one big all-encompassing action on your part as coach. It is enabled through constantly and continuously giving pieces to the coachee in presenting moments. You may ask how you can help a coachee reach his or her goals, but perhaps a more important question to answer is how you can acknowledge a coachee in any particular moment.

The Practice of Acknowledging

- Be unconditionally constructive in everything you say, yet say it all.
- Ask for far more than the person has done before.
- Create a wide enough gap between where the person is and where they want to be.
- Create possibility where there isn't enough—before you set goals.
- Eliminate all of the high, hidden emotional costs of your style of coaching.
- Acknowledge the ability of the coachee or team to solve their own problems.
- Endorse, endorse, endorse—this propels most people to be their best.
- Focus on the person's strengths, not their weaknesses.
- Get the person or group into action, not just discussion.
- Have the person take full responsibility for everything in their life, regardless of the outcome.
- Help the coachee to reframe what they are thinking or feeling.
- Make the coachee right because they are—even when they're not.
- Set up more than enough structure to support better behavior.
- Unhook the coachee from what is running them.

There are many ways to acknowledge a coachee; some will work better than others, depending on the coachee. You must listen carefully and respond with sensitivity to what the coachee needs in order to most effectively acknowledge the coachee into even more positive action.

There are eight important methods that are basic tools in the acknowledging process:

- Endorsement
- Focus on Strengths
- Wanting For
- Removing Barriers
- Holding the Vision
- Directness
- Silence
- Celebrating

Endorsement

Every coachee needs endorsement. Masterfully articulating support, confidence, or recognition of the coachee is invaluable to the process they are undertaking. Endorsement does not come naturally to most of us. Often, without the focused development of this method, endorsement sounds like we are trying to pump up the other person. Or we sound patronizing, certainly without meaning to. In general conversation, we tend to say nothing because we are afraid we will sound insincere if we are too encouraging. Endorsing coachees is essential in the developmental process, given the risks, uncertainty, and challenges the coachee will encounter as he or she enters new territory.

Focus on Strengths

Many people are so full of guilt or thoughts about what else they could be doing that they have yet to surrender to and be grateful for all they do have. This growth step (acceptance and gratitude) is essential for happiness and is an invaluable acknowledging phase. You help the coachee to get through this step by focusing on strengths and having these articulated strengths become enough for the coachee. The coachee then continues to develop more strengths, but only because he or she desire to build upon current inventory, not because they are dissatisfied with the ones they have.

Wanting For

Coachees often need to know that you are on their side, standing up for their success, even in the face of reality, problems, and diversions. Wanting a lot for your coachee helps to establish goals beyond what the coachee can see and reminds him or her that you are his or her advocate and supporter in his success. You may need to reveal these "want fors" to the coachee as a form of feedback based on careful listening. You become the coachee's champion for his or her success by wanting only the very best for your coachees.

Removing Barriers

Removing barriers is about identifying and eliminating (as much as possible) the obstacles that keep a person from being acknowledged or being able to embrace an acknowledgment. For each person there may be a number of these barriers, including:

- Limiting beliefs (typically with the coachee for a long time)
- "I can't" syndrome (can originate from real or imagined failure)
- Unwillingness to take risks (generally due to disempowerment and can become a cycle)
- Judgment of others (dodging responsibility)
- Blaming (more dodging of responsibility)
- Laziness (not willing to take action or do the work involved to succeed)
- Procrastination (always what they are "going" to do)
- Low self-esteem (a condition that tends to be a habit—can be broken)
- "Shoulds" (living the life someone else wants for you)

There are many, many other such barriers to being open and engaged in the practice of acknowledgment, but all of them can be labeled as tolerations. We tolerate certain people, circumstances, and behavior (in ourselves or others) on a daily basis. Your function is to enable the coachee to identify these tolerations and to find constructive ways to either eliminate them altogether, or reduce their ability to hinder growth.

Holding the Vision

By far the most acknowledging thing you can do for a coachee is to help him or her get in touch with a compelling vision—their own vision. When this happens, your job as a coach becomes easy and joyful because the coachee no longer leans on you for acknowledgment—he or she is generating their own acknowledgment. Acknowledgment is fueled by meaningful vision. The place to start this process is to help the coachee share, perhaps for the first time, what he or she most wants out of life. Through a series of conversations, the truth of their vision will be revealed, opening up the next level of awareness. Once the vision is known, you may need to hold onto it for the coachee, using it sensitively as a milestone and marker in their path of development. Keep in mind that in organizational coaching there can be a professional vision within a personal vision.

Directness

Coachees are paying you to share what you sense, see, and know. Your opinions and insights matter and are integral to a successful coaching relationship. Directness in coaching involves speaking your mind, using succinct phrasing and an honest approach that moves the coachee forward but does not blast him or her with the truth. Directness is not bluntness or speaking with no regard for the coachee's feelings. Directness can be a weapon without careful development. Coachees often need the nudge that directness brings to their progress. Master coaches are very direct, yet graceful and compassionate.

Silence

The natural universe always attempts to fill a vacuum and so will your coachee when you are quiet. Silence is an advanced skill, one that calls on you to have patience, faith, and willingness for the coachee to work things out for themselves. It is said that nature abhors a vacuum. It is our natural tendency to jump in and fix things. Although it may seem odd to include this concept here, the coach's practiced use of silence can be one of the most supportive tools of all. This can be a difficult skill to master, whether you are coaching in person or by telephone, but it is a skill worth mastering.

" You get the best effort from others not by lighting a fire beneath them, but by building a fire within. **"** | **Bob Nelson**

Celebrating

Celebrations have been an important element in human lives for thousands of years. Since ancient times, people have planned celebrations to rejoice in a successful harvest, to honor the return of warriors, and to enjoy the gift of the present. Unfortunately, our world has become so future-focused that we rarely stop to appreciate the fruits of our labor and the prosperity of today. Masterful coaches celebrate the many success steps that coachees achieve. Otherwise, coachees work toward the mega-solution or ultimate outcome, and focus on the inevitable problems that occur along the way.

Distinctions

There are subtle yet important differences in meaning between the following closely related terms. Understanding these distinctions allows you to perceive new layers of meaning and offers you new choices for shifting your thoughts, attitudes, and actions.

Acknowledge versus Endorse

Acknowledgment is the recognition and expression of the existence or truth of something. You acknowledge who they are underneath it all. Generally, you endorse a person's ability or capacity.

Strength versus Power

Power generally means you have power over something: yourself, another person, or circumstances. Strength implies no competition or need to have power over something because you are naturally strong. Coaches work to strengthen coachees more than to increase their power. Being naturally strong eliminates the need for power over anything.

Unconditionally Constructive versus Polite

To be unconditionally constructive is to phrase everything you must say to a coachee in positive, forwarding language and attitude. Polite is being nonoffensive, but may keep you from saying what needs to be said. Being unconditionally constructive is not a license for "dumping" but a tool for moving the coachee further on their path of development. Being merely polite will not motivate, inspire, and enliven your coachee.

Goals versus Shoulds

A goal is something that you really want. A "should" is a goal that you think you should want, or think you need, in order to reach another goal (a means to an end). An authentic goal allows choice and can be freely set, changed, or abandoned with little resistance or emotional reaction. A should is rife with risk, consequences, and potential condemnation. Many goals are actually shoulds; you as a coach must distinguish between these for the coachee and help him or her understand the differences.

Endorse versus Compliment

To endorse is to express approval and support of something or someone. To compliment is to praise or admire a certain behavior or the choice a person makes. Endorsement often implies support for the person, not just praise for a condition. While both are positive, the first one is stronger.

Reframe versus Reinterpret

To reframe means to step back and look at the situation from either a greater perspective or a totally different angle. Reframing does not change how something is viewed, but broadens the view and a person's awareness. Reinterpreting means thinking differently about a situation, to completely alter your judgment or interpretation. You must carefully determine which is necessary for the coachee and facilitate accordingly. Reframing is the easiest and most productive, but sometimes reinterpretation is necessary to rid a person of old shoulds and incorrect preconceptions.

Structure versus Parenting

You provide a structure of support for the coachee as he or she takes on new challenges and makes changes. However, the only experience of this type of support by some coachees has been what their parents provided for them as children, and the coachee may unintentionally try to put you in a parenting role. In addition, sometimes coaches want to help their coachees so much they put themselves in the role of quasi-parent. This is a delicate balance to which you should pay attention. You provide structure that includes such things as weekly calls, discussions, goals, reporting, and reminders. Parenting includes commiserating, getting too involved with coachees emotionally, shaming, patronizing, and considering your coachees to be immature children or emotionally disabled.

" The only person alive on this planet that can stop you from succeeding is you. " | **Aubry Padmore**

Compassionate versus Patronizing

Compassion is a genuine feeling of sympathy for a person and a desire to alleviate any suffering. Compassion is a gift. Patronizing is an offensive condescending manner, and is a way for you to feel superior. Compassion is feeling another's pain, having nothing but love for that person. When you see a person's weakness and make allowances for it, or you feel superior, or you judge them, you are patronizing.

Toleration versus Acceptance

A toleration is something that is put up with or endured; it is a burden and eats up time, money, and mental space. Tolerations can be eliminated. Acceptance is understanding that while something may not be pleasant, it is a fact of that person's life, and as such can become a positive factor with the right attitude and constructive planning for its presence. Often, the only difference between toleration and acceptance is in attitude and approach. Acceptance implies the condition or situation cannot be changed, except in the mind and future of the person. You acknowledge a coachee by helping to show the distinction and assisting in eliminating any harmful and hindering tolerations.

Application

> " My father gave me the greatest gift anyone could give another person, he believed in me. " | **Jim Valvano, Basketball Coach**

Methods of Acknowledgment

Endorsement

When coachees are growing and accomplishing, they need more endorsement than you may think. Anyone who is a pioneer, creative, entrepreneurial, making changes, or taking on big goals needs a great deal of encouragement. Some coaches simply aren't accustomed to giving high levels of endorsement and will find they need to stretch a bit in this area. Practice regular endorsing (not complimenting, fake-acknowledgment, seducing, or patronizing).

- *Encouragement*
  Keep going. You can do it! I believe in you.
- *Agreement*
  You are on the right track. Life is really hard sometimes.
- *Acknowledgment*
  You're strong enough to move through this glitch. I trust your judgment.
- *Advocating something your coachee wants or believes*
  It's time you reached this goal. Let's go for it full-tilt.
  It's possible and you're going to do it.
- *Empathizing*
  Feeling defeated is really tough.
  Reaching your first goal is a great motivator to keep moving forward.
- *Congratulations*
  Yay! You did it. Congratulations! I knew you would do it!

Endorsement is letting the coachee know that you recognize his or her strengths and desires. In a supportive way you tell the coachee reasons why he or she can do whatever it is they want to do. You endorse for the purpose of assisting coachees to acknowledge themselves, endorse others and encourage them to accept endorsement. A part of being endorsed is the acceptance of the endorsement. Coachees must listen carefully for this acceptance, and gain awareness of non-acceptance.

Focus on Strengths

All coachees have strengths and weaknesses. The primary focus of all coaching must be on the strengths of the coachee. Your coachee can be acknowledged by recognizing that his or her strengths are a valuable and vital part of who he or she is now, and what he or she can be in the future. Focusing on strengths does not mean ignoring the weaknesses. Weaknesses are addressed using unconditionally constructive language, but never becoming the focus. Your first step in this approach is to identify the strengths of the coachee through careful listening. Once you have determined your coachee's strengths, provide the informing feedback necessary to remind your coachee, or perhaps in some cases to newly educate him, of his strengths. It is likely you may discover a hidden strength the coachee was not completely aware of. You make the coachee understand the value and the resources of current strengths.

The discovery and building of coachee strengths can be through listening for clues and hints, or through direct questioning, using language such as this:

- In what areas of life do you feel naturally strong?
- True, you could use more training, but tell me what you're already good at.
- What is it about what you already have that is not satisfying to you?
- What is something you've always wanted to be extraordinary at?
- Given you're strong here, what's the next level of development with that?
- What do others think you're good at?
- Are you willing to not be strong everywhere? Is it okay to acknowledge this?

Put the coachee in touch with his or her natural strengths, the ones they may take for granted. People often need help to identify what they do very well naturally. Sometimes we get caught up with forcing ourselves to get better or stronger in weak areas. Identifying strengths may be the first step, but you must also suggest that coachees continue to invest in and develop their strengths. Keep after your coachees to go to the next level with their natural strengths; natural strengths can always use more development to become even stronger. Focus on and work with what the coachee already has. Show coachees how to identify existing strengths and resources and weave them together into a single unit—a group of things synthesized into a package, a powerful source for success. You might consider having your coachee make a list of 10 goals, and then develop a list of the resources that are available right now, whether seemingly related to those goals or not.

By weaving these two lists together, a coachee can determine what can be synthesized from this into an achievement. This is a highly creative process that is acknowledging because you are dealing with what you have instead of what you don't have or are striving to get. This process may reveal more of what you do not need, and already have.

Wanting For

You need ways to share ideas with coachees without inserting condemnation. These ideas may be new business opportunities, a change that you think is helpful for the coachee, or a message about life in general. You can do this without suppressing the coachee, making him or her wrong, or having a debate. The "What I want for you ..." approach helps the coachee to set attainable and desired goals and standards without feeling the pressure and deflating burden of past failures.

The following are samples only of virtually hundreds of "I wants" you can have for your coachee:

- What I want for you is to have your critical needs met so you can get on with your life.
- What I want for you is to be on a clear and conservative financial track that will allow you to be financially independent ASAP.
- What I want for you is to have the words and phrases you need to express your ideas clearly.
- What I want for your team is to work like clockwork so you can leave work at work.
- What I want for you is to find your vision and orient your life around it.
- What I want for you is to be fully restored so that you have time and energy to do the things that bring you joy.
- What I want for you is to start enjoying work so that this next year is effortless for you.
- What I want for you is to learn as much as you can from this unexpected situation.

Using the "What I want for you ..." approach leads the person to a higher place. It may take a day or 10 years for the person to take the actions required, but there is now a goal or standard worth having. You are establishing priorities. Specialize and be specific so that the standards are attainable. Choose carefully, because it will also be an expression of yourself that reflects both your and your coachee's values. Your message is like a gift handed to the coachee. As such, the coachee can accept it, reject it, ignore it or go with it. Give this gift freely, with no strings attached. How the coachee accepts it is up to them. Be sure to phrase your "want" for your coachee in positive language that reflects the improved future, not a poor past. What you want for your coachee should not become a "should" or condemnation of any kind. Notice the unconditionally constructive words used here:

What I want for you is:

- To be at your ideal weight, without having to diet.
- To have the peace of mind that strong financial planning provides.
- To enjoy your family as much as you enjoy your work.
- To run your company successfully and still feel free.
- To be at peace with yourself and the past.

Be sure you preface your want for your coachee with the words "What I want for you ..." Do not be tempted to use other phrases such as "What I see for you is ...", "What you should do is ...", "What you may consider is ...", or "What you need is ..." These will not produce the desired results because they are not free of judgment. They are not a gift anymore.

Removing Barriers: Identifying and Eliminating Tolerations

A great way you can serve your coachees is to help them identify and remove the most paralyzing barriers to self-acknowledgment: tolerations. Humans have made tolerating an abundant art form. We put up with, endure, take on, and are dragged down by people's behavior (including our own), situations, unmet needs, crossed boundaries, unfinished business, frustrations, and a myriad of problems. Tolerations are certain obstacles to self-acknowledgment. Most tolerations can be eliminated, but they must be identified first. Even the tolerations that cannot be eliminated are easier to handle just by our awareness of them.

You must ask the right questions to get the real truth about how much the coachee is tolerating, because the coachee may be so accustomed to the tolerations that they have become the standard. The following language and questions help identify and hopefully eliminate many tolerations:

- What are you putting up with right now?
- What have you been tolerating?
- It is all right to tolerate. We all do to some degree. You don't have to stop putting up with it. But it helps to say what it is, and whether you can or will do something about it.
- What is bugging you that you wish wasn't?
- What is it costing you to tolerate this?
- What is the benefit of putting up with this?
- Why are you really doing this?
- Why do you want to stop tolerating this?
- How is having this toleration serving you? How would you be served if you didn't have this toleration?
- What is the new standard that will handle this and other tolerations?
- Who will you have to become to stop tolerating this?

- How will you stop tolerating this?
- Who can help you stop putting up with this?

Holding the Vision

You hold the vision for your coachee when the coachee is feeling like "I can't," when the coachee is feeling discouraged, and when the coachee forgets or loses track of personal vision. You also hold a bigger, broader, more expansive vision than what the coachee sees. It is essential that you speak from knowing, believing, and seeing what the coachee can do. It is not enough, however, to merely hold the vision. You must impart the vision back to the coachee when you have determined the vision may have been lost. You hold the coachee accountable for his or her vision, reminding the coachee of what he or she has determined to be important. The process of coaching can take a coachee over many paths, covering a great deal of territory with many diversions and side trips. For this reason it is essential for you to hold on to the coachee's vision, re-establishing its prominence and importance for the coachee. Once again, careful listening and tracking of a coaching interaction, or a series of interactions, will allow you to keep the coachee appropriately accountable for his or her vision. Appropriately accountable in this instance means those reasonable and appropriate moments are used as opportunities to clarify the vision. It does not mean the coachee is beat over the head with his or her vision. This accountability may also mean revisiting, re-calibrating, and even resetting coachee vision.

Remember the vision belongs to the coachee, not to you. You merely hold it and keep it safe and accessible. Acknowledgment depends on vision. When the vision dies or is not immediately visible, self-acknowledgment ceases. You can use language similar to the following to hold vision and keep the coachee accountable to it:

- How does this (action, thought, shift) align with your vision?
- Does your vision match your values?
- I want to remind you of the vision you spoke of earlier. In light of your progress, does this vision still hold true for you?
- Considering this new development, does your ultimate vision require any recalibration?
- Does this mean you are expanding your vision?

Directness

People sometimes need a nudge to keep developing and rediscover their motivation. You must be sensitive to times when you see that the coachee is stalling, or waiting for a directive. Once the goals or immediate behaviors and activities have been established and clarified, you may need to be very direct and upfront by giving the coachee a verbal push. This push can be gentle, or more motivating, but cannot be condescending or judgmental. Don't back away from or be afraid of using directness with a coachee as a tool to acknowledge him or her. The directness of the coach can be phrased as follows:

- Yes, you can!
- It's time to get moving.
- It's not okay with me as your coach that you are not applying yourself.
- You must take action.
- Tell me how to coach you.
- When are you going to get serious?
- Why are you waiting, delaying?
- What are you truly dedicated to?
- How would you have to change in order to reach this goal?
- Are you discouraged?
- You are in a temporary slump; keep going.

" In order to become empowered, to become the co-creator in our lives, and to stop giving power to the belief that we are the victim, it is absolutely necessary to own that we have choices. **"** | **Robert Burney**

Silence

We have already discussed how the vacuum created by silence can support the coachee in filling it with new learning and self-discovery. In coaching, less talk is more opportunity for the coachee. If you talk too much or are too helpful, you actually do a disservice to your coachees. Allow them to find their own answers. This new freedom will let your focus be where it will do the most good. Using silence also informs coachees that they are doing the work, not you. You can use simple conversation "connectors" to enhance the flow of coachee talk around and through the silences, such as:

- (Total silence, no talk)
- Hmmm …
- Really?
- I see.
- Fine.
- What do want from me?
- What do you need to hear?
- Wow.
- Keep going.

While silence is useful and valuable in a coaching conversation, it can also be overused to the point that you are completely ineffectual, and your coachee is left hanging in the wind. Use your discernment and intuition to know when silence is appropriate, and when it is not. Some gaps definitely need to be filled.

Celebrating

Celebrating is an important element of a meaningful life. As we already mentioned, oftentimes cause for celebration is overlooked by the hurried and demanding world that we live in. Helping people shift from a struggling approach to a more effortless mindset creates an environment for the enjoyment of life. It creates a natural pull forward into a more fulfilling way of living. Celebration motivates people to continue with their larger goals.

Language examples of celebrating:

> I realize you have not completely attained your goal of completing this task. Let's look at what you have completed in the past three weeks. Write down the significant accomplishments you have realized. Now, what can you do to celebrate how far you have come and how will you celebrate it this weekend?

> The team has completed a major milestone. I would like each member to make a list of what stands out to you about the contribution of each other team member. Write this on an index card and give it to them in the next 10 minutes. Now let's go around the room and each person describe what you are grateful for and how you feel about this team after you receive your cards from other team members.

Benefits of Celebrating

- Reduces stress
- Motivates people to continue toward larger goals
- Reenergizes people
- Creates an opportunity to strengthen relationships
- Refreshes attitudes
- Allows people to pull back and see the big picture
- Improves health
- Allows people to enjoy a more balanced life

Five Ways to Celebrate

1. Encourage coachees to schedule a celebration—a massage, tickets to a game, trip to mall, lunch with a friend.
2. Give coachees permission to be good to themselves—sleep late, read a fun book, spend time with a favorite hobby.
3. Create a virtual party by inviting your coachees to an over-the-phone party. Ask each person to tell a joke and give a toast to the team.
4. Send electronic greeting cards.
5. When the coachee has a success, ask him or her to take the time to tell you what they did to contribute to the positive outcome.

Celebrating, acknowledging, and endorsing are a way of life, not just a coaching tool to help motivate or achieve goals.

Potential Perils of Acknowledgment

Acknowledgment is obviously, by its very nature, very powerful. It is a tool that can be used for great good, but also can be abused, causing the coachee great harm. It is vital that you understand your responsibility in using this tool, and as with any tool, have knowledge of its capacity for good or harm, depending upon how it is used. The following are mentioned as potential perils of acknowledgement so you understand and appreciate the responsibility, and know that balance in the use of this tool is an absolute must.

- Misunderstanding acknowledgment and using it to actually diminish someone
- Unwanted consequences that result from bold actions taken without enough information or preparation
- Coachee's uneasiness for the consequences
- Lack of information or preparation, ignorance, denial, and lack of understanding the consequences that may occur from actions taken as a result of acknowledgment
- False acknowledgment—misleading coachees, fooling them into thinking they can accomplish something they are not ready for or are unable to do
- Not telling the truth

Seven Ways to Acknowledge Your Coachee

1. *Advocate who they are.*
   - Point to their strengths, abilities, and qualities. Remind them who they really are and are becoming.
   - Endorse who they are and make them right for what they've done or attempted.
   - Do this more than you think you should. Growth requires more of this than we think.

2. *Stand up for what your coachees want or believe in.*
   - Reassure the coachee: You can do this; you will make it; you deserve this.
   - Hold the vision: You're doing this so you can be.... ; It is worth it, don't stop.
   - Have faith in them: I know you'll make it just fine.

3. *Want a lot for them.*
   - Know what you want for them, even if they don't, yet.
   - Challenge them to want a lot more for themselves than they currently do.
   - Evoke what they really want for themselves.

4. *Show that you care.*
   - Empathize; don't coach, when the coachees just need love and support. Care for them!
   - Spend extra time with your coachees who are going through a tough time.
   - Give gifts or tokens, cards, remember birthdays. Go out of your way for your coachees.

5. *Understand they are right—even if they aren't, they are.*
   - Everyone does their best; don't make them wrong for their mistakes or blocks.
   - Feel free to correct them, enforce your boundaries, and challenge them to do a lot more.
   - Know that you are right, too.

6. *Acknowledge their actions and results.*
   - Point out the growth, results, effort, and accomplishments that you see, even if the coachee doesn't.
   - Don't flatter, compliment, or over-acknowledge; keep it straight, simple, "right on."
   - No puffery.
   - Make it an acknowledgement, not a setup to push them hard, like, "Now that you've ... , you can ...."

7. *Have compassion and respect for your coachees.*
   - Honor that anyone working with a coach deserves extra respect.
   - Identify with their feelings, empathize, have compassion for what it takes to grow.
   - If you don't currently respect your coachees, make a huge request of them so that you can.

Acknowledgment Behaviors: Promoters and Pitfalls

The DOS are behaviors that promote success of acknowledging. The DON'TS are behaviors that limit the success of acknowledging.

Do—Remove barriers and simplify life. **Don't**—Assume you have to ADD something to the coachee's life.	Helping the coachee to remove or simplify something in his other life (such as tolerations) can be as acknowledging as helping them to develop, build, or add something. Often just the removal of a blockage results in immediate acknowledgment.
Do—Know the truth itself is acknowledging. **Don't**—Try to puff up the coachee or sugarcoat reality.	The truth, whether it is heard as good or bad news, is acknowledging. Being unjustifiably positive is usually more about you being uncomfortable with a coachee than acknowledging. You can be very positive, but if the coachee has a problem, label it a problem and not a challenge or some other sugarcoated lie.
Do—Understand that acknowledgment may be a new experience. **Don't**—Assume the coachee has been acknowledged before.	Acknowledgment may be a completely new experience for your coachee. If it is their first real experience, they will likely be a little clumsy with it initially. Don't expect perfection, and do be very encouraging. You may be the first person in your coachee's life that helps him or her to feel acknowledged.
Do—Actually acknowledge your coachees. **Don't**—Talk about acknowledgment.	Don't just talk about acknowledging your coachee—acknowledge your coachee. You can acknowledge by helping to create a situation in which they feel acknowledged rather than just understand the notion of acknowledgment. Make a big request, challenge your coachee to stop or start something, etc. This will acknowledge them a lot faster than talking about it.
Do—Help the coachee become self-acknowledged. **Don't**—Think it is the coach doing the acknowledging.	It is not about you acknowledging the coachee; it's about the coachee feeling and being acknowledged, from whatever source. You may need to jumpstart the coachee yourself, but it is better that you help the coachee to stay fully charged by his or her own system, not yours.
Do—Desire to acknowledge the coachee, not yourself. **Don't**—Dis-acknowledge the coachee.	You dis-acknowledge your coachee when you compete with them, belittle their development, label them incorrectly or in a demeaning way, keep yanking the rug out from underneath them. Genuinely desire your coachee's acknowledgment.

Do—Realize that not all coachees need to be acknowledged.	Not every coachee wants or needs to be acknowledged. Acknowledgment is not a tool to be used just because you have it. You must use careful listening and discernment to determine the signs that a coachee is either already acknowledged and just needs your coaching skills to move forward with structure, or is dis-acknowledged and does need acknowledging in order to advance. Your efforts at acknowledging may be an unneeded and unwelcome process for some coachees.
Don't—Waste time and offend the coachee with efforts to acknowledge when not needed.	
Do—Hear and do what acknowledges others.	You may get motivated and be acknowledged by excitement or a vision. A coachee may feel acknowledged by integrity. You may feel acknowledged by committing to a big goal; the coachee may feel most acknowledged by merely simplifying. It is very important to understand all of the things that acknowledge people and not just know what acknowledges you. Again, careful listening will give you the clues to what acknowledges your coachee.
Don't —Limit the coachee to what acknowledges you.	

Resources

Attention Readers:

Thank you for participating in the collective wisdom of Coach U. Together, we all continue to learn. Additional resources and forms can be found in *Coach U's Essential Coaching Tools: Your Complete Practice Resource* by CoachInc.com.

Attention CoachInc.com Students and Graduates:

CoachInc.com students and graduates may find additional and/or more recent resources associated with this module in the resource area of the student-only web site. If you are a student or graduate of one of CoachInc.com's ICF-accredited coach training programs, you can access these by searching under the name of the course. When the course description page appears you may find a link to the list of additional resources. Each item is a live link to its actual location on the web site. Click on the item to access the information.

Do remember to take the associated online self-test for this module once you have completed the course in person or by TeleClass. The tests are required for coach certification with the International Coach Federation. Throughout the course or anytime you find valuable resources for a particular course please feel free to add to the value of our curricula by forwarding the resource to revampteam@coachu.com.

www.coachinc.com

Part 3
Coaching Application

Chapter 10

Situational Coaching

Overview

By participating in this module you will gain a basic understanding of common personal or professional conditions experienced by a coachee. While coaching cannot be done based on a single formula or recipe, it is possible for a coach to use some of what is understood about various types of coachees to create a framework from which to develop a coaching plan.

Situational, situational coaching, coachee condition, entrepreneur, CEO/Executive, professional, career employee, sales professional, work team, creative, intellectual, leader, and parent.

What is Situational Coaching?

Situational coaching is about determining who you are coaching, what their personal or professional conditions or situations are, what they commonly need and want to work on, and how you can best address these issues. Even though CoachInc.com has only defined a limited number of situations, there may be literally hundreds of actual coachee conditions. We are providing a general overview of a few common conditions familiar to most coaches.

○ Distinctions
Go to Page > 303

Single operator versus connected, vision versus goal, leadership versus management, strategic versus tactical, expertise versus experience, marketing versus delivering, working hard versus producing results, internal desire versus external prompt, feature versus benefit, attraction versus promotion, self versus work, standard versus expectation, wise versus smart, interesting versus important, model versus peer, reserve versus just enough, taking care of self versus selfish, investment versus trade, in power versus in control, and influence versus affect.

○ Application
Go to Page > 310

Coachee Conditions: Situational Coaching

Coachee Type Profiles
1. Entrepreneur
2. CEO/Executive
3. Professional
4. Career Employee
5. Sales Professional
6. Work Team
7. Creative
8. Intellectual
9. Leader
10. Parent

Common Shifts by Coachee Type

Situational Coaching: Promoters and Pitfalls

○ Resources
Go to Page > 334

Benefits

By fully participating in the material offered in this module, you will gain a basic understanding of a coachee by identifying key factors. While coaching cannot be done based on a single formula or recipe, it is possible for a coach to use some of what is understood about various coachee situations to create a framework from which to develop a coaching plan.

This course is designed to:

O Allow you to identify and understand various coachee conditions

O Teach you how to determine traits, common scenarios, motivators, key coaching skills, important distinctions, and shifts for each situation

O Help you determine which tools will be effective for different conditions of coachees

O Impart the skills to develop an effective coaching plan, using methods and strategies based on who the coachee is and who the coachee wants to become

Definitions

The following are common words used to gain a better understanding of situational coaching.

Situational: Something that refers to the condition, state of affairs, circumstances, or position of something or someone with reference to the surrounding environment. Situational awareness is being aware and having understanding of how conditions, circumstances, and other environmental concerns affect a person's state of being and doing.

Situational coaching: Determining who you are coaching by identifying his or her situation or life condition, then understanding what the coachee needs or wants to work on, and how you can best help him or her reach their goals.

Coachee condition: One of ten generalized coachee situations, characterized by certain common distinguishable behaviors, needs, and circumstances.

The ten coachee conditions highlighted in this module are as follows:

Entrepreneur: Someone who undertakes a commercial risk for profit, often in the form of business ownership. Typically accountable to no one in particular, the entrepreneur is opportunistic, independent, driven, busy, and enjoys achievement.

CEO/Executive: Someone who has administrative authority over a company or division of a company that he or she does not fully own. He or she is accountable to the company owner, chairperson, board of directors, or stockholders.

Professional: Someone who has attained expertise in a particular field. Professionals often have completed advanced education in fields such as medicine, law, or business. Professionals are accountable to their clients and regulatory boards.

Career employee: The manager or employee who works for another person or company and wants to progress along a career path.

Sales professional: Someone who sells products and/or services to others. Includes brokers, account executives, sales representatives, insurance agents, inside and outside sales.

Work team: A group of individuals within an organization who are responsible for predetermined outcomes. Can include departments, divisions, manufacturing lines, boards, and committees.

Creative: Someone who is imaginative and generative. He or she is often characterized as a free spirit, on a nontraditional path, who is either working for him- or herself or primarily gaining income from contract work. Includes writers, artists, artisans, designers, and performers.

Intellectual: Someone who is engaged in or with an educational system or department and focuses on the development of theory and ideas. This includes educators, teachers, professors, researchers, philosophers, thinkers, sociologists, futurists, and commentators.

Leader: Those who are responsible for the successful future of an organization and/or the quality of the experience of those involved in a project or mission. Often, leaders are characterized by being motivational and inspirational to those they are leading. This includes executive directors, committee chairs, governmental leaders, ministers, project managers, and often presidents of organizations.

Parent: Those who by choice or default have become responsible for raising children. This includes biological parents, stepparents, adoptive and foster parents.

Concepts

What is Situational Coaching?

Situational coaching is about determining who you are coaching based on their life conditions or situations, their needs, what they want to work on, and how you can best address their issues. Even though CoachInc.com has determined only a limited number of situations, there may be literally hundreds of actual coachee conditions. We are providing only a general overview of a few common conditions familiar to most coaches.

Ten Coachee Types

- Entrepreneur
- CEO/Executive
- Professional
- Career Employee
- Sales Professional
- Work Team
- Creative
- Intellectual
- Leader
- Parent

These categories and definitions refer to roles that the coachee may fill, or situations a coachee may be confronted with, but you will find executives with an entrepreneurial spirit, creative professionals, and sales professionals running corporations. You may also find that a coachee plays various roles around particular issues or topics. We type them according to who they are being or needing to be as they interact with what is really happening (situation). As you read the symptoms and the situation, you can use the material fluidly, based on who the coachee is, as well as the role he or she may perform.

The Entrepreneur

Entrepreneurs enjoy creating, developing something new, and seeing if it can succeed. They thrive on the different, and spend a great deal of time and energy proving themselves. Few are truly successful in their entrepreneurial endeavors; some build a strong enough business to make a living, most do not. Many will continue to try different ideas as long as they can raise the capital to do so.

The CEO/Executive

The CEO/Executive is built to make companies run and be profitable. Each CEO/Executive has a unique style, based on the skill set he or she brings to the role. Responsibilities are likely to include people, projects, and financial resources of the company he or she runs. They are usually intellectual, but may need to work on interpersonal skills and leadership in general.

The Professional

The professional delivers a service to others that requires special education and/or advanced training. They include doctors, lawyers, dentists, chiropractors, accountants, therapists (physical, massage, mental health, etc.), and coaches. The professional understands the value of professional services and is usually a consistent coachee.

The Career Employee

The career employee is characterized by the fact that he or she works for another individual or company, and works to make someone else's vision a reality. They may have various levels of responsibility and authority based on their position in the company, but ultimately they are generally supervised or managed by someone else or at the very least have a direct report to which they are accountable.

The Sales Professional

The sales professional is a unique type of coachee for whom coaching can make a tremendous difference. Sales professionals are often seduced by possible income and fail to be realistic about actual income and the effort it takes to produce it. Facing frequent rejection and requiring numerous contacts, sales professionals tend to be extroverts and people-focused.

Work Team

The work team is a group of individuals within an organization who are responsible for predetermined outcomes. Can include departments, divisions, manufacturing lines, boards, and committees. In work teams, it can be helpful to coach both the team and members of the team individually, depending on the strength and cohesiveness of the team as well as the timeline and complexity of the goals. Work team members can experience challenges in general communication and managing multiple priorities with limited resources.

The Creative

The creative is imaginative and generative and is typically characterized as a free spirit who is usually on a nontraditional path. Creatives are often more spiritual and value aesthetic beauty. Pursuing the need to create is vital to their existence, though the need is seldom if ever fully met, since they are often dissatisfied with their lives and their creations.

Guiding Principle 1 | **People Have Something in Common.**
We return to the common ground of being by loving, honoring, and valuing self and others.

The Intellectual

The intellectual is someone who is engaged in or with an educational system or department and focuses on the development of theory and ideas. They deal with information and concepts and would rather not be wrong. The intellectual is accustomed to working with the big picture and often negates the details that can present a coaching opportunity. However, the bigger value for the intellectual is the collaborative partner that is looking out for where he or she is blind. Typically this is in the self-care and relationship area where intellectuals have to act from their heart instead of their head.

The Leader

The leader is someone who is responsible for carving out and creating a viable future for the entity or enterprise. Whether or not the leader created the vision, he or she is passionate about and responsible for keeping the team engaged and energetically moving toward that vision. The leader is often left to his or her own motivation and therefore seeks his or her own support outside the organization. Life can be lonely at the top.

The Parent

The parent is often extremely resourceful and is driven by unconditional love. This mix can be dynamic and valuable in one extreme or overbearing and enmeshed at the other. Nobody has the corner on the parent-training model and many people are struggling to deal with this life condition in the face of an everchanging world and set of guidelines. The feeling of failure is common and runs to the very heart and soul of this role. The parent needs to be regularly reenergized and assured that he or she is on a journey with no ultimate destination. You have to love your children unselfishly. That's hard. But it is the only way.

Mixed Conditions

Many subtypes or a variety of mixed conditions can often best represent the coachee's situation. For example, the creative profile can likely be found in other situations to some degree. The creative is often a soloist and can get caught up in his or her craft to a dysfunctional degree. This kind of behavior can be seen in other conditions. Besides the creative, the teen, and sales professional may also perform for the adrenaline rush. Learn to spot the characteristics of each condition in all the other situations, so that you can more quickly discern the needed course of action.

Distinctions

There are subtle yet important differences in meaning between the following closely related terms. Understanding these distinctions allows you to perceive new layers of meaning and offers you new choices for shifting your thoughts, attitudes, and actions.

When coaching each of these ten life conditions, you will discover certain common characteristics that must be distinguished from other behaviors. It is important for you to be sensitive to and listening for some of these common traits of each condition, and how certain characteristics and behaviors need to be distinguished from others. The following are key distinctions for each of the ten life conditions. Look for cross-over distinctions in other situations as well.

Entrepreneur

Single Operator versus Connected

The single operator may also be labeled as a "lone ranger" or "one person show." Single operators are capable of fast and decisive actions because they draw on their own areas of expertise and motivation. Being connected can widen the areas of expertise available to the entrepreneur, but requires the individual to be open and seek out supportive people to be involved in the decisions or offer counsel and guidance. Being connected is a beginning stage of building a team around which the business grows.

Vision versus Goal

A vision is what you see as being possible for the future. A personal vision creates excitement and ownership, and even inspires, toward accomplishing goals. A goal is what you want to accomplish, and is generally only part of the vision. A vision is something that pulls you toward the goal, and helps determine other goals. The coachee needs to understand this distinction when setting goals, and should be encouraged to explore his or her vision (for personal and professional life) first.

CEO/Executive

Leadership versus Management

Leadership in organizations involves influencing the activities of a group or team towards achieving specified goals. Managing is the process of marshalling, allocating, and coordinating existing resources, things, and people. As coaches, we want to be leaders rather than managers for our coachees. We want them to manage themselves so we can help them set new directions and priorities.

Strategic versus Tactical

A strategic approach starts with defining the expected outcomes or desired conclusions and then establishes the key milestones or actions needed over a long timeframe (typically two to five years) in order to best achieve the result. A tactical approach focuses on a much shorter period of time (typically one to four months) and focuses on the actions or options that can be taken now to best achieve the desired short-term results. The expertise is in the balance between the time spent on the strategy and the time spent on the tactical maneuvers.

Professional

Expertise versus Experience

Expertise is a collection of in-depth knowledge, extensive skills, rigorous training, and strong personal attributes that are focused in a specific subject area. It is a measure of the potential the individual has to contribute to the subject. Experience is often a collection of a wide range of knowledge, various skills, and differing types of training and personal attributes that allow the individual to know or apply the learning from past events to present circumstances. Expertise is what you know, experience is what you have demonstrated. Both need to be associated with an action, such as communicating, teaching, applying, and so on, in order to be effective or recognized by others.

Marketing versus Delivering

Marketing is a set of defined activities designed to attract new clients into the practice or business. Delivering is the actions required to fulfill the service or product to existing clients. Delivering can also be positioned or designed to attract clients via referrals, loyalty, retention, and so on. Marketing does not have the capacity to deliver the product or service. Both are needed in a practice or business and the balance between them can be a key factor.

Career Employee

Working Hard versus Producing Results

Working hard means the employee is making full use of his or her time and energy on the job. It may require multitasking, prioritization, teamwork, creativity, deep skills, and a variety of personal attributes in order to get the job done well. The results of hard work are recognized by the employee and may or may not be recognized or endorsed by the organization. Producing results occurs when the employee's time, energy, and work effort are aligned to the desired outcomes defined by the organization. It is the shift in the context of who is recognizing the work effort that becomes the critical distinction.

Internal Desire versus External Prompt

At its simplest level, internal desire speaks to being motivated from within to perform the task. External prompt speaks to being motivated from an outside source to perform the task. Both get the task done. In time, however, higher productivity can be sustained when the motivation is from within. This same distinction can be found in proactive and reactive perspectives. A reactive perspective will deal with the situation at hand as it occurs. A proactive perspective anticipates the situation and may in fact prevent it from occurring.

Sales Professional

Feature versus Benefit

A feature is a description of an inherent aspect or attribute of a product or service. A benefit is a description of how the feature may be of value to a customer. For example, a feature of coaching is the model used to conduct a coachee/coach conversation. Expressed as a benefit, the coaching model provides the coachee with a structure to clarify thoughts, formulate ideas, and develop effective actions. Explaining the feature leaves the interpretation of value to the customer. Explaining the benefit demonstrates the value. Guiding Principle # 5 shows us that people seek value.

Attraction versus Promotion

Attraction has many definitions and many sources but the inherent quality of attraction is its ability to pull in the desired resources and outcomes with minimal effort. Promotion is outbound, requiring energy to create an action that ultimately returns the desired resources and outcomes. In sales, the skills and actions required to create attraction and promotion are different. For sales professionals, attraction is all about the way they conduct themselves and who they are being as they perform the task of selling. Promotion is all about the product, the features and benefits, and what the product or service can do for a potential customer.

Work Team

In Power versus In Control

Some team members struggle with feeling like they have no control over their professional lives; the larger the team or organization, the last thing they want is to be controlled in any way. A useful shift to make with members of a team is to help them see that they may not have control of certain situations or timelines, as none of us do, but they do have the power to make good choices; to succeed or fail at what they attempt, and the power to be positive and contribute to the organization's vision. Power is a choice even when control eludes us.

Influence versus Affect

Most team members want to make strong contributions to their teams and organizations. They are looking to have an affect. The problem with having an affect is that it has a timeline that isn't lasting and often has consequences. Having an influence carries with it a long-term lasting impression. Typically an influence is subtler but there is more investment. Consider challenging work team members to have influence versus having an affect on something that is important to them.

Creative

Self versus Work

For the creative, the distinction between self and work can be blurred very easily. Self is the talent, the wisdom, the energy, and who the person needs to be in order to create the work.

Work is a tangible result of applying oneself. Work is what is visible to others and can be used to validate the qualities of self.

Standard versus Expectation

A standard is a defined set of tangible criteria that provides the ability to measure or judge subsequent actions, work, or behaviors. A standard can be communicated and therefore utilized by others. An expectation is a less defined set of criteria and can encompass more variable and emotional factors that can be modified for each situation. An expectation needs to be constantly communicated in order for it to be utilized or followed. Standards give us the ability for consistency and repeatable outcomes but can limit growth and change. Expectations allow us to modify the outcomes but can limit consistency of the outcome.

Intellectual

Wise versus Smart

There is a fabric created when one's knowledge is merged with experience—that is named wisdom. Being wise is the ultimate use of intellect and leaves the largest and most valuable impact on others and the world. The commodity of trade and value for the intellectual is the level of "smarts" that he or she has been able to attain and retain throughout his or her life. In communication intellectuals challenge themselves and others in intellectual banter to prove themselves and often win. Accumulating knowledge just to have it is an act of ego and selfishness. Weaving one's knowledge with living life to the fullest and sharing the outcome to positively impact others is an act focused on contribution of the highest level.

Interesting versus Important

We often speak of the rise of the information highway without a speed limit due to the Internet and ever-evolving technology. The ability to gain information is in the immediate hands of children who sometimes learn to search the web before entering school. Much of what is available to us can be very interesting but can just become an accumulation of disconnected pieces of knowledge. For the intellectual's development and success, he or she must learn to discern the important from the merely interesting. The important and useful can become the pivotal success factor to the intellectual. Organizations are competing over intellectual capital, and those that hold the key to this are recruited at high cost, becoming the linchpin to the company's competitive edge.

Application

Coachee Conditions: Situational Coaching

Determining the conditions, needs, and wants of your coachees, and how you can best address these issues, will enable you to evolve the *Who* of the coachee in a more informed manner. The following information is presented in tabular format to enable quick reference to the unique attributes, needs, and potential situations that may arise when coaching each of the ten conditions (entrepreneur, CEO/executive, professional, career employee, sales professional, work team, creative, intellectual, leader, and parent). Profiles have been created for each condition, and serve as a model around which to coach the coachee. These are models, containing common and solid information about certain conditions; they should not be used as rigid templates, but more as a guide to better informed coaching.

Coachee Type Profiles

For each type, the following is presented:

- How To Recognize
- Common Coaching Scenarios
- Motivating Factors
- Key Coaching Skills
- Coaching Tips

Common Shifts

A more detailed list of shifts common to each coachee type is presented after the coachee profiles.

Entrepreneur

How to Recognize

- Fast paced; may be loners because no one can keep up with them.
- Full of ideas; often need a coach to keep them focused.
- Creative.
- Confident, perhaps inappropriately.
- Resourceful; has a knack for solving problems, and sometimes for creating them.
- Persuasive; convinces others to trust them, buy into their ideas, and even invest.

Common Coaching Scenarios

- Their business is in crisis; they are in denial and/or paralyzed by it.
- They are successful, but work too many hours.
- They struggle more than necessary because of judgment problems related to projects, people, or methods.
- They are starting a new project.
- They are frustrated with the administrative side of the business.
- They are frustrated with the marketing side of the business.
- Their relationship to the product and/or service is skewed, either over- or undervalued.

Motivating Factors

- Dissatisfaction with the way things are currently.
- New ideas, methods, product, or service.
- Need for achievement and recognition.
- Need to prove something.

Key Coaching Skills

- *Be with the coachee:* Be obviously present with the entrepreneur. Relating in this way is a form of acknowledgment.
- *Support:* The entrepreneur is usually swimming upstream and needs support before, during, and after implementing changes.

- *Acknowledge:* And recognize the entrepreneur for both what was achieved and what it took to accomplish it. Help him or her develop the ability to acknowledge their own accomplishments.
- *Be respectful and developmental:* The entrepreneur needs a coach who is honest and upfront. By being direct and totally supportive (after asking their permission to do so), you move the coachee forward without diminishing them or comparing them to others.
- *Tell the truth:* Tell it as you see it, because the coachee is paying you to do this. By seeing an objective perspective and saying what is true, you allow the coachee to make better decisions. This truth helps the entrepreneur form a vision while reminding him or her of reality, which the entrepreneur often cannot see or prefers not to deal with.
- *Install structure:* This keeps the entrepreneur moving and helps ensure action, development, and results. Keep in mind that the new structure must be user-friendly (easy and usable).

Coaching Tips

○ Make the choice to value this coachee, no matter what.

○ Entrepreneurs need to talk and be heard; this a necessary part of their creative and problem-solving process. Let them talk and encourage them to say more.

○ Entrepreneurs are different and proud of it. Support their uniqueness; acknowledge it as their strength.

○ Entrepreneurs are catalysts and not managers; encourage them to do what they do well and turn what they do not do well (or do not enjoy) over to someone else. They still have to track it, but delegation will free up time and energy.

○ Understand what drives and motivates the entrepreneur so you can coach him or her effectively; the need to succeed, to prove him- or herself, to be different, to do something no one else has done. It will be different for each entrepreneur; be sure you have verified what is true for your entrepreneur coachee.

○ Entrepreneurs need a strong coach. Make huge, strong requests of the coachee and stick with them.

CEO/Executive

How to Recognize

- Linear thinkers; sequential, (think organizational chart) can easily miss breakthroughs and relationships between parts of the system (problem/solution).
- Object-oriented (data, money, results, performance).
- Define themselves through their work.
- Look to their work for fulfillment.
- Enjoy the status and power connected with being an executive.
- May be out of touch with some of the operational details of the organization.
- Controlling.
- Persuasive.

Common Coaching Scenarios

- Their company is not running smoothly.
- Their profit margins are inadequate.
- They are running on adrenalin.
- Their effectiveness is compromised by poor communication skills.
- Their industry change rate is leaving them behind.
- Their effectiveness is limited by their need to control.
- They are approaching retirement and want to leave a legacy.

Motivating Factors

- Winning is important.
- Increasing financial compensation as a measure of their success.
- Successes in the workplace— increasing share price and shareholder value.

Key Coaching Skills

- *Support:* The executive is surrounded by people who are taking from him or her and therefore needs support before, during, and after implementing changes. You benefit the executive by serving as a source of support so he or she is not drained by the constant outflow.
- *Acknowledge:* And recognize the executive, both for what was achieved and what it took to accomplish it.

- *Generate inquiry:* When a big issue is at hand, ask the right question—one without a quick answer (or no answer), that requires the coachee to really search for the truth.
- *Seeding:* Mention new ideas, distinctions, and goals, and allow them to select what to nourish into reality.
- *Strategize for big goals:* Strategy includes action plans and resources as well as timing, contingencies, leverage points, and delivery systems. Goals are what will be done; strategy is how it is going to be done.
- *Promote truth:* Help the CEO/Executive become aware of, recognize, consider, and articulate the truth. This is effective when he or she has enough reserve to accept the truth. Caution: Be sensitive to the CEO/Executive's ego.
- *Be positive, respectful, and direct:* Say what needs to be said and avoid comparing. The CEO/Executive needs a place to develop where he or she can be vulnerable without feeling threatened. The coach engenders trust and inspires a commitment to action.

Coaching Tips

- Let the coachee be in control of the relationship.

- As coach, your role is one of strategic partner to the executive. You are quite likely the only person he or she can discuss problems with who has no outside agenda.

- Do not criticize. CEOs /Executives don't get enough affirmation. Affirm them, point out their strengths, stroke their egos, but be honest. The trust level necessary for the relationship will not develop without honesty.

- Start with a big problem. Create a challenge and success early on, setting the pace to become a problem-free zone.

- Listen cleanly in the face of any judgment that may come up.

- Do not let the CEO/Executive delegate being coached to subordinates. This devalues coaching and often reduces the coach's effectiveness.

- Consider the CEO/Executive's coachability, willingness to change, and the likelihood you will be effective, before agreeing to accept the engagement.

- Recognize that the CEO/Executive has tough bosses (the board of directors and shareholders) and is under a great deal of pressure. Some actions will not be up to the CEO/Executive to choose; the board may dictate them.

Professional

How to Recognize

- Independent.
- Self-reliant.
- Consistent.
- Problem-solvers or need-satisfiers.
- Linear thinkers focused on question–answer, problem–solution.
- Information-, technique-, or project-oriented.

Common Coaching Scenarios

- Challenged with selling as well as delivering their services, time, and skills.
- Operating in a vacuum, lonely, need encouragement, a plan and a network for referrals.
- Unable to say no, many pro bono coachees, a customer base that produces little revenue.
- Successful but not fulfilled.
- Bored with what they are doing and how they are doing it.
- Overworked or overinvested in business.
- Finds the operational aspects of the business overwhelming.

Motivating Factors

- Being the best at what they do.
- Creatively solving problems and impacting people's lives.
- Knowing and/or learning about their field.
- Need to be someone special, need professional's acknowledgment.
- Autonomy and self-satisfaction.

Key Coaching Skills

- *Anchoring:* Remind the professional of who and where they are and what they are doing. The professional is growing so fast and is so busy doing everything that he or she needs the stability and security that anchoring offers.
- *Clarifying:* Verify you heard what you think you heard and it meant what you think it meant. Clarifying helps you to be clear, but also helps the coachee get

clearer as well. Listen for what is being said, what is not being said, what is congruent, and what does not make sense. You need to hear it all.

- *Requesting:* Ask the professional to do what you believe he or she needs to do. You must have the courage to ask, the wisdom to know what to ask, and the grace to ask it well. Requesting can be a clarifying tool with the professional.
- *Installing structure:* Existing structure (home, job, family) supports the professional and may need to be evaluated to keep the coachee moving and help ensure action, development, and results.
- *Strategizing:* Help the professional to develop a plan for how he or she will reach his or her goal. Include timing, resources, contingencies, leverage points, and delivery systems.

Coaching Tips

- ○ Needs to design a strategy to fill their practice. Include value-added services and attractive pricing. Focus on referrals.

- ○ Set financial and other goals 50 percent higher than required to cover costs, thus creating a reserve to cover coachee lags, vacation time, and turnover.

- ○ Help them build a reputation based on excellence. Have them identify what they are going to master that will set them apart; challenge them to work every detail of their practice to meet high standards.

- ○ Identify areas for coaching, including foundation (how solid is their relationship with their clients?), flow (how easy is it for them to work with their clients?), and future (are they building a relationship with the professional that will continue?)

- ○ Keep them focused on the actions they need to take; don't let them distract you.

- ○ Keep your professional coachee ahead in building a client base. Make sure they balance marketing and service delivery.

- ○ Do not tolerate crises or emergencies. Hold them to a standard of performance excellence.

- ○ Remember it is their business; the professional does the work. Don't let a dependency develop.

Career Employee

How to Recognize

- Linear.
- Task oriented.
- Focused on doing things the right way.
- Compensation may not be linked to performance.
- Implementer.
- Coordinator.
- Dependent and reactive.

Common Coaching Scenarios

- The company is reorganizing and the career type needs a strategy for protecting his or her job.
- The career type recognizes that his or her position is no longer a fit.
- The company does not acknowledge or recognize them and they feel that they need to change jobs.

Motivating Factors

- Security.
- Achievement.
- Advancement.

Key Coaching Skills

- *Anchoring:* Security and stability are important to the career employee. Anchors can provide a source of stability. This is particularly important if the coachee is growing quickly. Establish and affirm where he or she is now, where he or she was, and what's next.
- *Conditioning:* Ask the person if he or she sees what you see; discuss the change that is evident. Give the coachee time to get used to the idea, and then bring it up again. Conditioning the coachee to what is happening gives the mind and body time to adjust to new things.
- *Encouraging:* Tell them they are doing great, be excited for them, ask them to keep going, and tell them they can do it. Encouragement is always valuable,

even before the coachee needs it. The bigger the goal the sooner and bigger the encouragement is needed. Encouragement is a gift; give generously.

● *Single daily action goal:* By distilling the goal down to a single daily action, the career person will begin to see a result. Set the single daily action high enough to get the coachee's attention.

" Self-image sets the boundaries of individual accomplishment. **"** | **Maxwell Maltz**

Coaching Tips

○ Be linear when coaching career employees. Help them get clear on the action to take and develop a specific, step-by-step plan for action. A career plan will give them something tangible to work toward.

○ Give them lots of context so they can understand. They will usually want supporting information.

○ Use a proven researched assessment tool that supports a coachee to see who he or she is.

○ Encourage them to develop an ownership mentality and view themselves as entrepreneurs. Encourage them to work as though it was their company, and to consider the profit side—not just the accountability side.

○ Help them develop their communication skills and challenge and support them in developing a better relationship with their manager and/or supervisor. Encourage them to seek a mentor in their field or company.

○ Help them identify their values and create a vision, mission, and purpose for their lives. Challenge them to examine their current employment and to align what they do with who they are and what they value.

○ Career types are often challenged because they fail to get the support they need from their supervisors. Coach them in the skills of "managing up," so they can have a strong positive relationship with their manager or supervisor.

Sales Professional

How to Recognize

- Strong need to win.
- Frequently compares self to others.
- Optimistic; often willing to bet short-term security on the possibility of big gains.
- Often have a conflict about persuading or manipulating others.
- Driven.

Common Coaching Scenarios

- Adrenalin fueled, reactive, poor time management.
- Difficulty getting appointments; generates lots of activity, but little success.
- Wants to play a big game.

Motivating Factors

- Knowledge, learning new things—especially if it will give them an edge.
- Autonomy, independence.
- Recognition and accomplishment.

Key Coaching Skills

- *Being with the coachee:* Be obviously present with the sales professional. Relating in this way is a form of acknowledgment and models a skill he or she can use with clients and prospects as well.
- *The blitz:* Big games motivate the sales professional. Have him or her identify a big goal (make sure it is huge), then list everything needed to reach the goal: time, effort, tools, money, structure, and training. Set a daily action plan that orients their life around the goal and check progress as often as necessary to keep movement brisk.
- *Creating an action plan:* Include a list of steps that will lead to the result the coachee wants, with time lines for completion. This acts as both a guide and management system.
- *Gapping the goal:* Help sales professionals identify what they really, really want, and create a gap between where they are now and where they want to be. This creates a vacuum, pulling coachees toward what they want.

- *Installing structure:* Sales is, by its very nature, autonomous, and sales professionals can easily get lost in the freedom their job allows them. A structure is something you and the coachee create in order to support them in getting what they want. Be sure the structure is the sales professional's choice, well-designed and dynamic.

Coaching Tips

○ This coachee needs to set big, big goals.

○ Help sales professionals improve language related to features, benefits, and value. Challenge them to become an expert on the product and/or service, market issues, and trends.

○ Coach the sales professional to establish ongoing relationships in which they help customers get their needs met as an investment that will yield future success. Help him or her to be with their prospects, listen well, and hear their needs.

○ Referral generation and selling—joining a networking group and establishing strong circles of influence through which he or she can reach stronger prospects.

○ Sales professionals have very low reserves. They may be focused on their income potential instead of on what they are actually bringing home. Help them to create a sound financial picture—taxes up to date, realistic income projections, and strong reserves.

○ Sales professionals often need an adrenalin rush. They need help establishing other healthy sources of energy, withdrawing from the quick fix adrenalin offers and resisting relapse back into dependence on it.

Work Team

How to Recognize

- Two or more people working in collaboration to realize a common goal.
- A department or division, or multiple departments and divisions, working together to achieve predetermined outcomes.
- A group sharing a common vision.

Common Coaching Scenarios

- They want to learn more effective ways to communicate with others on the team.
- They are searching for better ways to communicate with their higher-ups.
- They are searching for their place in the team or organizational structure.
- They don't have others in their organization who they can talk to without being judged or being told what to do.
- They are struggling with multiple priorities with shrinking budgets, resources, and time.
- They are trying out new technologies and strategies.
- They are frustrated with change—or lack of change.
- It's cool to have your own coach, even if they are not really sure where they want to focus their coaching.

Motivating Factors

- They get to come up with their own solutions.
- New technology.
- Being acknowledged or recognized by their peers.
- Having a voice in the organization.

Key Coaching Skills

- *Be with the team, but keep the relationship professional.* Even if you can easily relate to the situation and understand their pain, keep the discussions action-oriented.
- *Support:* Find out what support each individual needs in the team to provide the most value to the team. Each individual team member has different needs, strengths, weaknesses, style of communication, and so on.

- *Hear the group* and be extraordinarily interested in who they are as individuals and as a team; they possess unique team dynamics. Don't assume you know them; let them tell you.
- *Be respectful and honest:* The group will be able to tell if you are holding back; they need a coach who is honest and upfront. You will need to be clear in your contract or agreement as to what is appropriate to share.
- *Tell the truth as you see it:* By having an objective perspective and saying what is true, you allow the coachee to make better decisions. This truth helps the individuals in the team create a plan for him- or herself while reminding him or her of the reality of the organization, which the individual often cannot see or prefers not to deal with.
- *Install structure in the coaching relationship:* It is imperative while coaching groups that structure is present. Additionally, it's a good idea to collectively come up with ground rules as a group at the beginning of the coaching relationship.

Coaching Tips

○ The group coaching relationship is a delicate partnership to build, and well worth the effort. They need to be in control of the pace of the relationship yet educated on the capacity of the coaching relationship. Building trust with a group takes a bit longer, but is essential to a successful coaching relationship.

○ Do collectively identify and clarify the desired outcomes. Also, collectively identify and clarify the strategies that will be employed. All team members must be aligned on the same vision.

○ Challenge the team members to acknowledge there is a world beyond his or hers. Although it's extremely helpful, they don't necessarily need to have 100 percent buy-in on a project or product, but will get further faster if they work to influence instead of affect.

○ Pick and choose which foundation work will most benefit the team. Everything you assign to members of a team must be immediately relevant, as there is often a shortage of time and resources.

○ Be clear that the team is eager to solve their own problems but does not always come up with viable solutions. Brainstorming and collaborative problem-solving could be helpful, especially with structure and ground rules to establish trust and respect in ideas that are shared.

○ Of course, you might want to refer to the other nine types in this section. No two teams are exactly alike, as different people with diverse backgrounds, personalities, and experiences will make up the work team.

Creative

How to Recognize

- Need space and support.
- Wear their talent as a badge of honor.
- Strongly identified with what they do.
- Define themselves by their need to create.
- Hard-working; exhausted from operating with no reserve.
- Will sacrifice much to accommodate the need to create.

Common Coaching Scenarios

- Creative coachees may consider their talent a badge of honor, but may also use it to avoid taking responsibility. If they are hiding behind their talent, coach them from expecting to be rewarded to taking responsibility for it.
- The concept of the starving artist might be dramatic, but is not very fulfilling. Many artists today make a very good living in their own lifetime with their art. Help the creative coachee get past their fear that they are not or never will be good enough and help them develop ways to make a living while creating (or better yet, from their creations).

Motivating Factors

- Acknowledgment (fame).
- Strong vision that needs to be communicated, shared.
- Desire (or need) to be special, unique, different.

Key Coaching Skills

- *Endorse thoroughly:* Give approval and support to who the creative is now and is becoming. Give the creative time to accept the endorsement (it may be strange to him or her at first).
- *Acknowledge, acknowledge:* What was achieved and what it took to accomplish it. Help the coachee develop the ability to acknowledge him- or herself. Acknowledge creatives for their implementation, rather than their vision.
- *Upgrade the energy:* Creatives run on adrenaline and often on fumes. Strengthening their personal foundation and helping them to let go of consumptive

324 | Coaching Application

people, problems, and situations will make it easier for creatives to adopt healthy sources of energy, such as reserve, efficiency, capacity, and satisfied needs.

- *Plug the holes:* Creatives use coaches because of problems or needs caused by holes in their foundation. Help them find and plug the holes with truth, integrity, responsibility, and personal foundation—whatever is needed—so they can create and maintain healthy reserves and become far more attractive.

- *Increase reserve levels:* Create high levels of reserve (110–200 percent more than needed) in a variety of areas (time, money, love, results, actions, opportunities, structure, awareness, and so on). It quiets the inner noise and fear, and frees the flow of creativity without concern about error.

- *Be direct:* There will be times when you will just have to tell the creative exactly what to do. When the coachee asks for this (or agrees to accept it), this can put him or her on a path.

Coaching Tips

○ The important objective with creatives is to wake them up to the real world. They live in a mirage of concepts and ideas, living the majority of their life in their heads.

○ Create discovery questions for the creative that challenge what they believe. Do not challenge creatives—be subtle and clear to shift their perceptions.

○ Help them strengthen their personal foundation. This will allow other needed changes to happen successfully.

Intellectual

How to Recognize

- They deal in information, ideas, and concepts.
- Self-reliant.
- They are right.
- Deal with the big picture.
- Love the intrigue of a question.
- Information is their currency.

Common Coaching Scenarios

- Under-earning for their position.
- Disconnected from significant relationships.
- Passed over for promotion by younger, more innovative colleagues.
- Never enough knowledge so cannot be satisfied.
- Various control issues.
- Legacy issues.

Motivating Factors

- Finding the right answer.
- Production oriented.
- They are right.
- New concepts and questions.

Key Coaching Skills

- *Build a collaborative partnership* with the intellectual. Brainstorming and generating ideas together will be key.
- *Subtly ask discovery questions* that challenge what they believe without challenging them.
- *Personal foundation issues:* Foundation work will be imperative to the intellectual's success; however, they may not want to invest in themselves because their focus is usually elsewhere. When they get the value of the investment they will take it on with a vengeance.
- *Requesting:* Ask for a shift in their perception, attitude, and behavior. The intellectual can be firmly locked down.

- *Strategizing:* Help the intellectual to develop a plan for how they will show value to their significant relationships.

Coaching Tips

- The intellectual seeks new information that they can immediately use or convert. Plant seeds and use messages.

- Help them set their sights higher, creating better goals and greater positions in their field. They need a kick.

- Never compete with the intellectual; you won't win. He or she must be right.

- Let the intellectual control the relationship. He or she needs control and in this relationship it is not a problem.

- Do not forget: Information is their currency; not people, love, peace, or spirituality. They need your ideas. Feed them.

Leader

How to Recognize

- They are in a position of authority and/or power.
- Motivational and inspirational.
- Typically driving a cause, holding a vision.
- Over-promises commitments.
- Can be ego-driven.
- It is all about them.

Common Coaching Scenarios

- They are running on empty.
- Relationships are strained.
- They are looking for the next opportunity.
- They need to become a better model.
- They need support in dealing with the demands of their position.

Motivating Factors

- Truly cares about making the vision a reality.
- Knows how to make things happen.
- Improving the quality of the experience.
- Is intuitive and can articulate what he or she senses with accuracy.

Key Coaching Skills

- *Be an understanding partner with the leader.* Relating in this way is a form of acknowledgment.
- *Support:* The leader really needs the support of someone who understands the demands of his or her position, but holds them accountable to succeed.
- *Make the leader right.*
- *Make sure that you stretch the leader beyond what he or she thinks they can do.* Leaders are already high achievers, but they can do more.
- *Encourage their strength* of being an original, forward thinker.

Coaching Tips

○ Do not try and impress or "do a good job." The leader wants exclusive focus on him or her, not you.

○ Help them strengthen their personal foundation. Their self-development will make them a stronger model.

○ Treat the leader as an equal while respecting their pressures and accomplishments. Don't become their fan club.

○ Hold the leader accountable for his or her promises. They often do not realize they are over-promising and under-delivering because they deliver so much.

Parent

How to Recognize

- Moving fast and frazzled.
- Extremely resourceful.
- Nurturing.
- Focused on others.
- Says yes first to almost everything they are asked to do.
- Multitasker.

Common Coaching Scenarios

- They have no time for themselves.
- Their children define them ("Oh, you must be Bobby's mom.")
- They struggle more than necessary because of trying to do it all.
- They are struggling in their intimate relationships.
- They are reentering the job market.
- They are frustrated with their children's behavior.
- They are grieving the loss of a parent.

Motivating Factors

- They love unconditionally.
- The family is most important.
- They have a strong support network.
- Success in this arena is their life work.

Key Coaching Skills

- *Build a unique relationship with the parent:* He or she has a strong support system of other parents but can really benefit from an objective point of view.
- *Support:* The parent needs to understand that he or she is making hundreds of decisions every day and not all of them are going to be good ones.
- *Acknowledge and recognize the job* it is to be a parent and the success they have achieved.
- *Be compassionate and developmental:* The parent operates out of love and expects love in return. They will also be looking for a developmental process where they can measure their success.

330 | Coaching Application

● *Ask them to remove half of their responsibilities to create time for self-care.* Encourage delegation and developing the skills and capabilities of the other family members.

Coaching Tips

○ The focus in working with parents is to get them to slow down the speed of their lives to allow room for joy again. In today's world, the parent cannot always keep up with their kids' schedules, and the little time that is not scheduled, and don't have opportunities to make decisions for themselves. No one is having fun.

○ Be a model for the parent in having a great life. They don't have another model.

○ Help them strengthen their personal foundation. This will allow other needed changes to happen successfully.

○ Challenge the parent to come up with solutions that minimize effort, time, and attention. They are good problem-solvers but don't realize that less is more.

○ Help the parent see the critical need to take care of him or herself first.

Common Shifts by Coachee Type

The following table illustrates shifts common to each of the coachee conditions listed.

Common Shifts by Coachee Type	
From	To
1. Entrepreneur	
● Operating on the edge financially	● Have sufficient reserves in place
● Crisis-reactive, frustrated	● Strong foresight, high standards
● Gets attached to ideas and results	● Takes self lightly, trusts self, associates
● Starting new projects continuously	● Limits number of projects, takes breaks between projects

Common Shifts by Coachee Type (*continued*)	
2. CEO/Executive	
• Anticipates and manages change	• Innovates, initiates change
• Solves problems	• Stops having problems
• Builds a team	• Creates a community of leaders
• Needs to be right	• Doesn't care who's right; is open
3. Professional	
• Loner, singular, not connected	• Close to circles of influence, top colleagues
• High overhead, expenses	• High profit margin (20–95%)
• 15–50% of time spent promoting	• 95% of time spent delivering service
• Rushes to meet deadlines; delays	• Under-promises, always ahead
4. Career Employee	
• Working for someone else	• Working for the joy of it
• Doing a job	• Moving along a career path
• Getting paid the same no matter what is done	• Enjoying the intrinsic rewards of a job well done
• Working for a promotion	• Increasing value at every level
5. Sales Professional	
• Unsatisfied needs, chasing	• Relentless self-care, responsible
• Highs and lows	• Consistency
• Could, should, would, wants-based	• Integrity, reality- and/or needs-based
• Overly optimistic, lives in possibility	• Realistic projections
6. Work Team	
• Independent	• Valued partnership
• Negative or frustrated	• Appropriately optimistic
• Overwhelmed and confused	• Clarity of next steps
• They are all that matter	• Care and concern of their impact on others

Common Shifts by Coachee Type (*continued*)	
7. Creative	
● Big break or lottery mentality	● Baby steps and/or process
● Entitled (because so talented)	● Education and/or growth
● I am my feelings	● I have feelings
● Victim/struggle, addict	● Reality check; responsible life
● Gets identity from creating	● Unique self—independent of creating
8. Intellectual	
● Always in their head	● Listening to their heart
● Being right	● Being happy
● Settling	● Challenging themselves professionally
● Oblivious	● Aware of their surroundings
● Controlling	● Collaborative
9. Leader	
● Over-promise	● Under-promise
● Controlling	● Powerful
● Running low	● High level of reserve
● Admired	● A model
10. Parent	
● Frazzled and harried	● More than enough time
● Constantly failing	● Setting themselves up for success
● No oxygen	● Regularly flowing air
● Saying yes first	● Saying no first

Situational Coaching: Promoters and Pitfalls

The DOs are behaviors that promote success of coaching various coachee conditions. The DON'Ts are behaviors that limit the success of coaching various coachee conditions.

Do—Understand that not every coachee will fit a condition perfectly. Don't—Try to make a coachee fit a situation.	The ability to read a coachee and fit him or her into one of the ten common conditions is valuable for both you and the coachee. However, resist the temptation to make the coachee fit the situation. Humans are unique. What is common to one CEO may not be common to another. Be sure to use the information learned in a loose and customizable manner. Listen to the coachee for who he or she is, not what category he or she is in. Allow the model to be flexible and adapt to the person, not the other way around..
Do—Remember that while most everyone fits into one category or another, we all share common ground. Don't—Forget Guiding Principle #1.	We all fit certain types, but we all also share greater commonalities. It is critical for you to honor, respect, and value others and yourself. Situational coaching is helpful for more informed coaching, and to alert us to potential areas of work for each coachee, but should not be used to pigeonhole or separate coachees from others who share common ground. Guiding Principle #1 addresses this primary factor of life: People have something in common. We return to the common ground of being by loving, honoring, and valuing one's self and others. The coaching process is a relationship that thrives on common ground, but be aware of the dangers of labeling.
Do—Coach the individual. Don't—Always assume the coachee should be coached according to the condition.	Coachee models and profiles are guides, and should be used to tailor your coaching—but all coaching is for the benefit of the coachee, not to prove a model. Use the models as tools, not weapons. Above all, coach the individual, not the model.

Guiding Principle 7 | **People Live from Their Perception.**
An inclusive, present-based perception of reality
is the platform for effective action.

Resources

Attention Readers:

Thank you for participating in the collective wisdom of Coach U. Together, we all continue to learn. Additional resources and forms can be found in *Coach U's Essential Coaching Tools: Your Complete Practice Resource* by CoachInc.com.

Attention CoachInc.com Students and Graduates:

CoachInc.com students and graduates may find additional and/or more recent resources associated with this module in the resource area of the student-only web site. If you are a student or graduate of one of CoachInc.com's ICF-accredited coach training programs, you can access these by searching under the name of the course. When the course description page appears you may find a link to the list of additional resources. Each item is a live link to its actual location on the web site. Click on the item to access the information.

Do remember to take the associated online self-test for this module once you have completed the course in person or by TeleClass. The tests are required for coach certification with the International Coach Federation. Throughout the course or anytime you find valuable resources for a particular course please feel free to add to the value of our curricula by forwarding the resource to revampteam@coachu.com.

Chapter 11

Establishing Yourself as a Coach

Overview

This module is a program designed to prepare you, as a new coach, for your first 3 to 18 months toward becoming or establishing yourself as a coach. This guide should be used as a reference manual to support your ongoing learning.

Coaching has become such an essential part of personal and organizational performance that coaching practices are now found inside organizations as well as in multicoach coaching groups and individual coaching businesses. New Coach Basics is intended to apply to coaches in any one of these three situations, though some of the information may be more relevant to one type of coaching practice than another.

This module will lead you step-by-step through the items essential to establishing yourself as a coach, introduce you to the new coachee process, and teach you the hallmarks of achieving ongoing coaching success.

Elevator speech, pro bono, scholarship, one sheet, referral, networking, leads group, and alliance.

Why New Coach Basics?

There are three distinct stages to a coach's development. New Coach Basics is designed to give new coaches the tools, information, samples, and basics needed for establishing themselves strongly. There are also eight basic misconceptions new coaches must understand in order to set realistic goals and targets.

⭕ Distinctions Go to Page > 345

Immediate wins versus long term shifts, source versus symptom, focus versus goals, community versus network, value of coaching versus coaching benefits, and niche versus specialty.

⭕ Application Go to Page > 347

New Coach Basics

> Part 1: Establishing Yourself as a Coach
> Part 2: New Coachee Process
> Part 3: Hallmarks of Ongoing Success

⭕ Resources Go to Page > 379

Benefits

By fully engaging in the material offered, this module will lead you step-by-step through the processes of establishing yourself as a coach, attracting coachees, and the new coachee process. Typically, coaches with private practices refer to coachees as clients. The module will also introduce you to the hallmarks of achieving ongoing success with your coachees.

This module offers a structured and supportive place to explore options, learn successful business practices, and develop materials to support your coaching activities for the first 3 to 18 months.

This course is designed to:

O **Present** the fundamental steps to establish yourself as a coach, including defining who and how you will coach, creating marketing materials, and developing offerings and fee structures

O **Define** the different methods of delivering coaching

O **Address** enrolling new coachees using the complimentary coaching session

O **Outline** the new coachee process, including the coaching services intake package and what you will need to cover in the first coaching session

O **Introduce** the tools and techniques you need to apply for ongoing success as a coach, including the coaching session prep form, tracking coachee progress and business growth

Definitions

The following are common words used to gain a better understanding of the coaching process, particularly in regard to coaching basics.

Elevator speech: One to three sentences describing what you specifically do as a coach. The elevator speech needs to be unique to what you do as a coach rather than a stock answer. For example, "I partner with small business owners to increase their profitability and the number of vacations they take per year" is much stronger than "I coach business owners." Also, try phrasing a short statement that invites the question, "Oh, how do you do that?" This allows you to then describe the benefits of coaching. For example, "I partner with people to help them gain promotion." ("Oh, really. How do you do that?")

Pro bono: Professional services provided at no charge.

Scholarship: Services delivered at a reduced rate to a coachee in financial need.

One sheet: An 8.5" × 11" or A-4 sized sheet of paper printed with your pertinent information, including name, specialty area, programs offered, short bio, and perhaps a photograph.

Referral: A potential coachee that contacts you because someone he or she knows has recommended your services. Referrals happen when someone else has generated the interest and encouraged a person to contact you. In order for you to have an abundance of referrals, you must create a pipeline for referrals that requires building a strong network. In a mature coaching practice, whether internal or external, most of your coachees will come through referrals or your network.

Networking: An interdependent relationship formed with other professionals, personal acquaintances, and colleagues that can be formal or informal. A leads group is a formal network. Colleagues, acquaintances, and business contacts are all part your informal network. Networking is valuable to you because it provides visibility, creates bonds between like-minded individuals, and provides opportunities for alliances and referrals.

Leads group: A structured organization of professionals who meet for the sole purpose of promoting their services and giving and getting referrals.

Alliance: An agreement between two professionals to promote or refer to one another. The arrangement may or may not include compensation. Some alliances bundle services for coachees or offer joint programs. Alliances are especially valuable when your coaching specialty complements the specialties of other coaches in your alliance. For example, a turnaround coach might form a complementary alliance with an executive coach.

Concepts

Why New Coach Basics?

Throughout the years, CoachInc.com has recognized there are distinct stages in a coach's development. Stage One happens in the first 3 to 24 months of building one's coaching practice, Stage Two takes place once a coach has become established, and Stage Three occurs when a coach achieves mastery of his or her coaching practice. The core skills courses teach the learning skills. This course is designed to give new coaches the tools, information, and samples—the basics needed for establishing yourself strongly.

Stage One
- Learning Skills
- Identifying Self as Coach
- Experimentation and Practice
- Building a Network
- Establishing a Presence as a Coach

Stage Two
- Credentialing
- Branding
- Adding Services
- Passive Income
- Maintaining a Network
- Increasing Profitability

Stage Three
- Mastery

Eight Misconceptions and Opposing Truths

As a new coach, it is useful to set realistic expectations for the growth of your practice. Like many people starting out on a new venture, you can have overly optimistic expectations, which may lead to misguided plans and early disappointments. These common coaching misconceptions and opposing truths will help you set realistic goals and targets.

1. Misconception: If I let colleagues and acquaintances know I am now a coach, I will have a full practice in a matter of months.

Truth: Building a coaching practice requires all the same skills and effort as building any other new venture. With continued promotion, networking, and marketing as well as dedicated focus, the average coach in private practice can create a full practice within 18 to 24 months. It may not take this long for coaches employed by and working within organizations.

2. Misconception: No one will want me as their coach if I don't have a web site.

Truth: Your coachees hire you because of who you are. Coachees do not hire you because of a shiny brochure, two-sided business cards, or an interactive web site. Keep your coach referral information on the CoachInc.com Find a Coach web site up-to-date and send people there if they request Internet information. Save the money you would spend on expensive marketing materials and invest them on yourself or on networking. The more people who know you, the more coachees you will attract.

3. Misconception: I can't start coaching until I have finished all my classes.

Truth: If you wait until you've completed your classes to start coaching, you'll miss out on the richness of many of the fieldwork assignments. These will ask you to practice the skills and tools you are learning with actual coachees. First, get confident in the basic skills, including foundation, listening, artful questioning, language, messaging, and acknowledging. Then take on coachees to solidify the learning. Many successful coaches begin coaching and build their coaching practices while still enrolled in a CoachInc.com program.

4. Misconception: I don't need to hire a coach right now. I'm just getting started.

Truth: Your attitude toward hiring a coach will color your prospective coachees' attitudes. When you are getting started is the ideal time to hire a strong coach. Creating a foundation for your business and developing yourself as a coach are key elements to success in this field. If you don't see value in coaching, how will you convey the value to someone considering you as his or her coach?

5. Misconception: I am doing personal coaching or business coaching, so I'm not going to participate fully in the courses that don't directly relate to my niche.

Truth: Both occur in a coaching interaction. The focus is on the development of the coachee. Coachees are multidimensional, and you never know when your personal coaching coachee will ask you to coach them on starting a new business. In addition, even if you are an internal coach, you are a small business. If you maximize your participation in this course, you will experience a richer learning and be able to coach a wider variety of coachees.

6. Misconception: There isn't a lot of overhead in a coaching business, so it's okay if I don't have a financial reserve.

Truth: If you are in need of money, you will reflect this when seeking new coachees, and you may come across as needy—not a positive characteristic for a coach. Before quitting your day job, be sure to have a minimum of six months' living expenses put aside, preferably a year. As mentioned before, it usually takes 18 to 24 months to build a thriving coaching practice.

7. Misconception: I can make $100,000 a year in my coaching business, which is great because I need to make that much this year.

Truth: From observations of CoachInc.com students over the past five years, most have between zero and 10 coachees per month during the two year period they attend classes, thus putting the average income around $25,000 per year. External coaches can and do make over $100,000, but only after years of mastering the craft and building their referral network.

It's also true that there is a much better success rate with coaches who have completed formal coach training by an ICF-accredited coach training organization, coaches who have invested in a period of time in working with a Professional Mentor Coach, and coaches who have a strong support network of other coaches.

8. Misconception: I have to give my coaching away for free in the beginning.

Truth: Engaging in pro bono coaching can be a great way to learn and practice your coaching skills when first starting out; however, giving away your coaching undermines its value, and yours. You may find it difficult to convert your coachees to a pay-for-service basis. Try trading coaching sessions with other new coaches so you can both practice your skills.

Distinctions

There are subtle yet important differences in meaning between the following closely related terms. Understanding these distinctions allows you to perceive new layers of meaning and offers you new choices for shifting your thoughts, attitudes, and actions.

Immediate Wins versus Long-term Shifts

Newer coachees often need quick results in order to get momentum in their lives and/or to believe in the effectiveness of coaching. Long-term shifts are generally more valuable; however, immediate wins provide quick results and specific outcomes for the coachee—perhaps what they were looking for in the first place.

Source versus Symptom

The source of something is its cause. The symptom is how the cause manifests itself. For example, being overweight is a symptom; bad eating habits or lack of exercise could be the cause. But the cause may go one level deeper. Someone's inability to manage his or her diet or fitness regime may result from low self- esteem. It's important to recognize the difference between source and symptom. Don't coach the coachee's symptoms; coach the source of the problem. Another example: Failure is the symptom and poor judgment may be the source or cause. As a coach, you want to become an expert at recognizing subtle symptoms and knowing what root causes are the source.

Focus versus Goals

Focus means placing your energy and attention in a particular area, such as money, health, or relationships. A goal is something specific that can be articulated and measured. So focusing on an area may seem to lead to achieving a goal in that area. Often though, once you start working toward a goal you see something even more worthwhile. Recommend that your coachees choose a focus first and then, once they have gotten into it, the goals will naturally flow from it.

Community versus Network

Your network is made up of the professionals or acquaintances in your life. A community is usually made up of people coming together with shared interests, relationships, or beliefs, for mutual support and encouragement. Some of your community might include people in your network, but in the community, the person and the relationship come ahead of the result or the business. Community is not based on need, whereas a network is usually intended to be an interdependent relationship. Your network is where you go to work; your community is where you go to learn, play, recharge, or relax.

Value of Coaching versus Coaching Benefits

The benefits of coaching can include more time, energy, income, and well-being. The value in being coached may include better judgment, increased awareness, greater perspective, improved communication skills, and so on. Help your coachees see both the value and benefits of coaching.

Niche versus Specialty

A niche defines whom you work with. It includes certain types of coachees, like entrepreneurs, professionals, or people in transition. A specialty means that you have developed a set of skills or proficiencies that can be used across many niches. Your coachees fall into the niches where your specialties apply. It's likely you'll develop a niche for yourself in your first 3 to 24 months as a coach. Later, you will likely specialize more.

Application

New Coach Basics

The following 10 steps are essential to create an atmosphere of success as a new coach, and are most effective when begun within the first three months of deciding to become a coach. These steps are designed to start you strongly so that through *consistent* action and ongoing support, you will have established yourself as a professional coach within 18 to 24 months.

Part 1: Establishing Yourself as a Coach

CoachInc.com recognizes that some new coaches are planning on being self-employed while others are, or plan to be, organizationally employed. Establishing yourself as a coach is equally important in either environment. As a self-employed coach, or as part of a coaching group, establishing yourself will assist with enrolling coachees and making money. As an organizationally employed coach, establishing yourself will create the credibility and trust necessary for fellow employees to rely on your coaching skills. Although several of the steps below apply to both types of coaches without modifications, other steps will look different, depending on your situation.

1. Begin Coach Training
2. Hire a Coach
3. Join a Community
4. Set Up Office
5. Design Your Practice
6. Create Fee Structure
7. Create Materials
8. Establish Your Presence or Practice
9. Introduce Yourself as a Coach
10. Enroll Coachees

1. Begin Coach Training

CoachInc.com's training programs prepare you to coach different coachee and client types, develop your coaching skills, set up and maintain a personal and/or business coaching practice, or take these skills into a corporate environment. For more information, go to the CoachInc .com web site (www.coachInc.com). Many of CoachInc.com's training programs are accredited with the International Coach Federation (ICF) to support coaches in getting the most respected certification designation in the industry.

Planning for a Transition to Coaching

If you are planning to transition into coaching from another profession, ask yourself these questions:

1. Do I want to have completed my training before leaving my current work situation?
2. Do I want to earn an International Coach Federation certification prior to leaving my current situation? If so, which one? (Be sure to visit the ICF web site for details on the requirements for each designation at www.coachfederation .org).
3. Do I need additional training for the niche I plan to serve?

2. Hire a Coach

It makes sense that if you want to become a coach, you experience being professionally coached first. It is important to recognize the difference a coach makes in your life for yourself. If you are unwilling to hire a coach, you may want to consider your resistance and what impact that may have on someone hiring you

Choosing a coach is a process. We recommend that you interview at least three coaches before choosing one. When hiring your first coach, look at what you first need to work on in yourself to achieve your goals as a coach. If you have many foundational items to handle before you can focus on your business, choose a coach who will support you in that area.

In order to apply for certification, you need to have been coached by an ICF-certified coach for a minimum of six months. Since it may take you a minimum of 12 to 18 months to complete the training hours required for certification, keep this timeline in mind when hiring a coach. You can find a list of coaches together with their areas of specialty at the CoachInc.com web site www.coachinc.com or at www.findacoach.com. Students and graduates of CoachInc .com's programs may participate in our mentor coaching program to hire a Professional Mentor Coach—these coaches are also ICF-certified. We recommend that CoachInc.com students and graduates hire a coach with one the following designations: PMC—CoachInc.com Professional Mentor Coach; PCC—ICF Professional Certified Coach, or MCC—ICF Master Certified Coach.

3. Join a Community

Coaching communities provide an outlet for you to learn about different types of coaching, create alliances, engage in ongoing learning, and find leadership opportunities. Coaching is a relatively new profession, and whether you are working as an internal coach or as an external coach, you probably spend the time you aren't coaching handling administrative tasks. Joining a coaching community allows you to connect with other coaches. The biggest advantage to joining a community 3 to 18 months into becoming a coach is to meet people and establish a presence.

Coaching communities can take many forms:

- Local Coach U Chapters
- CoachInc.com Special Interest Groups (SIGs)
- International Coach Federation local chapters
- Study groups
- Coaching consortiums
- Organized coaching practicums
- Networking groups
- Industry associations
- Other coaches in your organization, or internal coaches in other organizations

Considerations for Finding a Community

Since there are many options available and you want to choose communities that support you rather than drain you, answer the following questions and then seek communities that are tailored to your needs.

- What role do I want my community to play in my coaching career?
- Do I want my community to provide additional skills training?
- Do I want to create alliances with peers (other coaches) or with other professionals?
- What opportunities exist to get involved?
- How involved do I want to become in my community?
- Am I interested in volunteering or holding office?
- Do I need to be a member of a high-profile community to attract coachees or solidify credibility?
- What budget do I have for dues and meeting fees?
- What do I need from a community for value to have been provided?

4. Set Up Office

With so many options available, it is difficult to narrow down what you really need to set up your ideal coaching office, and very easy to blow your budget on "cool stuff" that is not necessary. Drawing on the wisdom of already established coaches, this list of office items is divided into essential and optional. If in doubt about whether you need something or it is not on the list, try operating without it for 30 days.

Absolutely essential is an easily accessible, always up-to-date filing system (paper or electronic), where you keep your coachee information and notes. Remember that accuracy and confidentiality are paramount.

Essential Items

- A work location—for in-person coaching you will want a quiet, private location, such as an enclosed office; for telephone coaching, a quiet space where you will not be interrupted is best.
- Phone line with voice mail—if you are an external coach, also consider using a low-rate long distance carrier or calling card.
- High quality phone and headset—high quality with mute button (for sneezes).
- Fax line—although e-mail is rapidly replacing it, a fax is still useful. Some phone companies now offer virtual fax, where incoming faxes are delivered as e-mail attachments
- Computer—any of the more popular office suites will offer what you need. Make sure programs are the most recent versions and that all software is integrated. (Be sure to load antivirus software.)
- Internet connection—choose a vendor that will integrate with your contact management software, and consider registering your own domain, so you can keep your e-mail address if you change vendors.
- Laser printer—documents need to be professional and clean.
- Contact management and calendar software—look for products that will integrate with handheld devices (if you use one).
- Bookkeeping software—may not be needed by internal coach; external coaches should check with an accountant, most prefer specific programs.
- File cabinet—get one larger than you think you will need; you will grow into it.
- Comfortable office chair—setting up your office space in an ergonomic way is a self-care practice.

❝ It is hard to fail, but it is worse never to have tried to succeed. **❞** | **Theodore Roosevelt**

Optional Items

Many coaches choose to purchase these optional items right away to aid in the running of their practice. If you opt not to purchase them right away, consider putting them in your business plan and budget to purchase them as your practice grows.

- Toll-Free number—you may want to offer toll-free calling if you are building a national or international coaching practice, or if you are doing business or corporate coaching.
- Fax machine—look for a plain paper one with a broadcast feature which will allow you to send the same document automatically to 50+ people, though bear in mind that many people now are resistant to junk fax; there can also be legal implications, so choose your audience carefully.
- Laptop computer—for portability.
- High-speed Internet connection—wireless, DSL or cable modems allow an always-on connection; be sure to install a personal firewall if using either of these connections.
- Copier.
- File labeler.

5. Design Your Practice

With the broader acceptance of coaching's vital role in organizational and staff development, coaches now find themselves inside organizations, or working in groups with other coaches. Managers are also now discovering the benefits of taking a coach approach in managing their staff. Of course, there are many coaches who have established successful individual coaching practices, working with people inside or outside an organizational context. Although coaching may take on a different appearance depending on the situation, the core values and methodologies remain constant.

Designing your coaching practice, whether it's your sole profession or part of your management responsibilities, means answering questions about who you want to coach, how you deliver your coaching, what type of coach you want to be, and so on. Who you want to coach is your target market or your niche. Your particular niche might be women, entrepreneurs, executives in a particular organization, or the staff in your department. Newly practicing coaches often find it easier to choose a niche to focus on rather than a specialty. (See Distinctions.) It is also often easier to market to a niche than to market to a specialty. Remember that even if your market is your work team, you still need to sell coaching to them. First, decide who you will coach, then choose how you will coach them. Then, decide the type of coach you want to be, though this may be dictated by your circumstances (in an organization, for example). Ways to deliver your coaching:

Telephone Coaching

Phone coaching offers the greatest flexibility for both you and the coachee. Sessions are generally 30 to 60 minutes. Most new coaches start by providing 45-minute sessions.

In-Person Coaching

In-person coaching works best when either you or the coachee has a private area to meet that is free from distractions. Most in-person sessions are approximately an hour long.

Electronic Coaching

Electronic coaching is done via instant messaging, e-mail, or using chat rooms. Some coaches even have video capabilities so their coachees can see them during a session. This method is perfect for the web-savvy coach and coachee and for working with coachees overseas.

One-on-One

This type of coaching involves just you and your coachee.

Group Coaching

Optimizing your time, group coaching works best when the participants are dealing with similar issues or pursuing similar outcomes.

Team Coaching

Similar to group coaching, team coaching involves coaching all members of a work team who are coming together on a project or assignment.

Collective Coaching

A collective is where a group of coaches who specialize in different areas form a team to be hired as one coach by the coachee. The coachee is coached by whichever coach handles what is going on with them the day of their session.

Just-in-Time Coaching

This coaching can use a number of different methods like e-mail or phone but is distinguished because there are no scheduled sessions. The coachee has access to the coach all month long and calls when he or she needs to be coached on something. This is often billed on a retainer versus a monthly cost.

Types of Coaches

Internal—hired as an employee of a coaching company who sells coaching to companies or individuals and assigns coachees to you.

Internal contract—hired by a company to coach their employees but remains an outside provider so that there is a greater level of objectivity; distinguished from an external coach because you only coach the employees in one large company and are under a long-term contract to provide services.

Internal employee—hired as an employee by a company to coach their fellow employees; although the number of these positions is growing, it is currently very competitive.

External—operates as a sole proprietor or small business owner, responsible for all aspects of business. External contract—operates as a freelance coach, taking work from one or more coaching companies. Integrated—you are not a coach by title but are weaving coaching skills and tools into the job you do.

6. Create Fee Structure

Coaching may simply be part of your job, in which case no fee applies. On the other hand, you may be required to account for time, and hence cost, allocated to coaching in your organization. For this purpose it's worth finding out what coaches in external coaching practices charge. If you are an external coach or internal contract coach, a credible and appropriate fee structure is important. Setting fees is a relatively simple process, because the market will determine what the appropriate fee is for your niche or specialty. Beyond that, you will need to set income goals that are in line with the number of coachees you would like to have and what they are able and willing to pay.

Questions to answer before setting your fees:

What is the market rate for the type of coaching you are doing? To find this information, do a search of coaches in your region on the coach referral sites; create a spreadsheet of services offered and prices charged. Tally the amount each coach is charging for each of the services they provide and then determine the average rate being charged. Remember that you may not be able to charge top rates if you are just starting out.

How much do you want and need to charge for your coaching?

To answer this question, first answer these questions:

> **A.** What was the initial cost of your infrastructure? Divide that number by 12. What is the monthly upkeep of that infrastructure? Add the divided number to the monthly number.
> **B.** What is the cost of your monthly marketing?
> **C.** What is the cost of your monthly phone bills?
> **D.** What amount of money do you need to make to support your life or contribute to your household?

After answering these questions, add up the amounts (F, below), then add 10 percent to 25 percent depending on the amount of taxes you will be required to pay on the income. This amount is how much you must make per month.

To then determine how much you need to charge for coaching, divide the amount you must make per month by the number of coachees you will have.

Formula: A + B + C + D = F × tax amount = G ÷ number of coachees = H

H = amount you must charge each coachee per month

Example: Joe is a new coach who has decided to work out of his home. He spent $1,200 setting up his office and the cost to maintain Internet service, web site hosting, and so on equals $150 per month. He has decided to spend $200 per month on marketing and his phone bills are $150 per month. He needs to contribute $4,000 per month to his household income. His equation would look like this:

$250 + $200 + $150 + $4,000 = $4,600 × 1.25 = $5,750

(4,600 + 1,100 in taxes) = $5,700

$5,700 ÷ 20 coachees = $287.50 per month

Joe needs to set his one-on-one fees at $300 per month if he wants to coach 20 people per month and meet his financial commitments.

Is the rate you would like to charge doable for the niche you have chosen? Answering this question requires you to do some market research. You already know what coaches in your region are charging. Using the same resources, you can determine what coaches in the same niche are charging. This will offer practical insights into what fee is appropriate. You could also determine the kinds of salaries people in your niche are earning, especially if it involves a particular profession. You can find much of this information on the Internet.

Remember that if you are offering coaching services to people who are employed, are in partnerships, or are self-employed, their employer may either meet the cost of coaching or they may be tax deductible.

Fee Structure
It is recommended that, to avoid confusion, you have no more than three fee options for coachees. Usually coachees will choose the middle option.

Sample fee structure:
- In-person coaching four times per month with unlimited telephone access to your coach in between calls for $400.
- One-on-one telephone coaching four times per month with unlimited e-mail access to your coach in between calls for $300.
- Group coaching twice per month for an hour with five other coachees for $150.
- You can set your own variations on these fees based on the information you have gathered.

7. Create Materials

The basic materials a coach needs to become established are:

- *Business cards.* A business card is nothing more than a handy way of providing contact information. It has no other specific marketing or sales role beyond brand recognition. If you are an internal coach, consider adding the title "coach" and any relevant qualification to your existing business card.
- *Biography or one-sheet.* A snapshot of who you are, what you do (including your niche or specialty), programs offered, a short bio, and (if appropriate to your niche), a photograph. Make sure all the information fits on one letter-size (8.5" × 11" or A-4) page. Include this sheet with an introductory letter; coaching services intake packet, marketing materials, and so on.
- *Coaching Services Intake Packet.*

Suggested Coaching Services Intake Packet Materials

Agreement
- List policies and procedures
- Request they sign it and return with payment or fax it back
- Invoice if appropriate—personal or internal coachees may require an invoice

Assessment Tests
- Coach U's Clean Sweep program
- One other, if applicable

Coachee Intake Form
The intake form should request comprehensive contact information, plus birthday (for keeping in touch) and referral information. It should also request:

- Relevant personal background information.
- Personal accomplishments and/or goals.
- Shifts or changes believed to be needed in a six-month timeframe.
- Habits, activities, or thought processes that need to be eliminated or modified in order to move forward quickly.
- A small number of burning short-term goals for the next 90 to 120 days, together with the changes necessary to make them happen.
- Long-term goals; a small number (two) to begin working on right away (wants, not shoulds).
- Areas of irresponsibility.
- Motivators, energizers.
- Other relevant information (for example: Is the coachee in therapy or a 12-step program or on related medication?).

- Why have you hired me?
- What does being coached mean to you?
- How will you know how effective our coaching has been?
- How might you sabotage our professional relationship?
- Do you understand that I stand for you, not your goals?
- Do you understand that hiring a coach is an investment in you?

Business Card and Promotional Material

- Brochure
- Bio or one-sheet
- Flier for upcoming class or program you are leading

Instructions

- What to Talk About with Your Coach sheet

Something unique

- A personal card
- A small gift or token of appreciation

(Access to the Welcome Letter, Agreement, and Coachee Intake form can be found in the resource book, *The Coach U's Essential Coaching Tools: Your Complete Practice Resource.*)

The Coaching Call Prep Form

Following the first call, ask coachees to submit a Coaching Call Prep form via e-mail or fax prior to your sessions. Most coaches choose three to five questions to place on their forms.

There are many reasons to have coachees use the prep form:

- It assists the coachee in organizing their thoughts before the call.
- It serves as a record of the coachee's accomplishments and progress.
- It provides the coach valuable information for guiding the session.
- Saving the forms and reviewing them quarterly allows the coach to easily complete progress report documents.

Common questions asked on the Coaching Call Prep form:

- What have you accomplished since our last session?
- What insights and shifts have you had since our last session?
- What are you grateful for since our last session?
- What did you intend to complete, but did not?
- What challenges and problems are you facing now?
- What opportunities are available to you right now?
- What do you want to use your coach for during the session?
- What do you want to commit to do by the next session?

8. Establish Your Presence or Practice

If you are coaching within an organization and being paid as an employee, then you may need to:

- Define your mission within the organization or your job role
- Communicate to others what you are now doing
- Establish funding for your programs
- Obtain an internal designation or executive sponsor
- Establish your presence inside the organization

If you are setting up an independent coaching practice, you need to register a legal business entity, as well as establishing your practice. Your country, state or province, region or county, and city or municipal laws may dictate what a small business needs to do to operate legally.

- *Obtain a business license.* Typically, a city or municipality will want you to obtain a business license. Your municipality may also have regulations about operating a business from a private dwelling, if that's what you are planning to do. You will need to check with your municipality regarding a business license and zoning regulations, but also check with your local chamber of commerce or other small or home-based business organizations for extra insight.
- *Register your business.* There are four common types of business entity: sole proprietorship, partnership, S-corporation, and limited liability corporation (LLC). Your country, state, or province will require you to register a business name even if you don't want to form a partnership or corporation. Either way, consult a business attorney or lawyer and an accountant.
- *Open a business checking account.* It makes sense to keep your business and personal money separate for lots of reasons, but especially for ease of book-keeping. Your bank will probably request some form of evidence that you have registered your legal business entity before allowing you to open a business account.
- *Buy business insurance.* Your business, including its assets like computers and office equipment, is your source of income, so it makes sense to insure it. If you are working from home, you may be able to buy business insurance as an addendum to your residential policy.
- *Get a separate business phone line.* Your phone is the vehicle through which most of your coachees will know your practice, so it must be professionally answered and operated. Extra phone lines are cheap and they frequently don't even need extra cabling. Either have a high-quality answering machine with a professional message or use voice mail with a separate mailbox from your personal line.

Other legal issues coaches may face include:

- *Copyright.* If you are sending out an e-newsletter, writing an e-book, or copying items from self-help books or business how-to books for workshops, you need to be careful that you are not infringing on copyright laws. Most sources state under what conditions the material can be reproduced. In addition, if you are using CoachInc.com materials, be sure to adhere to the guidelines. If you are creating original materials for publishing, make sure you print "Copyright," your name, and the date on each sheet. You don't need to register a copyright, because copyright exists in what is known as "prior art," which means that you created the document, words, and/or images before anyone else. If in doubt, consult an attorney specializing in intellectual property.
- *Confidentiality.* Some personal coachees, and almost all business coachees, will request written confidentiality statements, ensuring that any important information given to you will be kept private. Take signing these documents very seriously. Breaches of confidentiality can lead to lost coachees and legal action.
- *Trademark.* If you have a wonderful program name, company name, or product name, you may want to trademark it so that no one else can use it. Consult a trademark attorney for specific information.

" Far better is it to dare mighty things, to win glorious triumphs, even though checkered by failure … than to rank with those poor spirits who neither enjoy nor suffer much, because they live in a gray twilight that knows not victory nor defeat. **"** | **Theodore Roosevelt**

---

9. Introduce Yourself as a Coach

Numerous tools exist for you to introduce yourself to your network and announce to your community that you are now a coach. Once you have the basics, be creative in how you connect.

Basics

- *Business cards.* Start with something simple and elegant, or add "coach" to your existing business card if you are an internal coach.
- *Jane Smart letter.* This correspondence, which can be on paper or electronic, introduces you as a coach and explains what coaching is (see the resource book, *The Coach U's Essential Coaching Tools: Your Complete Practice Resource* for access to sample letters).
- *One-sheet.* This is the fastest way for someone to find out who you are and what you do. Typically, it is an 8.5" × 11" or A-4 size sheet of paper printed with

your pertinent information, including name, niche or specialty area, programs offered, and a short one-sentence description of each, a short biography and a professional photograph.

- *Elevator Speech.* One to three sentences describing what you specifically do as a coach, for you to use whenever anyone asks what you do. Remember, a statement that requires the response, "Oh really? How do you do that?" is very effective.
- *Coach referral site listings.* Placing yourself on listings gives you exposure, visibility, and a web presence. You can also edit the information easily. There is more information at www.findacoach.com.

Optional

- *Brochure.* You can create a brochure on your computer using your laser printer and paper, but remember that the finished product must look and feel professional. Brochure design is a skill that takes experience, training, and insight. Your local copy or print supplier can probably help you create an effective design and help you refine your content. Their advice is often free or available for a nominal charge if they print your brochure. Consider this as potentially a more cost-effective approach than designing your own brochure. After all, you're a coach, not a graphic artist.
- *Web site.* If you are working within a web-savvy coachee niche, creating a web site within your first two years as a coach may be imperative to your success. Otherwise, waiting until you have branded yourself will allow you to create a site that fully represents who you are and speaks to who you serve. As mentioned above, consider hiring a web designer for a professional looking website.

Tip: If your niche includes business professionals, consider hiring a graphic designer and a writer and then having the brochure professionally printed. Your brochure must complement your professional image.

---

10. Enroll Coachees

These are the five key stages involved in enrolling coachees:

1. Be Visible
2. Build Relationships
3. State the Value of Coaching
4. Provide a Coaching Experience
5. Close the Sale

1. Be Visible

This seems obvious; however, it takes intention and effort to be visible to those prospective coachees you are targeting. It is said that a prospective coachee must experience you seven times before he or she will hire you. This does not mean that they need to meet you seven times. It can mean that they see your name in a byline of an article, then hear from a friend who heard you speak at her networking meeting, and then see one of your business cards in the library, and so on.

First, choose ways that are easy and fun for you to be visible. When you are ready, challenge yourself by being visible in new ways.

Ways to be visible:

- Attend networking meetings.
- Be involved in your community.
- Call and connect with people you know.
- Submit articles to publications your market reads.
- Place TeleClass or event announcements in your newspaper's calendar section (calendar listings are usually not guaranteed, but they are free).
- Send your "Jane Smart" letter, and follow-up every three months with an update letter.
- Send postcards announcing a TeleClass, workshop, or coaching special.
- Write an e-newsletter and make a game of gathering subscribers.
- Create alliances.
- Put your business cards up on bulletin boards in coffee shops, grocery stores, and the library.
- Host an open house.
- Volunteer to speak at or for networking groups, industry associations, and at corporations during their lunch hour.
- List yourself in coach referral directories.
- If you have a web site, update the metatags frequently and submit to search engines often to keep yourself on the front page of retrievals.
- Join an Internet community through an e-mail group, newsgroup, and so on.

2. Build Relationships

All marketing boils down to building relationships. We build relationships by getting to know people and staying connected to them. How are you going to achieve these objectives in your business?

Getting to know people, collecting a business card, and putting someone in your database doesn't count as getting to know them. Set a goal for yourself to find out two personal details from whoever you come in contact with. After speaking with them, jot the information down on the back of their card. When you call to connect with them, you can refer back to the conversation and create an instant bond.

Stumped for what to ask? Try one of these questions:

- What challenge are you having in your business?
- What are you really excited about doing this year?
- What is your favorite thing about the industry you are in?
- What one block, if eliminated, would allow you to do what you really want?

Simply getting to know people helps you build a network, which, in time, will lead to bringing more coachees into your practice. People appreciate it when someone shows an interest in them, and they will likely also want to know what you do. This first contact is not an opportunity to sell. By all means talk about your practice, but don't try to sell to someone until you have developed trust and rapport over a number of contacts.

After the initial conversation, you should get a sense of what category the person falls into:

- *Prospect.* From the conversation you can tell that this person is a candidate for coaching with you.
- *Advocate.* This person may or may not be a prospect, but he or she is connected with a huge network of people who respect his or her opinion and they may be willing to recommend your services to that group.
- *Peer.* This person may be in the right network for you; however, you are unable to determine whether they would be a prospect or an advocate.
- *Acquaintance.* You and this person didn't click the first time, but keep an open mind for the future.

Make a point of connecting again soon with people you identified as prospects or advocates. You may invite them out for coffee or just call them on the phone. In any case, invite them to experience a complimentary session. The ultimate intention is to enroll the prospect and to give the advocate an experience of you so they can make referrals.

Guiding Principle 5 | **People Seek Value.**
Connection is the wellspring of creativity.

Staying Connected

The way you choose to stay connected to your network is a personal decision. Some coaches want the face-to-face contact, while others prefer more behind-the-scenes options. Whichever route you take, you will experience the most success when you are consistent.

Ways to stay connected:

- Phone campaign—This is where you set up a schedule in your network to make check-in calls once per month to everyone in their network. Keep notes so you can pick up the conversation next time. Be careful not to waste their time . . . (or yours).
- Attend networking meetings.
- Send e-newsletter or tips.
- Mail a "Thinking of You" card.
- Invite to coffee or lunch.
- Host an open house.
- Conduct a free discussion group.
- Send quarterly business update letter.
- Make referrals to them (don't underestimate the power of this one).
- Create an alliance.
- E-mail items of interest.
- Remember to call them on their birthday or send a birthday card.

3. State the Value of Coaching

One of the most feared questions by the new coach is "what is coaching?" New coaches are often nervous and unclear about how to explain such a complex relationship. However, a prospect that does not grasp the concept of what coaching is or who feels you are not sure what it is will not hire you. Here are three approaches to explaining coaching:

Approach 1: Sharing the Definition
This approach is the most direct and works well when you are in a group of people and feel that there may be different levels of experience within the group.

- Example 1: "Coaching is a partnership between the coach and the coachee where dreams, desires, and goals are objectively supported and challenged resulting in a positive, forward-moving experience for the coachee."
- Example 2: "Coaching is a synergistic relationship that grows and develops the coachee both internally and in their external environment."
- Example 3: "Coaching provides a confidential atmosphere to explore your authenticity, restore your integrity, and live a more fulfilling life."

Approach 2: Using a Metaphor
This approach works well when you know you have some time to paint a picture for your audience, whether it is a group or just one person. You will draw on their experience and interaction with other professionals.

- Example 1: "The easiest way for me to explain what a coach does is to draw some comparisons through a little story. Imagine that you are deciding to buy and learn how to ride a bike. First, you hire a consultant, who will tell you what kind of bike to buy, what the parts of the bike are for and other information that is their opinion of what bike is best for you. Next, you hire a coach, who listens to your experience of buying the bike with the consultant, and then walks you out to the bike, helps you on it, holds the back as you steady yourself, runs alongside you as you begin pedaling, and works with you to become proficient at it."
- Example 2: A sample conversation.
  Coach: "Have you ever had a coach for a sport or perhaps acting?"
  Prospect: "Yes, I had a football coach."
  Coach: "And what did that coach do for you? What did they provide?"
  Prospect: "Well, they supported me, cheered, yelled out corrections, pushed me really hard."
  Coach: "Believed in you to be your best?"
  Prospect: "Yeah, definitely."
  Coach: "Well, that's what I do for people in their lives and around their goals. I believe in people to be their best and then support them in achieving it by challenging them, offering ideas, and cheering them forward. In my coaching the game is life."

Approach 3: Do It

This approach works best one-on-one. Basically you are asking a probing question that allows you to coach the coachee on the spot.

Sample questions:

- What is one thing you would like to add to your life?
- What goal would you like to achieve in the next 90 days? What changes would you need to make to make it happen?
- What are the habits, activities, or thought processes that need to be eliminated or modified in order to move forward quickly?
- What is one long-term goal you would want to work on with a coach right away (wants, not shoulds)?
- What does being coached mean to you?

Remember Coach U's 123 Coach! Model. You can use this particular model in literally any situation—whether you're coaching or sitting at the dinner table with your family. This model foci on making sure that your coachee feels heard and understood. You have an opportunity to learn more, much more, while giving the other person some space to arrive at his or her own conclusions and strategies.

Coach U's 123! Coach Model

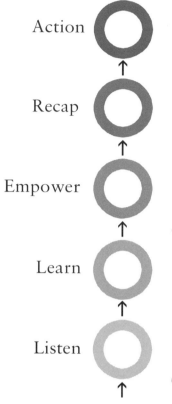

Action

Recap

Empower

Learn

Listen

○ Listen. When we listen to our coachees, we actively listen to what is being said and what isn't being said. We allow our coachees to fully express themselves.

○ Learn. We can learn about the situation, our coachee's perspective, previous experience with the situation, and more when we listen. When we immediately offer solutions we inadvertently disempower our coachees. Rather than jumping in with advice or a solution, we can encourage our coachees to evaluate the situation more closely. Here, you and the coachee both have a great opportunity to learn more so that you can address the source of the problem rather than the symptoms that are present.

○ Empower. Once you and your coachee have noticeably moved forward in the discussion, it's important to respond to the situation. Now would be a good time to further empower your coachee before aligning on a course of action. Let him or her know that he is or she is on the right path, that you understand where he is or she is coming from, and, briefly, what your perspective is or what your experience has been with something similar in the past.

○ Recap. The recap step is a necessary step. As you may have covered a lot of ground, or perhaps your coachee has jumped forward as a result of having the space to think out loud, it's crucial that you both know where you currently are before you align on a course of action. You will want to avoid a situation with which you might be familiar; finding out at the end that you're talking about two different things. The objective of recapping is for both you and the coachee to be clear.

○ Action. Accountability plays an important role in the coaching relationship. Coachees decide to hire coaches to support them in achieving their goals in the least amount of time and with the least amount of energy. Your coachees will expect you to keep track of their goals and commitments as well as to inquire into their status. And, for fun, many of them will test you here!

After you have fully discussed the current situation or problem, your coachee feels empowered and supported, and you have summarized and confirmed that you are both on the same page, it's time to align on a sound course of action. This can be to identify a short- or long-term strategy with supportive action steps, or to simply identify what the coachee will do by the time you next meet.

---

66 The highest reward for a person's toil is not what they get for it, but what they become by it. 99 | **John Ruskin**

4. Provide a Coaching Experience

For the self-employed coach, having a prospect experience the complimentary coaching session is one of the most important aspects of selling coaching. You want to allow the prospect to feel special. Using language such as, "I'd like to invite you to experience coaching—would you be interested?" is enticing.

One way to provide a coaching experience is the complimentary session. Don't be exclusive right away when presenting the complimentary session. Using language like, "I always make people do a free session with me before I decide if I want to work with them" is a turn-off. Granted, you will be evaluating whether you and the prospect are a good match, but the session is not just for you, it is mostly for him or her to experience coaching, specifically your coaching.

Once he or she agrees to the invitation for the complimentary session, set a date right away. About three days before the scheduled session, send a confirmation e-mail and give him or her instructions for the session. Many coaches ask a strong question or two and ask that the prospect bring the answer to the session. Their answer provides the topic for coaching.

50 questions you can ask prospective coachees:

1. What are you putting up with?
2. What are you really passionate about achieving in the next 90 days?
3. What block has kept you from achieving goals in the past?
4. What is your biggest unfulfilled dream?
5. In your company, who needs coaching?
6. What are you spending time on that is not adding value to your life?
7. What is your biggest fear?
8. What would you use a coach for in your life right now?
9. Whose life are you living?
10. What do you most need right now?
11. Where are you out of integrity?
12. What things in your life could you delegate to others?
13. What things in your life could you simplify?
14. What areas of your life are out-of-balance?
15. What is your unique talent?
16. Where do you want to be in a year? In five?
17. What's the biggest challenge you have?
18. What interests you most about coaching?
19. How perfect is your life?
20. If you could have anything, what would it be?
21. What are you looking for in a coach?
22. Would a coach help you earn more?
23. What are you wasting your time doing?

24. What's holding you back the most?
25. What is your business vision?
26. What is your most urgent problem?
27. Where are you falling behind?
28. What opportunities are you missing?
29. What changes can you make now?
30. What goal are you ready to achieve?
31. Are you earning enough?
32. What holds you back financially?
33. What needs immediate attention?
34. Are you up for a personal makeover?
35. What's the dream you've given up on?
36. What are you waiting for?
37. Is there a single change worth making?
38. What will your legacy be?
39. What does your ideal life look like?
40. What skill do you most want to learn?
41. Would you like to master the Internet?
42. Who is taking advantage of you?
43. What gifts are not being fully developed?
44. Are you coaching or managing?
45. What measurable results are important?
46. Have you worked with a coach before?
47. What gets you out of bed each day?
48. What's possible for you financially?
49. Would support make a difference?
50. Are you ready for the next level of your life?

5. Close the Sale

One of the places where many coaches get stuck is in "closing the sale." Closing means having the potential coachee agree to become your actual coachee. Although the idea of selling your services and closing a sale might seem removed from coaching, it is the only way to bring coachees into your practice. Remember, nothing happens until a sale is made. Two methods of closing that work well are the "assumptive" close and the "puppy-dog" close. As its name suggests, the assumptive close means proceeding on the assumption that the prospect has already become your coaching coachee, and that you need to handle the first steps in the relationship. For example, asking the following questions:

- Where should we start first?
- What is the next priority?
- What are the first 10 things you are going to do now that I am your coach?

... or clarifying the relating and/or coaching style

- How are you best coached?
- What should I do if you are having a rough time of it?
- How do you feel best supported?

... handling the business relationship

- How long will you be working with me?
- How do you want to handle the billing?
- What do we do if we have a problem together?

The complimentary session is a form of the puppy-dog close. ("Take the puppy home for the weekend and bring him back on Monday if it doesn't work out....") It's an opportunity for you to get to know your coachee better and to showcase your coaching skills. It is also when you ask the prospect to become a coachee. Since this is when you are closing the sale, this is where you will answer questions and field most objections as well.

Sample complimentary session outline:

- Welcome the prospect to the session
- Briefly outline how the session will work
- Listen as prospect shares the answer to the question you e-mailed him or her
- State back to the prospect what you heard, making a point to identify his or her strengths
- Allow the prospect to respond
- Remember to listen for blocks and passions
- Assign action steps for prospect to take immediately
- Allow prospect to accept and end coaching part of session
- Ask prospect what the experience was like for him or her
- Ask if the prospect sees how coaching could benefit him or her
- Invite him or her to become your coachee
- Allow him or her to answer; field questions and handle objections

Questions and Objections

Don't be put off if your prospective coachee has questions or objections. Both of these are "buying" signals. The prospective coachee is telling you "Yes, but...." Your responsibility is to answer their questions and respond to their objections in a way that leads them to "Yes." A trial close is a way of saying, "Have I handled all your questions and objections?"

Responding to Questions

Q. How do I know if I should hire a coach?

- Coaching works best when there is a significant gap between what you have and what you want.
- You need to be willing to change and to experiment with new ways of doing things.
- Is there a gap and are you willing to experiment? (Trial close)

Q. What should I look for in a coach?

- Experience: The coach should have worked well with someone who is where you are now.
- Compatibility: The coach and coachee should get along, naturally.
- Respect: The coachee should feel respect for who the coach is and for what he or she has accomplished.
- Would you start with me? (Trial close)

Q. What will a coach do for me?

- It is more like what you will do with a coach. The coach can provide direction, suggestions, support, and necessary structure, but it is best if you use the coach to help you get what you want instead of relying on the coach to make it happen for you.
- With a coach, you will do more than you will on your own.
- If you had a coach, how would you use him or her? (Trial close)

Q. What are your credentials?

- That is a good question. I have several:
  - My coachees' success. People hire a coach voluntarily, and don't keep him or her if it's not worth it. My coachees stay with me for an average of _____ months/year because they get more than enough value.
  - I have a degree in _____, which sometimes comes in handy.
  - I have worked with _____ coachees in the past _____ years, many of whom have goals and concerns similar to yours.
- Are you concerned that coaching is a gimmick?
- Is there any particular coachee of mine with whom you would like to speak?

Q. Is there a guarantee?

- No, because your success depends on you. But I do promise that my coachees will be satisfied, and if they are not, they may stop immediately. We don't try to keep anyone hooked in; that would not be good for either party.
- Are you concerned you might not get value from working with me?
- Does that mean you are willing to start coaching for a couple of months with me? (Trial close)

Responding To Objections

A laser message that speaks the truth is your best strategy.

I don't need a coach!

- No one really needs a coach. Being needy is not what having a coach is about. Coaching is about helping people who are already successful get more of what is important to them. I help successful people get more of what they want.
- Is there a particular reason why you think coaching wouldn't work for you? It works for most people.
- When someone responds that way, it sounds very defensive. Are you sure there isn't some way I could help you get what you want?

I don't think I'm interested.

- I know this sounds like a sales pitch, but why wouldn't you be interested in making a better future for yourself? Would you tell me why not?
- Then I'm sorry I bothered you. But if you change your mind or run across someone who can use a coach, can I count on you to pass on my name and number?
- Perhaps I did not do a very good job of explaining what it is I do. Would you give me another chance?

I don't think I understand what you do, exactly.

- Coaching is new, and we are just learning how to speak clearly about it.
- Do you have a sense of what coaches do? Good. How would you use me?
- What part don't you understand? Would you give me a chance to try another explanation?

I wouldn't know where to start!

- By having this conversation, we have already started. Why don't you tell me what you most want right now in your life and we will start making progress.

- We usually start with the things in your life that you are putting up with (tolerating) —things that take energy away and stop you moving forward. Can I help you make a short list?
- Where would you start if it didn't really matter where you started?

I just don't have the time right now to start with a coach.

- Being busy often means that you may be missing opportunities and needing to review priorities. That is something I can help you with.
- Why not?
- I can help you find a lot more time if you will let me.

For external coaches, or for internal coaches where there are budgetary considerations:

I can't afford it right now.

- Deciding what you can afford is really about making choices. Coaching is an investment in you and your future. Is there a goal that means a lot to you—that would be worth the investment to work with me?
- I know how hard things can be if money is really tight. But if you'll let me, I'll be happy to work with you to review your financial plan and suggest changes that would position you for a much stronger financial future. Would you trust me to be honest and not self-serving? (Consider also referring your prospective coachee to a money coach.)
- I fully understand. You know, I have a policy of providing full coaching services to five coachees who don't pay me. It is my way of serving and also creating goodwill for my business. Here's how it works: We get started this week and work together for two months. I will coach you just the same as my other coachees, if you'll be prepared to do the necessary work. If after two months you think you are getting value from our partnership, you hire me for three months at my regular fee of $200 per month. (It has been our experience that about 60 percent of folks who start this way convert to a fee-paying relationship.)

Part 2: New Coachee Process

1. Adding Value: The Follow-up
2. Send a Welcome Packet
3. Conduct a Strong First Session
4. Set the Stage for the Following Sessions
5. Introduce Coaching Support Structures and Tools

1. Adding Value: The Follow-up

Within 24 Hours

One of the things salespeople fear most is the follow-up call. They are concerned that the coachee may have had second thoughts and may want to back out of their commitment. The truth is, they are more likely to feel this way if you don't follow up. The follow-up call allows you to handle considerations, answer questions, and deal with logistical issues. Remember, an objection is just a way of saying, "Yes, but...."

It is important to validate and reinforce your new coachee's decision to work with you within 24 hours of his or her "Yes." After all, what they are buying is you, so it is in your best interest to stay in contact during this time. A phone call or e-mail stating that you are happy they have chosen you to work with and that you are looking forward to the partnership is as simple as it needs to be.

If you think your coachee may be weakening in his or her commitment to start coaching, try reclosing the sale. You can use some of the closing techniques listed in Closing the Sale, or you can try the following techniques.

... endorsing the coachee

- Steve, you have a very special way of ...
- Joan, one thing I like about you is ...
- Karen, it is going to be a pleasure to work with you because ...

... telling the coachee what you expect of them

- Jim, I'm going to need you to focus and ...
- Linda, for this to work, you will need to start doing ...
- Bill, all of my coachees.... Is that a problem for you?

2. Send Coaching Services Intake Packet

Your Coaching Service Intake Packet is another way of reinforcing and adding value to your coachee's commitment to work with you. It demonstrates professionalism, sets some of the ground rules for the relationship, and provides you with background information you'll use in your coaching calls or meetings. The packet can be sent regular mail or delivered electronically. Be sure to gauge how much information your coachee prefers. If you are not sure—ask. The Coachee Intake form is your way of collecting a lot of information about the coachee in a short amount of time.

Within 48 Hours

- Send your coaching service intake packet
- Request the agreement be signed and returned with payment before the first coaching session

3. Conduct a Strong First Session

Review the Coachee Intake Form

- Thank your coachee for completing the form
- Acknowledge the coachee for his or her successes
- Get clarity around vague areas
- Establish an atmosphere of trust and compassion

Focus on the Next 90 Days

- Select one to five goals that are reachable in the first 90 days of your coaching
- Set up a structure to support your coachee and receive frequent reports during this time

Help the Coachee to Eliminate Tolerations

- Ask the coachee to make a list of approximately 100 tolerations
- In the second call, set up a structure and plan for eliminating those tolerations

4. Set the Stage for the Following Sessions

Bonding with your coachee and building his or her trust in you during the first month will assist with retaining him or her as a coachee. One of the most effective ways to do this is to take a genuine interest in their personal journey, ask them to tell you their story, listen and really hear what they are saying. Remember to use active listening techniques.

If you have followed the guidelines for the first 60 days' coaching, your coachee can expect to see real results turning up in his or her life by the end of three months. This should ensure that he or she will continue as your coachee for some time after that.

Overall, though, manage the relationship with your coachee like the professional you are. Be properly prepared for each meeting or call, use your skills and intuition, and polish your integrity. Do what you say you will do, don't over-promise, and do use direct communication.

Also consider following these suggestions:

1. Double up your contact for the first month
- Do spot, check-in-how-are-you calls
- Put your coachee on a business builder or other extra call
- Take a genuine interest in them

2. Step over nothing
- If coachees are late on calls or payment, deal with it up front and resolve it. Make this an ideal relationship.
- Respond to everything they are doing or not doing. Correct bad habits immediately.
- Show them how to be on the coaching call and how to best use you (most don't know).

3. Build a strong coachee information base
- Put the coachee on Coach U's Clean Sweep and other 100-point programs
- Set them up with 10 strong daily habits
- Use other analytical tools as appropriate (don't overdo it—choose carefully)

4. Make solid requests
- Take more actions
- Make huge shifts
- Strengthen their personal foundation

5. Identify focus areas
- Help the coachee to accomplish immediate goal results
- Convert bigger goals into focus areas
- Use the Ready-Set-Goal form

" Without goals, you become what you were. With goals, you become what you wish. **"** | **James Fadiman**

---

5. Introduce Coaching Support Structures and Tools

This section explains the following tools you can use to guide you through your first few coaching sessions. As your experience builds and you develop your own coaching style, you may rely less on these structures, but the underlying principles are common to all coaching. Their value is in getting you started as a coach in a sound, structured, and professional manner.

- How I Coach My Coachees
- How to Get the Most Out of Your Coaching
- What to Talk About With Your Coach
- The Coaching Call Prep Form
- Focus Worksheet
- 10 Daily Habits

Coaching structures provide the coach and the coachee with organized ways to work together. Structures are used to make the coachee's life easier and the coaching more effective. The informational sheets, *How I Coach My Coachees, How to Get the Most Out of Your Coaching,* and *What to Talk About with Your Coach* provide a structure for your relationship with your coachee during the first few coaching calls.

The Coaching Call Prep form and Focus Worksheet are tools that benefit both the coachee and you, the coach, by outlining an agenda and focus for coaching. The 10 Daily Habits and eliminating tolerations processes help coachees get maximum benefit from the coaching process by optimizing their physical and mental preparedness, and by eliminating emotional distractions.

Programs such as Coach U's Clean Sweep are also considered coaching support structures and can be used to guide the coachee in incremental upgrades in key areas of their lives while the coaching itself foci on other items or areas.

(See the resource book, *The Coach U's Essential Coaching Tools: Your Complete Practice Resource,* for where to find these information sheets, structures and tools.)

Part 3: Hallmarks of Ongoing Success

1. Grow the Relationship
2. Track Coachee Progress
3. Record Information for Certification
4. Hone your Skills and Stay on the Path of Personal Development
5. Practice Maintenance

1. Grow the Relationship

Relationships are like gardens; they need regular maintenance to bloom. Here are some suggestions:

- *Keep ahead of your coachee.* Spend 15 minutes a month looking at each coachee file and determine what's next for each one. Discuss all of this with your coachee.

He or she will be impressed and will want to play. Ask your coachee what both of you should be working on. With prompting, he or she will tell you.

- *Make huge requests.* Don't ask what you think your coachee is capable of. Ask what you really want for him or her. Ask "What is the biggest request I should make of you"? (Yes, this works.) Ask your coachee to come up to your standards; don't go down to theirs. If it is important to you, it should be important to him or her.
- *Keep giving perspective.* Coachees grow quickly with a coach and they need to keep getting new bearings to feel confident. Say something like "Here's where you are now. What may be next is ..." Remind them that they are doing fine. Even with good growth or results, coachees get scared.
- *Ask your coachee to articulate the value of your coaching.* If the coachee can say in his or her own words what he or she is getting, it sinks in better, and the coachee is better able to share with others what he or she has understood and done. Finally, it is important for the coach to know what the coachee feels he or she has received. Good feedback.
- *Accept nothing but your coachee's best efforts.* Don't carry a stick; yet don't accept anything less than the coachee's best efforts. Don't fall for diversions, disappointments, or other coachee–ego tactics. You're the coach. It helps to not accept anything less than the best in your life, too.
- *Want more and more for them.* Advanced coaches are able to want huge amounts for their coachees; they are "generous." Keep sharing what you really want for the coachee, not just what you think they can hear or handle.
- *Be a model instead of just an expert.* It is important to model the behavior you want to see in your coachee. If you are living your life in such a way as to be proud of yourself, your coachees also grow. You attract better coachees when you are a model.

2. Track Coachee Progress

Keeping an accurate, objective record of your coachees' progress is important for a number of reasons:

- It helps you make sure your coachees are moving forward.
- It can help you identify blocks or recurrent themes in their lives.
- It can reinforce for the coachee his or her progress, and therefore the value of being coached by you.

Conducting a progress review at least quarterly can be an effective way of sharing information. A progress review should include, at a minimum, the following:

- Coachee's goals at the beginning of the recording period
- Progress toward those goals

- New goals set as a result of achieving previous goals
- Areas where progress has been slow or become blocked, and insights into the reasons
- Assessment instruments completed and the insights gained
- Progress with 10 Daily Habits, tolerations, and Clean Sweep

3. Record Information for Certification

Not all coaches may choose to seek certification. However, if you think you might want to be certified in the future, look at the requirements now, inform your coach of your decision, and begin compiling the information necessary right away.

You should keep accurate records, with independent verification where possible and appropriate, in the following areas:

- List of coachees, past and present
- Hours spent coaching each coachee and aggregate coaching hours
- Training taken
- Own coaching hours
- Related involvement in coaching, such as TeleClasses, ICF chapter involvement, and so on
- Community and network involvement
- Classes and/or seminars led or participated in

4. Hone your Skills and Stay on the Path of Personal Development

Although this module is focused on the nuts and bolts of establishing yourself as a coach, it is important to mention that, as a coach, you are a role model, and your ability to attract coachees will be affected by how you treat yourself.

Make a commitment to hone your skills. Practice coaching at every opportunity, whether in a formal coaching relationship or not. Take as many courses as possible, including TeleClasses. Remember, the best way to learn is to teach. Offer to lead TeleClasses, or participate in role-plays.

Stay on your personal development path. The more you know about yourself, the better you will be able to understand your coachees and their needs. Read books, take courses, and ask friends and colleagues (and especially your coach) for constructive feedback and insight.

Ensure you have a strong personal foundation. Before asking your coachees to use any of the Coach U self-assessment tools, make sure you have completed them yourself. What did you learn about yourself? How are you scoring on the Clean Sweep? How are you doing on your 10 Daily Habits? What are you tolerating?

Ask your coach to keep you accountable for always being your best.

5. Practice Maintenance

Practice maintenance covers several key areas:

- Maintaining coachees (or customer service management)
- Maintaining records (or administrative management)
- Maintaining focus (or coachee management)

Maintaining Coachees

Within your first years of coaching you will notice what is referred to as the "three-month wall." This wall describes the lull that tends to happen between coachee and coach after the first three months of coaching that can result in the coachee leaving. The best way to prevent hitting the wall is to follow the instructions provided for starting the coachee strongly and for setting the stage for following sessions. Additionally, schedule a call during the third month to review the progress made and define what's next for the coachee. This extra contact reminds them of their immediate wins and creates the momentum to move forward into the fourth month. The value of progress review is covered previously; see "Tracking Coachee Progress."

Extras: Consider also offering your coachees extras to reinforce the value of the relationship. However, don't let these dominate your life or get in the way of the basic work of providing excellent, professional coaching for your coachees.

- Offer a toll-free number to allow your coachees to call you easily if they travel.
- Offer extra coaching time or sessions, but not to the point where the coachee expects this. Don't ever let sessions run over. Simply schedule another time for additional coaching. Step in heavily sometimes and offer a daily five-minute pep talk during a difficult time.
- Offer business builder programs. A business builder is a 30-minute chat and/or pep talk with two to six coachees each business morning for a week. Package or use a CoachInc.com program like Personal Foundation to give extra time on a group basis.
- Develop a newsletter. Keep it simple, but professional. A monthly typewritten letter will suffice. It should be about you, your practice, your success, and your direction. Keep it newsy and positive. Don't be too intimate, or talk about your personal growth; keep it about the practice. Remember, though, that the downside of starting a newsletter is that you must keep it going. Don't allow the newsletter to take up all your coaching and preparation time.
- Use assessment tests like Coach U's Clean Sweep worksheets. Most coachees

find a couple that they like and use, but don't make it compulsory. Don't give them all out; pick the ones you think will work well for your coachee.

- Refer coachees to your network. If a coachee is having a specific problem, find the professional who can solve it and put them together. If a coachee needs a different coach, fire yourself and put them with someone who can better help.
- Offer seminars and trainings. If appropriate, conduct weekly support groups for your coachees. Set up seminars for the public and offer complimentary entrance for your coachees. Set up "coachee only" seminars each month or quarter. Even if they can't come, they will talk about you.

Coaching can confront issues coachees are not ready to look at or handle, and it seems they realize this fact around month three. Even if you do everything right, they may still leave after three months because they are no longer coachable. Keep in touch with them periodically; many of these coachees will return when they are ready to overcome their obstacles.

Maintaining Records

As well as keeping accurate and timely records of coachee progress, even if you are a coach in an external practice, you will need to keep business records. Most jurisdictions require you to keep financial records for up to seven years. Even of you are an internal coach or belong to a multicoach practice, you should still keep records so that you can demonstrate your success. And, keep track of progress towards your own goals.

" What we have done for ourselves alone dies with us. What we have done for others and the world remains immortal. **"** | **Albert Pine**

Maintaining Focus

If your coachee seems to be losing interest or is stuck, it may be because his or her focus and possibly even your focus has wandered. Handling things that come up, dealing with current issues, and creating new goals can all take focus away from the original issues—those which you may have been hired to help with in the first place. Take time to review goals with the help of the review tools already mentioned in this section, and help the coachee back to his or her original focus. At the same time, review progress toward those goals, as it may have been more than you or the coachee realize.

Resources

Attention Readers:

Thank you for participating in the collective wisdom of Coach U. Together, we all continue to learn. Additional resources and forms can be found in *Coach U's Essential Coaching Tools: Your Complete Practice Resource* by CoachInc.com.

Attention CoachInc.com Students and Graduates:

CoachInc.com students and graduates may find additional and/or more recent resources associated with this module in the resource area of the student-only web site. If you are a student or graduate of one of CoachInc.com's ICF-accredited coach training programs, you can access these by searching under the name of the course. When the course description page appears you may find a link to the list of additional resources. Each item is a live link to its actual location on the web site. Click on the item to access the information.

Do remember to take the associated online self-test for this module once you have completed the course in person or by TeleClass. The tests are required for coach certification with the International Coach Federation. Throughout the course or anytime you find valuable resources for a particular course please feel free to add to the value of our curriculum by forwarding the resource to revampteam@coachu.com.

Index

Coach U, Inc. Intellectual Property Rights

The following are the intended guidelines as to what you may and may not do with the Coach U, Inc. created materials, concepts, tools, processes, and programs. We encourage you to use many of the Coach U, Inc. programs and materials in ways that benefit you, your coachees, and your business. We are committed to your satisfaction and support as someone who is interested in Coach training and the profession of Coaching, so please read these guidelines with that in mind. If you have further questions or need additional support, please email licensing@coachu.com with your question or request.

THE BASIC INTELLECTUAL PROPERTY RIGHTS:

As an original purchaser of this material you are granted a license to use, not ownership of, specific materials and programs that are a part of Intellectual Property of Coach U, Inc. A license grants permission to use the selected programs and materials in approved ways.

Individual Use:
Coaches may use/duplicate/share/teach all of the "Coachee Coaching Programs" to anyone, group or individual, in a TeleClass, onsite, live workshop or live presentation, with no royalty due to Coach U, Inc. or permission required. This includes programs such as the Clean Sweep, 25 Secrets, Personal and Professional Foundation, and Irresistible Attraction, etc. When using the material, the integrity of the material needs to remain intact and the creation/copyright/contact information for Coach U, Inc MUST be included in use of the material (sample: copyright, 2005 Coach U, Inc.com, all rights reserved. www.coachu.com).

Use for the Training of Coaches:
If it is your intention to use these materials as curriculum for the training of coaches we ask that you request permission from Coach U, Inc. as original authors of this intellectual property. Our intention in making this request is not to restrict the use of the materials in any way but to support you in creating training programs that maintain the integrity of our intellectual property. Such requests can be made by sending an email to licensing@coachu.com.

Interested in Learning More?

We primarily provide coach training to individuals wishing to become certified coaches. We also offer other coach training, personal development, and professional development programs to individuals and organizations in person and through distance learning using the internet and TeleClasses.

Interested in Bringing Coaching to Your Organization?

If you would like to learn more about creating a coaching culture within your organization or having us speak at one of your organization's events, we would be happy to discuss this with you. We are experienced in providing customized coach training programs, individual and group coaching services, and can also consult with you to develop other customized programs.

Interested in Hiring a Coach?

Our International Coach directory contains listings of hundreds of Coach U and Corporate Coach U trained coaches located throughout the world. For information on how to hire a coach or to view profiles of coaches complete with contact information, please visit www.findacoach.com.

Don't forget to request your complimentary copy of our book *Becoming A Coach*.

Contact Us Today

1-800-48COACH
admissions@coachinc.com
www.coachinc.com
www.ccui.com / www.coachu.com

CoachInc.com
P.O. Box 881595
Steamboat Springs, CO 80488-1595

We Want Your Feedback!

We appreciate the opportunity to act upon your feedback. Whether you would like to share a positive review, provide constructive criticism, offer suggestions, or would simply like to share how this publication has made an impact on you or your organization, we want to hear from you. Thank you in advance!

Jennifer Corbin
President of Coach U and Corporate Coach U
jennifer@coachinc.com
1-800-329-5655